UNIVERSITY OF
WINCHESTER

Martial Rose Library
Tel: 01962 827306

To be returned on or before the day marked above, subject to recall.

THE MEDIATED CITY

THE NEWS IN A POST-INDUSTRIAL CONTEXT

Stephen Coleman, Nancy Thumim,
Chris Birchall, Julie Firmstone, Giles Moss,
Katy Parry, Judith Stamper and Jay G. Blumler

ZED
Zed Books
London

The Mediated City: The news in a post-industrial context was first
published in 2016 by Zed Books Ltd, The Foundry, 17 Oval Way,
London SE11 5RR, UK.

www.zedbooks.net

Editorial copyright © Stephen Coleman 2016
Copyright in this collection © Zed Books 2016

The right of Stephen Coleman to be identified as the editor of this work
has been asserted by him in accordance with the Copyright, Designs and
Patents Act, 1988.

Typeset in Plantin and Kievit by Swales & Willis Ltd, Exeter, Devon
Cover design by Michael Oswell

A catalogue record for this book is available from the British Library.

ISBN 978-1-78360-818-8 hb
ISBN 978-1-78360-817-1 pb
ISBN 978-1-78360-820-1 pdf
ISBN 978-1-78360-819-5 epub
ISBN 978-1-78360-821-8 mobi

Printed and bound by CPI Group (UK) Ltd, Croydon, CR0 4YY

MIX
Paper from
responsible sources
FSC
www.fsc.org   FSC® C013604

We dedicate this book to the people of Leeds: a population that is never without stories to tell, hear and circulate.

CONTENTS

FIGURES AND TABLES

Figures

Tables

ACKNOWLEDGEMENTS

The authors would like to thank John Lloyd for supporting this research project from the outset and recognizing its originality. We thank Ramon de Juan for helping to set up scoping interviews; Dr Steven McDermott for his valuable contribution to our early network study of the Leeds news ecology; Matt Lund and his colleagues from Leeds City Council for giving thoughtful answers to our many questions and helping to facilitate our city-wide survey; Gary Blake from Voluntary Action Leeds for helpful research contacts and for conducting a key interview on our behalf; BBC Yorkshire, ITV Yorkshire, Yorkshire Post Newspapers, the National Housing Federation, members of the public and the many journalists, producers, bloggers, community workers, activists and media managers who gave their time generously and answered our probing questions with refreshing honesty. We are most grateful to our news content analysis coders, Joseph Dempsey and Josh Herbert; students in the School of Media and Communication at the University of Leeds who helped us monitor a week in local news media in Leeds; and to Charlotte Elliott for her diligent and intelligent editorial work.

We owe thanks to our many colleagues in the School of Media and Communication at the University of Leeds for listening to us, commenting upon various presentations and generally encouraging us to pursue this project. We are most grateful to Zed Books for their commitment to our research and to our anonymous reviewers for insightful and thoughtful comments on the manuscript.

ABOUT THE CONTRIBUTORS

Chris Birchall is a lecturer in digital media at the School of Media and Communication at the University of Leeds. He has a background in computer science and extensive experience in professional digital media production, and his current research interests include the relationship between digital technologies, interpersonal communication and citizenship.

Jay G. Blumler is an emeritus professor of public communication at the University of Leeds and emeritus professor of journalism at the University of Maryland. A past president and fellow of the International Communication Association, he designed the survey instrument for the Leeds News Ecology research.

Stephen Coleman is professor of political communication in the School of Media and Communication, University of Leeds. His most recent book is *How Voters Feel* (2013). Recent co-edited collections include *Can the Media Serve Democracy? Essays in honour of Jay G. Blumler* (2015), *Handbook of Digital Politics* (2015) and *Deliberation and Democracy: Innovative processes and institutions* (2015).

Julie Firmstone is associate professor at the School of Media and Communication, University of Leeds. Her research investigates a range of issues in the fields of sociology of news, political communications and audience research. Researching the role of the news media and digital forms of communication in engaging citizens in democracy at a local level is one her main research themes.

Giles Moss is lecturer in media policy in the School of Media and Communication, University of Leeds. He is co-author of *Understanding Copyright: Intellectual property in the digital age* (2015) and co-editor of *Can the Media Serve Democracy? Essays in honour of Jay G. Blumler* (2015).

Katy Parry is a lecturer in media and communication at the University of Leeds. She is co-author of *Political Culture and Media Genre: Beyond the news* (2012) with Kay Richardson and John Corner. Along with Stephen Coleman and Giles Moss, she co-edited a Festschrift, *Can the Media Serve Democracy? Essays in honour of Jay G. Blumler* (2015).

Judith Stamper is associate professor of broadcast journalism at the School of Media and Communication, University of Leeds. She is a former BBC television journalist for *The Money Programme, Newsnight* and BBC Yorkshire's evening news programme *Look North.*

Nancy Thumim is a lecturer in media and communication at the University of Leeds. Her book *Self-Representation and Digital Culture* was published in 2012.

INTRODUCTION: A NEW NEWS ECOLOGY

In recent years, and particularly since the emergence of the internet and social media networks, there has been much debate about the future of local news. This debate has been dominated by two contrasting narratives. One is a story of decline and degradation, characterized by a failing business model, massive job losses within local media organizations, a diminished quality of investigative journalism, increasing dependence upon unscrutinized sources, and a dangerous blurring of lines between authoritative, credible news and the ad hoc observations of lay reporters. The other is a story of vibrant reinvention, powered by communication technologies that make possible the networked diffusion of pluralistic accounts, reports and perspectives that move beyond the limitations set by mediating elites and open up localities to a new mode of speaking to and for themselves. The narrative of decline focuses upon loss and deficit, pointing to a crisis of trustworthy channels of public knowledge. The narrative of reinvention emphasizes democratic potential, seeing the emergence of diverse and cross-cutting flows of autonomous, vernacular expression and insight, as a new means by which local experience can be articulated, shared and negotiated.

It is not our aim in this book to subscribe to, or seek to refute, either of these popular narratives. Both are grounded in some truth. In some countries or regions, one narrative seems to possess more explanatory force and relevance than the other, but in no context do either of these accounts do enough to problematize their object of study, which is news itself. It is as if 'news' were a taken-for-granted, known entity; an ontological phenomenon so obvious that it need only be discussed in terms of its enhancement or demise. The displacement of mainstream media by citizen-generated journalism augments the civic quality of 'news', claim the digital enthusiasts. The decline of old media arrangements leads to a news deficit, lament the traditionalists. In neither case do observers question what it is that is flourishing or languishing. The pictures of news to which such accounts give rise are always incomplete, for they exclude a range of communicative practices involved in the making and reception of what might count as news. Researchers who study news have tended to be remarkably confident that they know what it is and how it comes about. The aim of our study has been to resist such certainties and to regard our object of study as a much less stable feature of contemporary culture than it has sometimes been taken for.

This book arises out of research collaboration between a group of scholars who set out to monitor and explain the mediation of news within a major British city. We seek to demonstrate in the chapters that follow how news is a feature of local culture and culture is, in part at least, a product of the stories that circulate within local news. Both the stories that a city tells itself and the practices whereby such stories circulate constitute a dynamic definition of local news.

We are not only interested in understanding local media, but processes of local mediation. As Silverstone (1999: 13) argued, mediation involves 'producers and consumers of media in a more or less continuous activity of engagement and disengagement, with meanings that have their source or their focus in those mediated texts, but which extend through, and are measured against, experience in a multitude of different ways'. The pulsating experiential texture of the city is both source and product of mediation. The playing out of that dialectic is the central theme of this book.

The account we offer here is not, we hope, peculiar to one British city. We are well aware of the dangers of generalizing insensitively on the limited basis of UK or US studies, but we are also reasonably confident that what we have to say about our city tells a story about the conditions, changes and challenges of making and receiving local news in many post-industrial, socially fragmented contexts.

We begin our study by acknowledging that cities are conglomerations of people who can neither know nor ignore one another. The circulation of local news is one of the ways by which relations of enduring coexistence are maintained. Both the normative importance of such shared urban narratives (Dewey 1927; Stamm 1985; Kaniss 1991; McLeod et al. 1999; Oliver and Myers 1999; Friedland 2001; Couldry and Markham 2006; Kovach and Rosensteil 2006), and their empirical forms (Ball-Rokeach et al. 2001; Shah et al., 2001; Paek et al. 2005; Heider et al. 2005; Franklin 2006, 2013; Anderson 2010; Costera Meijer 2013; Dickens et al. 2015), have been the subject of scholarship for almost a century.

Employing a multi-method approach, we have set out to identify and make sense of a *news ecology*. What exactly does this term mean? The metaphor of the city as a *media ecology* has an illustrious history, connecting back to a long tradition of media and communication research exemplified by the Chicago School of Sociology (Nielsen 2015: 28). Milberry (2012) offers a definition of this rather amorphous concept:

> Broadly defined as the study of complex communication systems as environments, media ecology has emerged as a metadiscipline that seeks integrated and holistic accounts of the consequences wrought by the collision of technology, culture, and consciousness. While there are some texts that offer a thorough exploration of media ecology as a field, these tend to be in shorter supply than detailed treatments of its various and particular elements.

Media ecology studies have witnessed something of a theoretical resurgence in recent years (Strate 2006; Lum 2006). This revival has been enhanced by a number of empirical studies, which not only seek to explore media connections within localities, but have taken full account of the new effects of digital communication. For example, Anderson's seminal study of news in Philadelphia and the Pew study of news in Baltimore (Anderson 2010, 2013; Pew Research Center 2010) were inspirational models in the formation of our own approach.

The remit of our study is news within one specific media ecology: the city of Leeds in the north of England. To describe and explain that media ecology per se would have been a much more ambitious project than we were able to undertake. It would range from a vast body of non-news-based mass-media content to a sweeping gamut of personal media practices, such as interpersonal text messaging and the creation of YouTube videos produced with a view to making people chuckle. In studying a local news ecology, we are motivated by a simple civic concern: unless people know what's going on in the areas where they live and work, what hope is there that they will form wider social attachment, awareness and engagement?

We set out below first an account of *why* we have adopted an ecological approach and how we think it can enhance our understanding of contemporary news practices, and second *how* we conducted our research by weaving together methodological approaches that are rarely combined within a single study.

Why study news ecologies?

Urban cultures are vast repositories of stories, forever circulating. Some local stories make their way through a maze of winding urban pathways to reach public attention, while others remain peripheral or unheeded, destined for the communicative margins of 'gossip' or 'mere noise'. The circulatory energy that constitutes newsworthiness is not a natural force. Despite sometimes naive journalistic claims, major news stories do not arrive with their objective meaning transparent and their headline size already determined. News is made and driven; it travels because people and institutions make it move.

Understanding the relations, convergences and tensions between the institutions that produce and transmit news; the contexts within which news sticks or slides away; the uses that different people make of news; and the environmental conditions that shape and drive news is an ecological exercise. That is to say, it involves a sophisticated understanding of the ways in which communities are communicatively integrated through 'a range of communication activities that link networks of individuals, groups and institutions in a specific community domain' (Friedland 2001: 360). The most promising approach to community integration has been advanced by McLeod (1996) and his colleagues at the University of Wisconsin, who define the concept as 'a multidimsensional, multilevel phenomenon' involving 'the exchange of communication and influence directed toward social control and/or social change'. Nardi and O'Day (1999) refer to an information ecology as '... a complex *system* of parts and relationships, It exhibits *diversity* and experiences continual evolution. Different parts of an ecology *coevolve*,changing together according to the relationships in the system.'

In this book we employ the ecological perspective to describe three sorts of relationship. The first is between individual-level interpersonal communication and city-wide-level shared knowledge. Without some degree of micro–macro integration, the conversations, grapevines and idiomatic expressions that occur in the context of interpersonal communication would be unrelated to the circulating stories transmitted by local media. As McLeod et al. recognize, 'On an individual level, integration is the presence of intrapersonal feelings of local attachment (as a source of motivation) and maintenance of interpersonal relationships in the community (as a basis of participation)'.

Communication theorists have long been interested in this

relationship. Simmel's work on webs of group affiliation (1922) and Lazarsfeld's studies of the role of 'personal influence' in the diffusion of publicly circulating ideas were foundational. More recently, Huckfeldt and Sprague (1987, 1995) have demonstrated empirically how political information is encountered within social networks comprising crossovers between personal interaction and media exposure:

> ... political information is processed and integrated not by isolated individuals but rather by interdependent individuals who conduct their day-to-day activities in socially structured ways and who send and receive distinctive interpretations of political events in a repetitive process of social interaction. Thus, political behavior may be understood in terms of individuals tied together by, and located within, networks, groups and other social formations that largely determine their opportunities for the exchange of meaningful political information. (1987: 1197)

An impressive (but neglected) example of this sensitivity to the dialectical interpenetration of interpersonal and mediated local information is Davison's 1989 study of the Kingsbridge community in New York's Bronx borough. Davison argues for the importance of word-of-mouth communication as a primary level of news circulation:

> Each retail store is potentially a communication center, and some merchants play an active part in keeping neighborhoods informed about developments that affect them. Store windows are a favorite place for public service announcements of many kinds. The schools will provide a variety of channels that link the institution with the community and members of the community with one another ... Block and apartment house associations also maintain various channels, including newsletters. (Ibid: 15)

A key question for our research, then, relates to the role of interpersonal communication in the circulation of Leeds news. Are the same centres still serving as portals to local information or have these changed? Has the advent of the internet, as a hybrid channel of interpersonal and mass communication, replaced or augmented these local grapevines? Has the much-celebrated interactivity of contemporary media made it easier for people to use technologies to interact with one another and/or with institutional news providers? What sort of vernacular translations take place when citizens talk among themselves about messages emanating from the media? And what sort of concessions are mainstream news producers making to new modes of civic expression, information-sharing and collective action? These are questions best examined ecologically; that is to say, in terms of the co-evolution and adaptation of different forms of communicative practices rather than the evaluation of one in terms of the other.

Second, the ecological perspective has long been utilized to explore the ways in which different communities within a city read and speak to – or ignore – one another. The seminal research in this context was undertaken by Robert Park in his Chicago studies. Exploring the 'moral distances' between 'cities within cities' which turn a city into 'a mosaic of little worlds which touch but do not interpenetrate', Park undertook a detailed empirical inquiry into the ways that coexisting communities and populations managed to avoid one another's interests and values. Park maintained that

> What is achieved by communication is understanding and the
> ability of one individual to understand another is the measure of
> the distance between them. This differing ability to understand
> one individual or another is a matter of observation but it is also a
> matter of feeling. We can see the distance that separates A from B,
> but we can *sense* the distance that separates us from others. This
> individual seems reserved and distant and insofar incomprehensible.
> There is always a certain amount of vague apprehension of the one
> we do not understand; but we are at ease with the person who is
> completely understandable. This sense of being at ease and at home
> or the absence of it is what we mean by distance.

This notion of distance is highly relevant to Leeds: a city in which 170 languages are spoken; particular communities and their events are widely associated with ethnic or religious traditions; and the local Member of the European Parliament at the time of our study represented the racist British National Party. How do people in Leeds come to terms with these differences and distances? How do they come to know the strangers who are their fellow citizens? How well do communities feel that their stories are told and received? What efforts are made by local media to translate stories across cultural distances? In what sense is the local public sphere characterized by the ease of the 'completely understandable' or the apprehension of the culturally uncomprehended?

Third, much valuable research has been conducted on changes in the diffusion of local news, especially since the advent of the internet. Whereas the path from source to journalist to audience was once fairly linear (one might say industrial), it is now the case that a range of media technologies, practices and genres are available to people hoping to make, circulate and receive news. Anderson's (2010) excellent study of one local news story in Philadelphia suggests that sources are becoming increasingly 'savvy' about the best ways to gain public attention by utilizing different media. While media organizations might perceive themselves to be in fierce competition with another to 'deliver' the news, an ecological perspective suggests that different media fulfil different functions in the bid to reach public attention. For example, news blogs might seem to be very weak competitors in relation to well-resourced mainstream news providers, but as a means of reaching the latter some of them are highly significant. The overall news ecology is becoming more like a division of informational labour than a war of each against all.

As the process of producing, filtering and circulating news becomes less industrially monolithic, so do patterns of news consumption. In their study of media effects on civic life, McCombs et al. (2011: 61–2) observe how citizens use news media to complement one another. Media scholars and commentators need, they argue, 'to abandon the idea that the various news media are in competition with one another for the attention of the news audience'. They refer to the 'unequivocal empirical fact' that 'most members of the audience engage multiple information outlets in order to remain up-to-date on public affairs ... It is necessary to understand these relationships among different types of media use.' The breadth and eclecticism of these relationships are borne out by a 2011 survey, conducted by the Pew Research Center's Project for Excellence in Journalism and Internet & American Life Project in association with the John S. and James L. Knight Foundation, which found that its American respondents relied upon a range of media sources to find information about their local communities:

> Americans appear to discern significant differences in the
> strengths of different information sources. They recognize that

there may be more information about their child's school on a parent-run listserv than on television or even their neighborhood weekly paper. They recognize that if they want information about zoning or local government, it may be more available in the newspaper they do not regularly buy than on the television station they watch many days for traffic and weather.

Indeed, it may well be the case that, as the mediated news ecology becomes more differentiated, there is an emerging rationale for specific parts of it to stick to performing the roles that they are best at rather than for all players to try to serve all public information needs. Might it be that radio or television news are bound to break news faster and more effectively than newspapers or news blogs and therefore the latter should cease to aspire to become news-breakers? Might it be that council websites are capable of providing certain kinds of local service-related information, but that public discussion about council service provision or policy is more likely to be open and trusted when it takes place on third-party blogs or discussion fora? Might it be that local radio is well placed to invite public comment about news stories, via phone-ins and user-generated content, but that they will never be as good as newspapers at conducting the kind of investigative journalism that takes time and probing expertise? There are not simple, generalizable answers to these questions; and the local contingencies and practices of media ecologies from one locality to another might suggest quite different responses. In the context of our Leeds study, it is clear that while a great deal of effort is being made by a range of actors to produce and circulate local news, the resources and public attention available to be shared between the various outlets are limited. If there is evidence that certain media organizations are best at serving particular local information needs, would it not make sense for the entire news ecology to play to its constituent strengths, thereby enhancing the overall public interest? Might there be organizationally and economically efficient ways in which greater synergy between local news providers could serve the local public sphere? We discuss the strategic and policy implications of these questions more fully in the final chapter, while much of the empirical evidence set out in the following chapters points to ways in which the production and circulation of news have become an ecological enterprise, transcending the interest of any single information provider.

How we studied a local news ecology

During the early stages of the study, we conducted extensive online research as a means of charting and understanding the diffusion of news within the city that we were exploring, Leeds. During our one-week intensive study of the Leeds news ecology (see below), multiple methods of data collection were applied.[1] This research proved

---

1 Steven McDermott was the researcher who completed this digital research. For Twitter, we used Google Reader to make a search request that included a geolocation target for Leeds tweets only. The geocode uses the latitude and longitude of Leeds city and was extended to a 25-kilometre radius. This geolocation request was altered each day to include particular query words that were 'trending' in the Leeds area. Trending words were acquired by following Trendsmap (trendsmap.com/local/gb/leeds) for approximately twenty-four hours a day during the seven-day period. However, using the Google Reader method did not capture a high enough percentage of local tweets as Twitter limits the number it returns and the frequency at which the search requests are returned. We therefore used Your TwapperKeeper (version 0.5.5), which allowed us to archive certain Twitter accounts and all Twitter accounts that follow them. We compiled a list of key Twitter accounts by using Archivist Website (archivist. visitmix.com/). In the months approaching our intensive data collection week the term 'Leeds' was entered into the Archivist, which then generated a list of Twitter account users who most frequently used the word 'Leeds'. The top twenty Twitter account names were entered into NodeXL on a daily basis returning their followers, who they followed, any mentions of other Twitter accounts and the last tweet that they posted. This resulted in 50,000-plus accounts being accessed daily. This archive can then be downloaded onto a spreadsheet to extract information beyond the text of the tweet. It also contains the user name, the date and time of the tweet and on some occasions the location of the sender at the time of posting the tweet. This enabled us to generate graphs or maps of the accounts most associating themselves with the term 'Leeds'. As will be seen in Chapter 2, the limited use of Twitter by people in Leeds made it unwise to draw too many conclusions about news interests or habits by studying this population. We were also interested in mapping the Leeds blogosphere. We compiled a list of blogs associated with the city of Leeds, using Google blog search and the Guardian Leeds sites. These URLs were collected using Issuecrawler, targeting the front page of blogs and websites and also conducting crawls of entire blogs and websites, in search of hyperlinks between these sites. For blogs and websites this returned approximately 480 sites, websites and blogs. A map of the Leeds blogosphere and web-sphere was produced, identifying network centrality and betweenness. We also followed forty publicly accessible Facebook accounts relevant to Leeds news. Google Reader was used to collect the RSS feed updates for those sites as well as manually copying and pasting those that did not have RSS feeds available. For Forums and other RSS feeds (approx. 221), a search was conducted in the months in the run-up to the intensive data collection week and these were added to Google Reader.

valuable in identifying relevant sites of local news. It confirmed that news was presented and discussed not only in expected places like the BBC local news website, city-wide blogs and Facebook and Twitter networks, but also in less obvious corners of the internet, such as football supporters' forums and informal neighbourhood groups. Network analysis helped us to identify connections between dispersed sites and actors within the news ecology. But it could not possibly provide us with a meaningful overview of the Leeds news ecology, because only a limited section of the population were accessing it (and fewer still producing its content) and because the circulation of news stories within the city was clearly taking place within a much broader environment than could be captured by the concept of 'online news' or the method of 'network analysis'. To adopt Mejias's (2010: 612–13) term, limiting our study of the news ecology to prominent nodes on a network map would risk ignoring the 'paranodal': those actors and spaces that do not conform to the organizing logic of the network. While social network analysis helped us to see how people's experience of news often took place in between and beyond the recognized pathways of news circulation, it could not explain how and why some stories kept to the mainstream routes, others meandered across diverse social practices and others were lost without trace.

Alongside our digital network research, we conducted seventeen 'scoping interviews' to help us develop a more qualitative map of the Leeds news ecology. Employing a snowballing sampling method, we asked interviewees where to go next, both within established networks and off the grid. Interviewees included mainstream news providers, including senior editors from the local BBC television and radio news programmes, the ITV (commercial) news provider and the main local newspaper (the *Yorkshire Evening Post*). As well as these we spoke to a range of more peripheral, sometimes eccentric, local mediators, such as a local artist who (among other things) draws pictures and writes poems about local events on people's shopping bags, the director of an evangelical Christian radio station and several niche bloggers. These interviews were invaluable in giving us a sense of how news practices often transcend the limits and routines of conventional journalism. They reminded us of the importance of sites of hyper-local news circulation, such as neighbourhoods in the poorer peripheries to the east of the city for whose inhabitants 'going to Leeds' is regarded as a major excursion.

Through these scoping interviews, combined with the information garnered about nodes in the digital networks, we developed a map of the news ecology of the city. While our picture was necessarily incomplete and defeasible, it gave us a strong sense that a city's news ecology is inherently complex and fluid. A network map might help us to orient our subsequent research, but only in order to more deeply acknowledge its unsettled nature. Indeed, even the very shape and size of the city we were observing – which seemed so clear to us in our initial mapping – turned out to be contested. ('Leeds' is defined in multiple ways, but we eventually settled on the outer ring road of the city as its most significant boundary.)

Inspired by the Pew (2010) study of Baltimore, we decided to monitor the news in Leeds over the course of a single week. Focusing on a single week was limiting in some respects: there was no guarantee that the week we selected would be 'typical'. However, studying news in a more concentrated and comprehensive way over a shorter period offered us an opportunity to trace and categorize the issues that were covered; to explore how news spoke to certain groups, while ignoring others; to see how different news producers explained, defended and understood the news they were constructing and disseminating; and to understand how media audiences related to news, taking into account the diversity of people in the city as much as the diversity of media outlets. Achieving these goals in a credible way required a range of methods, *none of which would have offered us adequate explanatory material on its own.*

The first aspect of our research involved recording and analysing the news produced over the course of the week by a wide range of local news providers. During the week itself, the research team monitored news output and identified and tracked stories and emerging themes. Then, in the weeks that followed, we conducted a more systematic content analysis of a broad range of these news outlets. The results of this analysis are reported in Chapter 2.

Our content analysis of a week's news pointed to the variety of news channels and sources calling for public attention within the city, but also the ways in which a range of quite different forms and narratives are fused together as 'news'. Within the context of 'the glocal city', wars in the Middle East compete with ice on local roads for significance as shared knowledge; the fate of the Leeds United football club, long regarded locally as a victim of commercial neglect, helps to frame an understanding of irresponsible global bankers creating a crisis that has to be paid for by the poorest local citizens. Urban stories do not emerge or circulate within discrete bubbles; they inform one another and contribute to an aggregate social mood – or, more accurately, a range of distinct, but intersecting, local moods.

The second aspect of the research examined the views of media users and audiences. Eight focus groups provided valuable insights into how people make sense of the news, relate it to their own lives and fit it into their everyday routines. We discuss these focus groups in Chapter 4. Above all, the focus groups helped us to capture the sense in which local narratives are often defined by miscommunications and misunderstandings. More than through content analysis or survey research, focus groups reveal the ways in which the seemingly absent, unsaid or even taboo features of the city contribute greatly to people's sense of where they live. Surveys tap into what people can remember about their own and others' actions; focus groups often stumble upon what is forgotten, misremembered or systematically distorted. A survey of a representative sample of the Leeds population, which we discuss in Chapter 3, complemented the focus groups, enabling us to understand how prevalent different practices and views were and to explore differences among socio-demographic groups.

Far from delivering a neat picture of 'how the city gets its news', the combination of survey data and focus group transcripts allowed us to explore the multiple ways in which individual citizens make sense of their collective experience – what news is as much as where it is found. In asking our respondents how and when they accessed news, it became very clear that people do so in countless ways, sometimes using several media sources and platforms to piece together a version of local reality; sometimes trusting some sources or platforms more than others; sometimes looking for different emphases and perspectives to the ones on offer; sometimes regarding the news as a kind of background white noise that assures them that nothing too awful is about to disrupt their lives; and sometimes using the news as a basis for personal action, such as talking to others, challenging media accounts, protesting or engaging in the formal political process.

It is in response to this inchoate, pluralistic, fragmented approach to local news that the notion of the media ecology of a city really comes into its own. The media themselves and the audiences to whom they speak (and now increasingly speak to one another through social media as well as in other ways) are both interdependent and uncoordinated. How they relate to one another depends upon a complex set of actions that, we suggest, are best studied in all their rich, qualitative detail and then joined together to create a picture of an ecology through which various kinds of news travel – which is greater than any of its units.

The third aspect of our research aimed to understand the perspectives of different news producers about the news they constructed and circulated over the course of the monitoring week. These interviews are discussed in Chapter 5. In analysing the transcripts, we were struck by a discrepancy between what news providers thought (and claimed) they were doing and what they actually delivered. This led us to probe what we regarded as fundamental tensions between a set of genuinely meant public purposes and the capacity to implement them.

As well as interviews with mainstream news providers, we interviewed six local alternative news providers with a view to understanding how mainstream and non-mainstream norms converge, conflict and fit together. We explore these interviews in Chapter 6. It was clear by this stage in the fieldwork on news in the media ecology of the city of this medium-sized UK city that we were not witnessing a transformative displacement of mainstream local media, in the way that some, mainly US, studies have suggested is prevalent. In Leeds, alternative channels and sources appear to perform a supplementary role, providing much-needed information for minority communities and playing some part in challenging dominant news agendas. Yet news sources reaching small audiences can, our research suggests, have an impact disproportionate to their reach across the broader news ecology (e.g. one political blogger was mentioned as a significant actor to us by local council representatives, even though they probably constituted a significant proportion of his readers). Our analysis of alternative news providers moved away from a conventional focus upon competition for public attention and pointed to some emergent news practices that challenge traditional notions of news as the circulation of packaged stories.

Finally, and also inspired by the Pew study (2010), we identified two 'news stories' to explore in more depth. These stories not only dominated the headlines during our monitoring week, but raised important issues in response to our overarching research questions concerning news in the media ecology of the contemporary city

In our first case study (Chapter 7) we looked at news surrounding the annual Chapeltown Carnival, which is the longest-running African-Caribbean carnival in Europe, having been going since 1967. The carnival is held in the Chapeltown and Harehills area of Leeds every August bank holiday weekend and regularly attracts crowds of around 150,000 people. We wanted to explore the role of local media in bridging distances of 'race', ethnicity and class in their coverage of this event – questions of distance are key to ecology studies of the city, as explored in Chapter 1.

In our second case study (Chapter 8) we set out to focus on Leeds as a democratic city, governed by an accountable elected council. We wanted to ask questions such as: How well is local representation mediated? What does democratic accountability look like at the parochial level? Our case study considered media coverage of a series of major cuts in council services, specifically related to residential care homes for elderly people. We were interested in exploring how this story became known and understood by local people. The decision to close local care homes (in response to swingeing cuts in public expenditure imposed by the national government) had been preceded by a public consultation, but few people had heard about it or taken part. Only when news stories about the effects of the cuts became headline news were most local people engaged by it in any meaningful way. But that was rather too late. We found that, despite much professed commitment by the city council to engaging with the public, this notion had several contested meanings, ranging from a one-way flow of information from government to citizens to the creation of a citizenry that is not only listened to through consultation, but empowered as partners in decision-making. This uncertainty about the meaning of public engagement left both local government communication strategists and journalists somewhat confused about their roles in relation to local civic participation. Where does that leave norms of accountability, and could we, by means of this case study, propose ways in which it could be strengthened? After much reflection, we decided to conclude this case study with a counterfactual account of how a city facing such financial dilemmas could establish a more conversational mechanism for public involvement in the policy process.

Mapping the Leeds news ecology and the actors involved in it was a challenging task, but explaining what difference it makes to people's lives was more difficult still. Achieving these goals, as we have argued, required the use of multiple methods. And we think the approach we have taken here might usefully be replicated in other cities. If we are to understand the complexities of what news is, how it matters to people, and how it travels across space and place, we need to employ more than the banal generalities of those who claim that 'the digital revolution' has displaced the need for journalistic mediation or its rearguard echo that nothing can improve upon the journalistic traditions of yesteryear. It is to the implications of our ecological approach that we turn in the final chapter.

1 | MAKING SENSE OF/IN THE CITY

Communicating community

How does a city come to imagine itself? How does it tell itself stories, circulate news, create events, store its memories and come to terms with difference and diversity? Unlike the simple communities of pre-modernity in which everyone stood a chance of knowing everyone else, modern cities are vast, spatially dispersed and culturally fragmented clusters of attachments, interdependencies and institutions. More than just a *place*, the city is a way of sensing the zones and boundaries of potential and permissible social interaction. Simmel (Frisby and Featherstone 1997) famously regarded the city as a space of inexhaustible temporal acceleration and affective overstimulation: 'With each crossing of the street, with tempo and multiplicity of economic, occupational and social life, the city sets up a deep contrast with small town and rural life, with reference to the sensory foundations of psychic life.' The contemporary urban sociologist Richard Sennett, reflecting upon the sensual over-abundance of the city, observes that 'if something begins to disturb or touch me, I need only keep on walking to stop feeling'. Cities, for Sennett, are labyrinths of overwhelming impressions in which 'The eye sees differences to which it reacts with indifference ... My senses are flooded by images, but the difference in value between one image and another becomes as fleeting as my own movement: difference becomes a mere parade of variety.'

In small-scale communities, the social is conspicuous and events are hard to miss. Cities, in contrast, are spaces of overexposure, where experience is fragmented and every impression must compete for attention. It is impossible to 'take in' the city as a whole. The vastness of the city is apprehended through a series of encounters with 'no-go areas', which are avoided by all, except those who must live or work in them, 'must-go' areas, such as the centres and intersections that claim to connect and define the city, administrative areas, which are constructed by bureaucrats in order to manage discrete populations, and 'outside' areas from whence come strangers. City dwellers learn a range of strategies for attending and avoiding; being seen and remaining invisible; acknowledging, evading and resisting the rules. Among the most significant of these tactics for urban living is the acquisition of local knowledge: knowing what you need to know because everyone else knows it; knowing what others do not know, thereby giving you an advantage in relation to them; knowing how to maintain personal boundaries; knowing how to socialize; knowing how to search for a better quality of knowing.

As well as working, sleeping and engaging in the intimacies of family and friendship, people in cities spend their time looking for, responding to and creating knowledge about their environment. They are information hunter-gatherers, foraging for knowledge, just as their ancestors chased after food.

Dewey's (1916: 5) assertion that 'There is more than a verbal tie between the words common, community, and communication' provides a useful theoretical foundation for this book, the main purpose of which is to try to understand how a city talks to itself about what is new, what matters and what needs to be done. The ecological interrelationships between the environment people share (common), their connectedness (community) and the mediation of this mutual reality (communication) is the focus of our study. An ecological perspective acknowledges that cities as places are not simply uncovered or exposed through communication. On the contrary, they are products of communication; the urban space as context is made present through the contextualizing work of communication. In saying this, we are not claiming that cities are somehow inventions or fictions, engendered by strategies of communication. Nevertheless, to speak of places such New York City, Calcutta or Leeds as being real is not to say that the nature of their reality is objective or clear cut. Only through what are often competing and contradictory communications do communities emerge as meaningful places rather than dots on a map. Adopting such a constructivist perspective, we might say that cities are both a product and shaper of collective imagination. And the best way to access the collective imaginings that constitute a city is through the stories that people tell themselves, about where and how they live and the practices they pursue, as they go about making their lives in the city.

In thinking about the mediated city as being both context-dependent and context-shaping, we focus in this book upon a specific city at a particular time. The city is Leeds in the north-east of England. The time is the summer of 2011. Our aim is to bring place and time to life and connect them meaningfully to the news ecology through which they are apprehended. We begin to do so in this introductory chapter by first locating Leeds and pointing to the fluidity that surrounds its apparent fixity as a place. We then turn to the timing of our study, attempting to place it within both a long-term and more immediate historical context. The concluding sections of this chapter explore what it means to speak of a news ecology; how such an ecology has taken shape over time in Leeds; and the extent to which this ecology is in the midst of a radical transformation.

A place called Leeds

In his 1971 book *Portrait of Leeds*, Brian Thompson suggested that 'Leeds is much more a generalised concept place name in inverted commas; it is the city but it is also the commuter villages and the region as well' (1971). In the 2001 census, the city of Leeds was described as an 'urban subdivision' comprising an area of 42 square miles (109 square kilometres), with a population of 443,247; making it the fifth-largest city in the United Kingdom. Just over a third of the city's residents live as married couples; just under a third of residences are one-person households; and one in ten households are inhabited by lone parents. Eighty-five per cent of the population are white; 7.7 per cent are Asian (mainly from Pakistan and India) and 3.5 per cent are black (with twice as many of African than of Afro-Caribbean descent). Most people in Leeds describe themselves as Christian, but 3 per cent are Muslim, 16.8 per cent say they have no religion and the city has the UK's third-largest Jewish population, after London and Manchester.

Delineating the borders of the city is not easy. When combined with the ten surrounding towns (effectively, outer suburbs) of Farsley, Garforth, Guiseley, Horsforth, Morley, Otley, Pudsey, Rothwell, Wetherby and Yeadon, Leeds becomes a Metropolitan District, with a population of 715,402. Beyond this 'greater Leeds' conurbation is the bigger still West Yorkshire Urban Area, which includes the cities of Leeds, Bradford, Wakefield and Huddersfield, with a population of 1.5 million. Within Leeds there are eight parliamentary constituencies (but the European constituency of Yorkshire and Humber is much larger than all of these put together), thirty-one civil parishes, thirty-three council wards and five administrative 'wedges', each with its own 'inner and outer area committee'. In short, to speak of Leeds is to refer to a somewhat amorphous entity; a jumble of overlapping territorial and administrative spaces and boundaries. Of course, people living and working in Leeds make their way through and around these confusing spaces and boundaries, experiencing Leeds as 'a generalised concept place name in inverted commas' in much the same way as they come to make sense of themselves as part of a multinational United Kingdom or European Union. As we discovered in our focus groups with Leeds residents (see Chapter 4), it is to the locally known places in which they live and work from day to day that people's deepest attachments are formed. The rest are little more than places of officialdom or passing through.

Beyond topographical or demographic conceptions of place, which reduce the city to contours and statistics, there is a historical sense of place that seeps through the built environment. To stand for a few moments in Millennium Square in the centre of Leeds is to be surrounded by iconic reminders of the city's Victorian grandeur: the City Museum, built in 1819, the Town Hall, built in 1858, the General Infirmary, built in 1869, and the Carriageworks, built in 1848 as the home of the West Riding Carriage Manufactory. These imposing edifices evoke memories of the city's former glory as the capital of Yorkshire's newly industrialized West Riding and global centre of the prosperous wool industry. Leeds was the first industrial city in the world's first industrial nation and traces of that imperial grandeur are everywhere, both in terms of the now incongruent arrogance emanating from the institutional architecture of a rising ruling class, and the urban chasms opened up by the ruins of post-industrialism. As a classical manufacturing city rooted in the dynamics of mass production and distribution, Leeds was hit hard by the demise of an economic infrastructure geared to making tangible, durable commodities. Its replacement by an amorphous financial services sector, prone to the vagaries of boom and bust cycles, the decomposition of once-cohesive neighbourhoods and the absorption of their populations into the soulless inner city, and the cumulative reconfiguration of the local by global forces that can be neither controlled nor avoided, have left Leeds, like many other large Western cities, facing something of an identity crisis. Its monumentalized red-brick confidence casts a shadow over the sprawling city, or 'urban subdivision', or 'metropolitan district', somehow rebuking it for its post-industrial inertia.

The elusiveness of a singular Leeds identity generates a sense of disorientation. Asked to say what characterizes the city, the manager of the local BBC radio station could only point to its indeterminacy: 'It's really broad ... we have diverse communities. We have a diversity of rich and poor. It's an amalgam of lots of different things. And it's not like a place, like Otley or Ilkley or ... even Bradford ... It's very eclectic.'

Cities like Leeds, which once thrived because of what they made and sold, are now increasingly dependent for their positions in the world upon how they are imagined, both by those living within them and others who might be magnetically drawn to their aura. The creation of city reputations has become a major industry, turning geography into a performative project. Local governments pursue 'urban branding' strategies at huge cost with a view to making their city appear to be the coolest, smartest, most connected, cutting-edge or upwardly mobile place to be. Thrift (2008: 172) has observed astutely that 'As cities are increasingly expected to have "buzz", to be "creative", and to generally bring forth powers of invention and intuition, all of which can be forged into economic weapons, so the active engineering of the affective register of cities has been highlighted as the talent of transformation.'

The project of semioticizing (Law and Urry 2004) Leeds as a city has been taken up by an organization called Marketing Leeds, which 'aims to raise the profile of Leeds as a vibrant, dynamic, internationally competitive city and as the gateway to Yorkshire and the UK' by creating 'innovative marketing and promotional campaigns and events to support the delivery of real economic impact and the creation of wealth for the region'. Their 'Live It Love It' campaign is an attempt to engender symbolic capital by working on the image of Leeds to the point that its representation overwhelms what is being signified. As the campaign website puts it,

> The brand reflects an overarching simple proposition based
> on people's passion for their city. Particularly for the people of
> Leeds – there is no arguing with the sentiment. What is common
> with all Leeds advocates is a shared pride and passion for their

city. All who experience Leeds – its diversity, lifestyle, warmth, people and quality of life – share the same belief: if you spend time in the city, you grow to love it. Our brand serves many purposes: it is a promise, a call to action, and a statement of pride. How it is interpreted will depend upon who we are talking to, and where we are talking to them. Within Leeds, it is a proud vindication. To our wider audiences, it is an intriguing promise, and a call to action.

However, Emma Bearman, who produces one of the city's most popular blogs, is uncomfortable with such branding, and especially its themes of rhetorical and semiotic focus upon retail and finance: 'Where does that leave us? Because, as citizens, we don't actually feel that the marketing message which is pumped out externally resonates with what we experience.'

The gap between slick representations of the branded city, with their inevitable suppression of the eyesores, deprivations, anxieties and conflicts that nobody is ever likely to 'grow to love', and the messy coexistence of everyday lives rooted within parts of the city that are sometimes unknown to one another, is the space in which mediation is paramount. Many different actors, with varying explicit and tacit interests, are involved in defining Leeds as a place. No single definition will ever emerge. But the success or failure of images, stories, worries, aspirations and evasions in circulating, gaining attention and taking root depends upon technologies and practices of mediation that give place its history and flavour. Local news is the first layer of such a history, the first lick of an enduring flavour.

Leeds: a post-industrial city

Cities exist not only as places in space, but also as histories in time. All across the city clocks display the passing of time. Seconds tick away, marking and maintaining an inescapable urban rhythm. At bus shelters electronic signs announce, sometimes over-optimistically, how many minutes passengers will have to wait. As each hour turns into the next, events begin and conclude. Millions of imperceptible glances at watches and mobile phones ensure that people are attuned to time. Time pervades the city. Not only local time, but the 'phantasmagoric' (Giddens 1990: 19) presence of distant events and absent actors is experienced through technologies of temporal connection, which simulate a kind of global simultaneity.

In its heyday as the first industrial city, Leeds had to learn to accommodate itself to the strange phenomenon of clock time, which, as Giddens (1991: 17) states, 'facilitated, but also presumed, deeply structured changes in the tissue of everyday life'. With the emergence of the industrial city, time ceased to be regarded as natural, irregular and task oriented, as it had been in the pre-modern economy. It became instead a standardized currency through which labour was bought and regimented, profits calculated and efficiency measured. Clocks provided a universal standard of ontological stability; symbolic evidence that amid the volatile social forces of the market, there was a regular beat to the conduct of life.

While the clock as a container of time and the city as a temporally bound space characterized industrial culture, post-industrial cities find themselves implicated in multiple, asymmetrical flows of time. Sociologists and cultural geographers have noted that with the emergence of global telecommunications networks 'voice, data, image, and video signals can flow ... at *instantaneous* velocity because of the near speed-of-light flows of electrons and photons' (Castells 1994). Not only are more people in touch with distant others, but there is a sense in which the instantaneity and asynchronicity of message flow is producing a temporally destabilizing effect, making the city 'disappear into the heterogeneity of advanced technology's temporal regime' (Virilio 2005: 19). While this postmodernist perspective, most commonly associated with Virilio's work on 'the over-exposed city', is suggestive insofar as it captures the disruptions to place-centred temporality generated by global networks, its more excessive rhetoric sometimes fails to register local, empirical experience. For the average resident of Leeds, life is still dominated by clock time, and when it is 9 a.m. in the affluent suburbs of the city, it is exactly the same time in the more deprived housing estates. Buses and trains run according to local timetables and local news is most commonly received from *daily* newspapers, *hourly* radio bulletins or *fixed-time* television programmes. Mobile phones and online social networks might be 24/7 services, but they continue to be used by most people within the contexts of their parochial daytime routines rather than as ubiquitous connectors to global society (Lenhart et al. 2010, Lenhart 2012). Indeed, one of the key findings that we report in this book is that people in Leeds are still primarily conscious of and concerned about the local and immediate aspects of their everyday lives. Living within a 'financial city', dependent upon critical decisions made in distant time zones, they might be faintly aware of tremors emanating from Frankfurt or Wall Street. As members of diasporas, they might tune in to news and entertainment from lands where the hour hand is at a different point on the dial. As long-distance commuters they might need to juggle their commitments to fit in with externally regulated timetables, and as international travellers they might suffer from various forms of jet lag, but these interconnections and mobilities do not undermine their more settled preoccupations with affairs of home and family, the streets along which they walk and drive, the places of local work and consumption, and the local institutions of authority that affect their lives. In short, experience continues to be filtered through the familiarity of the local, even if it is shaped by indirect and asynchronous forces.

Although time, like space, might seem to be fixed and objective, as with place it is experienced differently depending upon people's subjective temporal orientations. How people come to comprehend and respond to the passing of historical time will depend not only upon what is happening around them, but upon how they have come to experience and feel about the world and their capacity to control relationships between past, present and future. The demise of industrial greatness for one person might be perceived by others as a welcome evolution from squalor and regimentation. The dazzling prospect of urban regeneration for one might for another feel like an assault upon a settled way of life. An economic crisis might be experienced by investors as a challenge to move swiftly to more fertile fields, while for another it heralds the repossession of their home. As news circulates, it mediates between these conflicting perceptions and interests, or fails to do so, thereby leaving some people feeling neglected or misrepresented. So, in placing our study within the context of a specific time, it is important to heed Aminzade's (1992: 469) advice that 'studies of temporality that ignore subjectivity are incomplete'. Just as there is not a singular Leeds, multiple temporal registers coexist within the city.

Following the approach of the historian Fernand Braudel (1980), we might say that Leeds in the summer of 2011 was in the midst of both a long-term and more immediate history. The *longue durée* (long-term) account tells of the transition of Leeds from being a mighty industrial conurbation to a post-industrial city in search of a clear identity. For some, this transition was a process of simple decline, whereas for others it was an opportunity for urban reinvention. For most people, though, the *longue durée* has been experienced as a confusing and ambiguous path into the unknown, transcending lives and generations, and neither erasing traces of the industrial past nor establishing contours of a certain future. In short, people find themselves in the midst of history, frequently baffled by why once-stable aspects of life have had to change and worried about where change might lead. Episodic news reports, characterized by brevity and ephemerality, add to this uncertainty, for, while everything that happens is an effect of other things that have happened before, these antecedents often remain unexplained. So, for most people who are not historians, the experience of living through an historical transition is like feeling the jolts of turbulence on a bumpy voyage, but never being quite certain where the aeroplane left from, who controls it or when or where it will land.

In the *longue durée*, Leeds in 2011 was in the midst of accommodating itself to its post-industrial condition. The prosperity of the city had been built on the wool and worsted industries, augmented in the early twentieth century by a highly profitable engineering sector. Dating the beginning of the city's industrial decline is problematic. A first phase of decline occurred from the 1950s to the early 1970s, with the loss of 37,000 manufacturing jobs in the city. However, this was to some extent compensated by growth in the business and service sector, which cushioned against significant rises in unemployment. It was between 1971 and 1981 that manufacturing in Leeds collapsed, falling by a third and leading to a marked rise in unemployment. Global market deregulation in the 1980s and 1990s added to economic instability, as several of the leading local companies were taken over by foreign investors. These included Tetley brewers by Carlsberg, the Yorkshire Bank by the National Australia Bank, and Asda by Wal-Mart; while the financial services sector grew by two-thirds. Leeds ceased to sell what it made and increasingly devoted energy to selling itself: by 1990, more people in Leeds worked in tourism than in the textile industry. By 2008, Leeds had three times more people working in the business and finance sector than in manufacturing. As in the rest of the United Kingdom, the heady rhetoric of urban regeneration and the financial boom of the early 2000s suggested that post-industrial prosperity lay in the provision of intangible services; the so-called weightless economy. There was excitement in Leeds as banks, legal and insurance companies moved there to establish their non-London bases. Reskilling to become part of a seemingly ever-expanding white-collar workforce came to be an increasingly compulsory offer for the long-term unemployed, who were urged to roll with the flow of the new economy, whether they wanted to or not. By the middle of the twenty-first century, Leeds seemed to be more successful than most other northern cities in adapting to the economic priorities espoused by all three major political parties. It was frequently cited as a city that had made a success out of post-industrial adaptation, one which made itself at home in the global marketplace.

Had we conducted our study in 2007, this mood of urban confidence would have been hard to miss. But between then and 2011 the *courte durée* (short term) got in the way. The immediate backdrop to our study was economic crisis and urban riots. The financial bubble burst. In the autumn of 2008, four British banks nearly collapsed and had to be kept afloat through costly government intervention. This, together with simultaneous collapses of the stock and housing markets, led to a massive fall in tax revenue and an unprecedented need for the government to borrow money. This economic catastrophe was not confined to Britain: its roots and effects were truly globalized, destabilizing most advanced capitalist economies, from the United States to every single state of the European Union, some of which found themselves on the brink of bankruptcy. Having to spend so much to save the banking sector from total collapse, governments were left with far less money than ever before to spend on the services that they had long been expected to provide. Massive cuts in expenditure led directly to a fractured social infrastructure, pervasive insecurity, accelerated unemployment and unmet social needs.

In the context of Leeds, these effects were exacerbated by its strong dependence upon financial services. Unemployment increased at a higher rate than in most other northern post-industrial cities at a 14 per cent increase above the levels in 2006. Fifteen thousand jobs in the financial sector alone were lost in the years between 2008 and 2011. Initially, the percentage of the Leeds workforce working in the financial sector was overtaken by those employed in public services, but once local and national governments introduced austerity budgets, entailing swingeing cuts to public services, that area of employment also contracted. Facing a £50 million cut in government grants and a £40 million rise in costs, in 2011 Leeds City Council introduced an austerity budget which involved the closure of leisure centres, day centres, hostels for the homeless and residential homes for the elderly, a 6.8 per cent increase in council house rents and service charges, and the axing of 3,000 council jobs within four years. The council leader, Keith Wakefield, described these as 'staggering and unprecedented cuts'.

By the summer of 2011, when our study was conducted, the city was in a state of shock, with rumours circulating everywhere about swingeing cuts yet to come. But the feelings of fear and vulnerability were not evenly spread. As ever, the poorest, least formally educated and least organized were the most likely not only to feel the effects of the cuts, but also to be preoccupied by anxieties about what might happen next. As Stillwell and Shepherd (2004: 128) noted in their study of social inequality in Leeds, even during the boom years:

> A substantial proportion of the local population ... remained excluded from the opportunities that economic growth and prosperity ... brought. Levels of unemployment, poverty, health, crime, educational performance and environmental quality vary widely between localities across the city, with problems being particularly acute in some inner city areas.

They go on to state that 'The affluent suburban communities in the northern suburbs contrast starkly with those parts of the inner city where social problems across several dimensions are at their worst.' Objectively, these northern suburbs and the most deprived inner-city areas shared the same clock time, but in subjective terms their experiences of the present and confidence in the future were markedly different. This became very evident when urban riots broke out across the United Kingdom in the summer of 2011. These riots provided a backdrop to our study, having dominated the news both nationally and locally in the weeks and months during which we were conducting the initial, scoping phase of our research. The riots were widely regarded as the most serious cases of urban disorder that Britain had witnessed in a century. While debate still continues regarding the relationship of these riots to poverty in general, and the post-2008 austerity cuts in particular, the fact that 58 per cent of those appearing in courts on riot-related charges lived in the 20 per cent most deprived areas of England would seem to imply that there was at the very least a strong correlation between the desperation of long-term poverty and the willingness to riot.

Unlike several nearby northern cities and towns, Leeds escaped full-scale rioting. Several commentators have suggested that this was a result of the remarkably productive collaboration between the police, youth services and local community leaders in Leeds. Despite the high-profile shooting of an Afro-Caribbean community leader in the Chapeltown area of Leeds and ensuing skirmishes between young blacks and Asians, appeals to youth to keep calm and for the police to maintain a low-level presence on the streets succeeded in averting any significant rioting in Leeds. However, as we shall see in Chapter 7, in people's minds fear of urban disorder and assumptions about its cause were far from absent, and different fears and assumptions prevailed in different parts of the city. How these perceptions of past, present and future came to be acknowledged, or not, has been a central question for our study. How do these perceptions come to be formed, mediated, shared and revised within an urban news ecology? How far does local news shape or reflect the different world-views that coexist within a city like Leeds, and how far does it contribute to a sense of common understanding?

The coexistence of past and future within the news ecology

Too often declarations of excitement about the changes precipitated by 'new media' fail to relate to the long history of communicative reconfiguration that came before. Contemporary news practices are themselves products of social evolution and transformation. Rarely in history is one form or practice simply replaced by another. Understanding a news ecology entails an archaeological appreciation of its foundations as well as a sensitivity to the symbolic significance of emerging architectures. Thinking about the common ambitions of very old and very recent news outlets might help us to become more cautious social historians and more modest observers of the shock of the future.

When the city's red-brick embodiments of industrial confidence were first erected, Leeds received its news of empire, commerce and municipality via steam presses and weekly newspapers. The process of news circulation was characteristically industrial, commercial and linear. News, like other industrial commodities, emanated from conspicuous centres, producing tangible products, targeted at a mass audience. As an industrial process, the news was assembled in large-scale, dedicated centres, operating much like other places of manufacture, along the lines of efficient, machine-assisted production, standardized quality filtering and mass distribution to a clearly targeted market. As with other industrial operations, news production was strictly driven by sale and profit, with little regard for civic or public interests of a non-commercial nature. Moreover, it was a linear process, in which the stories, messages and values of the news sender were inscribed in the product, and news receivers had little or no influence upon the editorial content. Above all, news was deeply embedded within a physical ecology of place, comprising buildings, monuments, factories and districts. The distinction between 'here' and 'there' was rarely problematic for industrial news consumers.

The *Leeds Mercury* was established in 1718, one of approximately a hundred provincial newspapers existing at the time in England. The local press in those days was an offshoot of commercial printing businesses, which also sold stationery and patent medicines. The *Leeds Mercury* had no journalists working for it. News gathering was a matter of cutting and pasting stories from the national press. Parliamentary accounts were always several days old and there was no coverage of local council meetings or municipal events. Advertising was the principal source of revenue; the *Leeds Mercury* was making a profit of around £3,000 a year by 1830, and local political organizations wanting to insert an opinion in its pages had to pay for the privilege.

The *Mercury*'s main competition came from the Tory-supporting *Leeds Intelligencer*, but the latter's circulation never grew beyond 4,000, whereas sales of the *Mercury* increased from around 750 in 1801 to 5,500 in 1833 and 10,000 in the 1840s, making it the most popular city newspaper in the country. The *Mercury*'s political and cultural outlook was summed up by its owner, Edward Baines, in an article published in 1843. He regarded the city of Leeds with undisguised economic pride, for it was 'the main source of all the foreign commerce of England', purchasing 'raw materials, luxuries, and necessaries from other countries' and 'animat[ing] the industry of every quarter of the globe, as well as enrich[ing] our own island ...'. But, as for the culture of Leeds, its people and environment, Baines could not conceal his distaste:

I admit that the manufacturing districts have a repulsive exterior. The smoke that hangs over them, – their noisy, bustling and dirty streets, – the large proportion of the working classes seen there, many of whom have their persons and clothing blackened with their occupations, – the hum and buzz of machinery in the factories, – the flaming of furnaces, – the rude earnestness of the 'unwashed artificers', – and their provincial dialect, – are little calculated to gratify 'ears polite', or to please the eye accustomed to parks and green fields.

This split between civic pride and barely concealed contempt for the population was unlikely to damage the *Mercury*'s local reputation, for its readership was largely confined to those with 'ears polite' and 'eyes accustomed to parks and green fields' rather than the 'hands' who worked for them. This view of the city as both an efficient economic enterprise and an uncouth culture, best avoided, represented a form of class-based mediation that reported the city from the minority perspective of those who owned most of it.

Not surprisingly, then, when the Chartist movement emerged in the 1830s, demanding votes for all men, the *Mercury* was wholly opposed to such a measure. This stimulated the establishment of a new Leeds-based (but nationally circulating) newspaper, set up to expound strikingly different values from those of the *Leeds Mercury*. The *Northern Star* (officially called the *Northern Star and Leeds General Advertiser*) was established in 1837 and edited by the radical Chartist Feargus O'Connor. Within two years, it was selling 30,000 copies per week, although not all of these copies were sold in Leeds. Copies of the paper tended to be shared between groups of workers and read aloud in factories and beer shops, leading O'Connor to claim that seven people on average read each copy, which pushed its real readership well into six figures. Then, as now, the news that circulated in Leeds varied greatly depending on its source. Major local news stories would appear in the *Leeds Mercury* or the *Northern Star*, but rarely in both.

By the mid-nineteenth century, the radical working-class *Northern Star* ceased to exist. The Conservative *Leeds Intelligencer* was bought by the Yorkshire Conservative Newspaper Company and became the *Yorkshire Post*. The *Leeds Mercury* continued to expound the views of the liberal mill owners, plodding on until 1923, when the *Yorkshire Post* acquired it. Ascendant for the next few decades as the only daily newspaper in the region, along with the Leeds-based *Evening Post*, produced from the same press, the *Yorkshire Post* is now a fading newspaper. In 2012, its owners fired its editor and replaced him with a financial director. As one veteran journalist on the *Post* put it:

> When I started, going back to '72, circulation of the *Evening Post* was two hundred and fifty to three thousand a night. Today it's forty thousand a night, and the *Yorkshire Post* is similar ... We used to do nine editions of the paper a day and I could book up a story at two o'clock in the afternoon and have it on the streets by five, which was how fast we used to be. Today we are an overnight newspaper ... the deadline for tomorrow with the *Yorkshire Evening Post* is six o'clock tonight and ... it will be sold at half past eight tomorrow morning.

The morning and evening local newspaper were the main daily providers of mass-circulated local news until the advent of local radio and the regional television news slots. By the 1960s, broadcasting was the emergent channel for local news, forcing the mainstream local press into a new role as commentator and, occasionally, investigator. Beyond the leading local press and broadcast providers, the *Post*, BBC and ITV, there exist a number of other channels. These ranged from community radio stations catering for minority groups and tastes, to independent producers creating local content, to neighbourhood newspapers and newsletters and city-based websites and blogs; not to mention less conspicuous communicative outlets such as graffiti, discussion circles, social media networks, mobile-phone exchanges and physical noticeboards. This then moves the discussion to a very recent addition to the architecture of the local news ecology and considers how it symbolizes a notion of publicness that builds upon, rather than displacing, the mainstream news media.

At the turn of the present century, in a bid to reinvent the city for a post-industrial era, Leeds City Council, with support from the UK

Millennium Fund, invested £12 million in the development of what is now Millennium Square, conceiving it as 'one of Europe's most innovative multi-purpose city centre spaces ... a multi-functional live event venue [that] has a standing capacity of 8,000 persons in its concert configuration'. A conspicuous feature of this new urban hub is a 26-square-metre 'Big Screen' that towers over the square with the avowed aim of reflecting the events of the world into the city as well as the city to itself. Funded jointly by Leeds City Council and the BBC, its primary ambition is to display content produced by local artists and community activists. A camera embedded within the screen serves as 'a giant mirror upon which passers-by can view themselves': to some, a way of capturing the mundane movement of and through the city, thereby immersing the media space within the lifeworld; to others, a feature of ominous surveillance. As for locally produced content, Chris Nriapa, who manages the Big Screen for the BBC, says that he has shown material by 'hundreds of local groups' who seem to be 'very interested, as it's a free to use public platform unlike no other'. On its website, the Leeds Big Screen announces an exciting vision for a new kind of urban publicness:

> As the range of public information, events, entertainment and interactive services continue to develop it is possible to envisage a world in which a public space broadcasting screen, operated in the interests of the public, becomes a standard part of the urban infrastructure. A network of screens could interact with each other, sharing content and experiences. Creating a new urban focal point, a new gathering place and a new events arena, it is already being suggested that PSB screens may have a key role to play in the regeneration of UK urban life.

It is not our intention here to investigate in any empirical detail the success of the Leeds Big Screen in realizing this impressive vision of public space. Despite its localist ambitions, the vast majority of the content shown on the Big Screen comes from the national BBC rather than autonomous, grassroots sources. Clearly, it is a one-off, developing project offering ephemeral stimulation to passers-by rather than captivating a fixed audience, connecting with other public contexts or providing a new urban focal point. Rather than explore the success or failure of the Leeds Big Screen as a site of urban regeneration, we are interested in what it represents rhetorically as a notion of publicness. Far beyond the promoters of the Big Screen, scholars, practitioners and policy-makers have been rethinking the shape and scope of the public sphere in response to what seem like transformative changes in technologies, techniques and cultures of social communication (Thompson 1995; Iveson 2007; Castells 2008; Dahlgren 2009; Coleman and Ross 2010; Williams and Delli Carpini 2011; Baym and Boyd 2012). The suggestion emerging from much of this work is that the mediation of everyday life is increasingly ubiquitous. Where once the centres of information transmission were conspicuous (newspaper offices, broadcasting studios, press conferences), the means of producing and circulating information are now widely dispersed and inexpensively accessible. While in the past public address to a nation or a city tended to be vertical (top-down), linear and monological, the scope for interactivity weakens clear boundaries between information producers and what once seemed like a natural and enduring entity: the audience. Whereas the architectural grandeur and solidity of the nineteenth-century city was experienced through a vivid consciousness of physical place, the 'liquid modernity' (Bauman 2000) of twenty-first-century social space is best understood in terms of what Castells (1989: 146) has called 'the space of flows': the mediated entanglement of propinquity and distance, spatiality and time, tangibility and virtuality, the personal and the social.

The notion of publicness that lies behind the Big Screen is but one manifestation of a new way of thinking about urban communication. Unlike the Town Hall, whose Victorian power lay in its enduring solidity and exclusive interiority, or the BBC studio, from which messages are transmitted with a view to reaching a mass, targeted population, the power of the Big Screen does not rely upon a single, static, receptive audience. It is quite clear to anyone spending more than ten minutes standing in front of the Screen on most days of the week that it draws only transient attention from people passing through the city centre. But its symbolic significance depends far less upon the 'capture' of a mass audience than upon the breadth of its connections to the thousands of tweets, blog entries, emails, mobile phone calls, text messages and broadcast 'media events' (Dayan and Katz 1992) that circulate around it. In short, the Big Screen overshadows the city, not in terms of its inherent influence, but insofar as it makes visible a network of linkages that are now the most active molecules of urban cohesion.

The news ecology of a city like Leeds might best be understood as a complex process of coordinated and accidental circulation. Much of the common knowledge that circulates in Leeds is produced and transmitted by the mainstream media with a view to reaching an audience and telling them stories about the world in which they live. This kind of news production comprises a coordinated attempt to narrate the city: to set its public agenda, distinguish stories worth telling and voices worthy of being heard from the mass of competing signals, and to retain audience trust by providing a consistency of approach to social reality. Other aspects of common knowledge are generated and communicated in a less coordinated fashion. From verbal grapevines to social media networks, word gets around; people talk about the media and act as their own media. Much of this non-mainstream circulation is accidental. It revolves around communicative practices that people have developed as ways of making sense of the ubiquity of mediation. Most studies of urban communication have focused upon either mainstream or alternative news production; either by the stories told in the name of common knowledge or by the practices engaged in by people seeking to engage with public knowledge on their own terms. This book focuses upon the ecological interdependence of these aspects of public communication.

2 | A WEEK IN NEWS

In this chapter, we present a profile of the reported news in Leeds over the course of a single week. By itself, content analysis can be a limiting technique, partitioning aspects of new stories into predetermined measures and categories, in a verifiable yet fragmentary manner. However, in keeping with our perspective on media news ecology, it is our intention to use such data as an initial resource through which to explore the stories that are told, and the stories that people tell themselves, about their local area. A content analysis across media forms and genres allows us to track the trajectory of such stories as they interweave within and recede beyond the news ecology. When this is combined with the survey data in Chapter 3 we start to build a picture of how such news is encountered, experienced or disregarded in everyday lives. Local news informs us about those events closest to us in physical and experiential terms; about which we are perhaps most likely to have our own opinion. In its routine assumption, even constitution, of a shared sense of economic woes or community anxieties, local reporting reflects back to us our immediate social world, usually recognizable in some shape or form even if it's simply the background landscape or cityscape. Although written almost a century ago, Walter Lippman's observation that we judge the credibility of a news source 'by its treatment of that part of the news in which we feel ourselves involved' speaks to the importance of considering how such news is presented: 'And by its handling of those events we most frequently decide to like it or dislike it, to trust it or refuse to have the sheet in the house' (1922: 191). In examining those stories that play a role in reaffirming our everyday realities, 'in which we feel ourselves involved', we can start to explore the variations in presentation and treatment of such realities across the Leeds news ecology.

There are, then, compelling reasons to chart the news ecology in empirical terms: What kinds of stories are covered by which local media? What is the nature of their coverage? Where do we see similarities and differences? How are cultural or community events perceived within the local news ecology? In this chapter we delve into the coverage of news from within and around the Leeds area, which we gathered during one week in 2011, from 29 August to 4 September. Our findings suggest that the perspectives of local people are well represented in the news, in the sense that 'ordinary people' are the most common type of source for quotations. But with a preponderance of crime-related stories in broadcast news, the inclusion of citizen voices does not necessarily indicate that they are holding officials to account in their frequent appearances. Our specific measure for political or campaigning stories reveals a mixed picture when it comes to reporting on initiatives designed to influence policy or service provision. Likewise, by combining our measures for 'story subjects' and 'tone of news', we are able to capture how the celebratory coverage of cultural activities and civic opportunities provides a significant counterweight to the reporting of crime and accidents. The next section provides an overview of the media monitoring undertaken and the findings from the resulting content analysis. A copy of the coding scheme can be found in Appendix 1.

News content analysis: approach and sampling

Our codebook is designed to capture the format and content of local news media. The unit of analysis is a news item: defined as a segment of news dealing with a discrete subject matter, usually following the same format. As Lewis et al. (2006) have observed, determining what counts as a separate news item is not always a straightforward matter; our coders are guided primarily by the theme rather than format. So, for example, where an outside report is followed by a studio interview regarding the same event, this would be considered the same news item. Radio news could present difficulties here, given that news bulletins might be assembled entirely out of short headline-style news-bites with no follow-up extension to the story. Coders were encouraged to make notes on any difficulties related to format or content and we held regular meetings to discuss potential discrepancies and develop coder instructions and conventions. For example, following a pilot study we added 'human interest' to the 'story topic' measure while other coding conventions became apparent only during the main coding period, but were consistently applied (e.g. war veterans coded under the 'Armed forces').

Each news item is coded for a number of measures, in some cases requiring open text-based contributions (e.g. headline/summary) and, in other cases, an appropriate variable chosen from a drop-down list, or a simple 'yes/no/not applicable' tick-box. The coding is conducted using an Access database, allowing textual as well as numerical data to be stored, and the querying of such data in cross-tabulated results and keyword searches. In this way, we coded for elements related to both news format (for instance, whether an item was 'news-in-brief', whether it appeared on the front page, or whether it included direct quotations from sources), as well as the thematic concerns and treatment (story topic, type of actors quoted, whether the story was 'celebratory' in style). Questions of style and substance overlap, of course, with the opportunity for a more explanatory or analytical reporting style and the use of outside sources for quotes requiring sufficient time or space in the available 'news hole'. Our measures are designed to capture a holistic sense of the news as it is presented across a range of local media outlets, while also allowing us to focus our attention on particular stories of interest.

As a discrete set of results, the data represent relatively sturdy foundations upon which we can build a more nuanced and interpretative appreciation of the news values and thematic concerns of local news. Few studies have attempted to capture patterns of local news coverage across television, radio, print and web-based media in such a manner, although the Pew Project for Excellence in Journalism's (PEJ's) study of the 'news ecosystem' of Baltimore offers a similar cross-media approach (2010). Anderson (2010) offers an ethnographic news diffusion study of Philadelphia's local news ecosystem; in his case following how one particular news story of activists' arrests, dubbed the 'Francisville Four', 'emerged, exploded, and then quickly faded away' over one week in June 2008 (ibid.: 290). With only one week of news captured, albeit covering a range of media forms, it is not our intention to overplay the broader significance of our results, but we do contend that this initial mapping of news stories offers a rich and broad basis from which to start our exploration of the Leeds news ecology.

For broadcast media, we included news bulletins from two mainstream television channels (*Look North* on BBC1 and *Calendar* on ITV1), and two local radio stations (BBC Radio Leeds and local independent provider Radio Aire, now part of Bauer Radio's network of local radio stations). On television, the local news slot follows the national and international news bulletin at regular intervals throughout the day: our sample includes news items from the lunchtime, teatime and late evening bulletins. For radio we coded the 10 a.m. news headlines and a comparable later evening slot, where stories often receive extended attention. This allowed us to track which stories are repeated throughout the day, in addition to those items receiving coverage across news outlets. With an average of sixteen pages devoted to news each day (i.e. excluding classifieds, sports news, business, letters page), the *Yorkshire Evening Post* (YEP) served as our local daily press example, supplemented by four weekly newspapers (*Morley Observer and Advertiser*, *Weekly News Leeds*, *Wharfedale Observer*, *Wharfe Valley Times* (owned by Johnston Press, who also own YEP)) and a hyperlocal newsletter produced every four months (*Kirkstall Matters*). Additionally, our sample included a number of popular local blogs, (*southleeds*, *holtparktoday*, *culturevulture*, *beyondgdnleeds*, *blottr Leeds*, *theleedscitizen*, *northleedsnews*); see Chapter 6 for more details on the 'hyperlocal' media providers in Leeds. We initially collected blog posts over a longer period (with an additional week-long period either side of our 'core' week), owing to the irregularity and infrequency of posting in a number of the blogs. This list represents our 'core sample' of media materials: conducting a content analysis on the preceding outlets allowed us to gain a picture of the spread of news stories during our selected week, but we did not necessarily restrict our study to this primary sample, because we recognized the diversity and changeability of the news ecology. For example, we also recorded phone-in shows and 'drive-time' on the radio stations – spaces where stories can gain new life and prompt variations in communicative expression and conversation. Likewise, blogs often operate as both discrete, chronologically organized spaces for authored opinion and as a fragment of a wider conversation within the hyperlinked space of the worldwide web.

We applied a range of measures to each news item, as outlined above, and in more detail in Appendix 1. The next section presents aggregate figures based on these measures and variables. Our research design enables comparison across media forms and genres while recognizing the different affordances and constraints of each type. For this reason, we present both actual numbers and percentages in our tables. The figures for a single week of news might not warrant extended statistical analysis, but they do reveal points for comparison and further examination.

Broadcast media content analysis: 'And now for the news where you are'

We start with the most consulted locally based news source after national providers: broadcast media. So what are the notable features we can record through comparison of local news bulletins? Our first measure concerned the extent to which the news focused on local, national or international events. As noted, our broadcast sample allows us to compare the local BBC news with the equivalent main independent provider. Table 2.1 shows the results for television:

For television, the majority of stories have a regional focus – this is not surprising given that both *Calendar* and *Look North* cover a larger region than the Leeds city area. Both are broadcast from Leeds

TABLE 2.1 Geographic focus for television items

Geographic location (number of stories and as a percentage of all stories for each outlet)	Television	
	BBC *Look North*	ITV *Calendar*
Hyperlocal (within Leeds wards)	20	10
	20.4%	16.9%
Leeds city	4	2
	4.1%	3.4%
Regional (Yorkshire)	65	31
	66.3%	52.5%
National	7	14
	7.1%	23.7%
International	1	1
	1.0%	1.7%
N/A/Not sure	1	1
	1.0%	1.7%
Total	98	59
	99.9%	99.9%

but with supporting news rooms in York, Sheffield and Bradford for *Look North* and Sheffield, Hull and Lincoln for *Calendar*. In many cases, stories coded as 'regional' were those concerned with cities other than Leeds; for example, Doncaster's mayor announcing the he will 'wage war' on antisocial behaviour (BBC *Look North*, 30 August), or the UK School Games opening in Sheffield (both channels, 1 September). Other items reported the regional impact of new policies; for example, the news that pregnant women in Yorkshire would no longer have the choice of a Caesarean section for non-medical reasons. On both channels, at the moment when the national broadcast switches to its regional newsrooms, the section of local news is introduced with the phrase 'And now for the news *where you are*', or 'the news *where you are* follows the national weather'. The audience is addressed directly and identified as part of a community at a regional level. As our survey suggests, *local* news, rather than national or international, is valued for its relevance 'to me' and for being 'easier to understand'.

The preference for hyperlocal through to regional news focus is clear for both television bulletins: 91 per cent of items for *Look North* and 73 per cent for *Calendar*. The fact that they are scheduled to follow the main national news bulletins means, of course, that they are not required to include nationally and internationally focused items, and would risk unnecessary repetition in doing so. If we likewise consider hyperlocal, city and regional news together for radio, such items comprise 55 per cent of Radio Leeds' output; compared to only 38 per cent for Radio Aire (see Table 2.2). The propensity to report on national and international stories to such a degree makes Radio Aire an exception in our study of mainstream local broadcast media, and its lack of *regionally* focused items is in stark contrast to Radio Leeds (12.7 per cent for the former compared to 34.7 per cent for the latter). In numerical terms this represents forty-one stories for Radio Leeds, as opposed to only seven for Radio Aire. The stories in this 'regional' category are thematically similar, even if not reporting the exact same events. For example, reports from the law courts – a judge ordering three members of a Yorkshire car gang to pay back a total of £120,000 (Radio Aire, 1 September), or a twenty-four-year-old man appearing in court charged with murder (Radio Leeds, 3 September) – in addition to budget cuts, cultural events and accidents.

TABLE 2.2 Geographic focus for radio news items

Geographic location (number of stories and as a percentage of all stories for each outlet)	Radio	
	BBC Radio Leeds	Radio Aire
Hyperlocal (within Leeds wards)	8	12
	6.8%	21.8%
Leeds city	16	2
	13.6%	3.6%
Regional (Yorkshire)	41	7
	34.7%	12.7%
National	37	21
	31.4%	38.2%
International	15	12
	12.7%	21.8%
N/A/Not sure	1	1
	0.8%	1.8%
Total	118	55
	100.0%	99.9%

In the case of Radio Aire, then, three international stories received coverage: the war in Libya, including speculation on the health of the so-called 'Lockerbie bomber'; air flight disruption in New York due to Hurricane Irene; and R&B singer Beyoncé's pregnancy announcement at the MTV music awards. Developments in Libya also formed the main international story for Radio Leeds, whereas the television broadcasts had only one item each in this category, for reasons mentioned above. In fact, on 29 August, the failing health of the 'Lockerbie bomber', Abdelbaset al-Megrahi, formed the lead news item for both radio stations, prompted by CNN footage showing him to be 'at death's door', and with a local academic from Huddersfield University providing expert commentary in an interview for Radio Leeds. The point here is that the news mix or 'recipe' is not always predictable. In this case, we have a *leading* news item for both stations based on footage from a distant war-torn country, involving a controversial figure who had spent many years in prison in Scotland and was given renewed newsworthiness owing to footage from a US television channel, along with a local expert brought in to comment on the issue. In this way, the intersecting dynamics between 'international', 'national' and 'local' elements in the news are not always clear cut, predictable or easily distinguishable.

In the cases where international events made a rare appearance on BBC television news, it was due to a local angle, such as the Sheffield-based hepathlete Jessica Ennis failing to win gold at the World Championships. For radio, national stories often remained just that: nationally focused in the reporting of, say, new statistical figures for property ownership, convictions for child sex abuse offences, or the final repatriation ceremonies at Wootton Bassett. For our television news bulletins, the reporting of such events would generally include a regional angle – for example, the funeral of an RAF Red Arrow pilot taking place in his home village of Morcott in Rutland, or Yorkshire schools involved in a national fitness campaign in the run-up to the Olympics. ITV's *Calendar* also included stories with a less obvious local position, such as a ceremony being held for the families of fourteen military servicemen who had died in 2006 when their Nimrod plane crashed in Afghanistan, or the announcement of lay-offs for armed forces personnel. Offering no apparent local angle, what these examples do possibly reveal is a particular interest in military-related stories.

Reporting the local: celebrating culture and recording crime

Focusing now on the hyperlocal and Leeds-based news items, we are able to cross-tabulate these results with our measure for noting 'celebratory' coverage or, alternatively, that which focuses on 'disorder' or crime. To expand a little further on our celebratory and disorder stories, we present our instructions for coders (see Table 2.3).

While fewer in number compared to regional news overall, proportionally speaking, local stories were *more likely* to be coded for a celebratory or disorder character in tone across our broadcast media outlets: ranging from celebratory cultural events to crime and accident-related news. Considering those stories placed within the city space, there is a noticeable tendency to include both the positive-active and the negative-passive: from reporting what people

TABLE 2.3 Good/bad news

This is recorded on a three-point option bar – only one option can be selected

(a) Celebratory	(b) Neither celebratory or disorder	(c) Disorder
Celebratory of Yorkshire/ Leeds: its character(s), heroes/ achievers, scenery, reasons for local pride/products, charity achievements, cultural events, positive nostalgia, people/ places overcoming obstacles/ disadvantage. Coders should bear in mind this is not simply 'good news' but celebratory in nature.	If the item is neither explicitly celebratory nor focusing on disorder issues. This is likely to be the default option for descriptive news reporting.	Crime and corruption, rape, fires, accidents, bad weather (e.g. floods or drought), drunkenness and disorder in town, environmental degradation.

are *doing now* (cultural events), to the terrible things that have *happened to* people (crime and accidents). Here there are notable differences between news providers: for Radio Aire, eight out of fourteen city-based stories were coded for 'disorder' (57 per cent) with only one celebratory story; whereas Radio Leeds balanced six positive stories (25 per cent) with five negative (21 per cent), out of a total of twenty-four. Although these are admittedly small numbers, this would indicate a markedly dissimilar approach to the selection and treatment of those news stories closest to home for Leeds-based citizens.

There is a similar but less pronounced pattern in television news: BBC *Look North* balances nine celebratory news stories (37.5 per cent) against seven 'bad news' stories (29.2 per cent) out of total twenty-four, while all twelve of ITV *Calendar*'s local stories have a celebratory or disorder tone – four positive (33.3 per cent) and eight negative (66.7 per cent). It would appear that BBC broadcast news (TV and radio) is not only more likely to focus on positive local events, but also to report them in a celebratory manner. This finding is supported by our 'story topic' measure discussed later, where crime stories attract most coverage across all broadcast media, but the mix with other themes and stories can differ, as we will show. It is only at the regional level that the pattern for BBC news becomes similar to that of its independent rivals. So what do these figures start to reveal?

Turning to celebratory stories first, we can chart a number of events throughout the week: the 'Oldest West Indian Carnival in Europe', in its forty-fourth year, taking place on 29 August in Chapeltown and Harehills; and the end of the annual Leeds Music Festival, which had also notably passed with very little trouble. Other cultural highlights include an allotments showcase, a ballet show and a 'traditional rush bearing' festival, demonstrating a range of interests in culture and crafts. Local news providers also allocate airtime to publicize their own achievements; for Radio Aire, this is a celebration of its own birthday, and for BBC *Look North* a story on how their programme helped raise money for charity with the successful sell-off of leftover camping equipment from the Leeds Music Festival. In these stories, the radio station and television programme both promote their own integral role within the local community. Indeed, Radio Aire celebrates its significance as a local media outlet by reporting that it is the 'top trending topic' in Leeds on Twitter, with named personalities also celebrating its birthday (1 September).

At the other end of the spectrum ('disorder'), the week starts with the news of a stabbing in Leeds, and the eventual arrest of a local man for murder. On the Wednesday, the bodies of two young people were found at the bottom of a block of flats, sparking an investigation into the circumstances of their deaths. By the Thursday, another murder inquiry was launched after the body of a man was found with brutal head injuries. Each of the stories prompted calls for information, tributes from family or neighbours, and updates on the investigations throughout the week. Such stories invoke shock and horror at violent deaths and unexplained events within the city ward districts. Outside of Leeds, at a regional level, other accidents add to coverage of this nature: a woman loses her leg after an accident at a funfair, a boy dies after falling into a canal, and young man is killed in a motorbike accident. Indeed, accidents accounted for most of our stories coded as 'other' under our 'story topic' measure, their distressing regularity a factor we had not been fully prepared for in the development of our categories. The additional presentation of voices from those immediately affected or simply stunned by events offers an emotional bridge to the 'overhearing audience' of broadcast news (Heritage 1985; Scannell 1991).

It appears that the above-detailed stories provide the stock substance of local news, which is geographically close and emotionally resonant. The ratio of Leeds-based 'bad' to 'good' news on Radio Aire is 8:1, and on *Calendar* 8:4, while BBC news bulletins tend to balance 'bad' with 'good' with a 5:6 ratio for Radio Leeds and 7:9 for *Look North*. Again, we stress these are small numbers, but they offer comparable data during this same week of news selection, for broadcasters who are making decisions on news items often lasting only thirty seconds or a minute. With such tight time constraints, the orientation of each short item quickly adds to an emerging picture of priorities and concerns.

Prominence of 'story topics'

Our 'story topic' and 'actors quoted and cited' measures provide further elucidation on the kind of news encountered. Each news item was coded for a 'prominent story topic': the main theme for the story, selected from a selection of twenty variables. Where coders felt that the sense of the story would be better represented with a secondary subject code, they also coded for a 'subsidiary story topic'. For television, around half (53.5 per cent) did not require a secondary subject code; for radio it was 58.4 per cent (and for press the average was around 44 per cent, but with greater discrepancies between news titles). We present figures for the 'prominent story subject' as our main findings; however, we will also comment on whether the inclusion of subsidiary subject topics, which were applied to around half the news items as shown above, greatly alters the sense of story subject dominance or diversity.

Presented in order of overall occurrence, we can see that, for television, news items relating to crime or legal processes were predominant for both the BBC and ITV (see Figure 2.1). The general patterns of coverage are roughly similar, but we can point to a number of differences. As noted earlier, the 'other' category largely represented reports of accidents, such as the drowned boy mentioned above, various car accidents and an Oxfam warehouse burning down. Such stories were more frequent on *Calendar* (20.3 per cent as opposed to 11.2 per cent), whereas BBC's *Look North* gave more attention to cultural events (17.3 per cent compared to 6.8 per cent). It is notable that 'human interest' stories are also much more likely to appear on ITV (13.6 per cent to the BBC's 2.0 per cent),

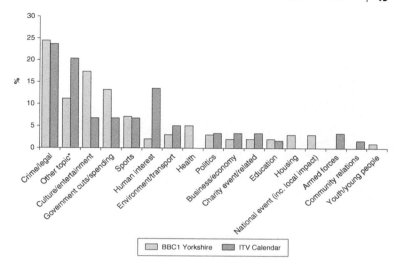

2.1 Television: prominent story topic (as a percentage of all stories)

Note: * 'Other topic' mostly refers to accidents, with one celebratory story, and one interview with the Duke of Devonshire. No stories coded for: 'Scandal'; 'International event'; 'Welfare'; 'N/A/Not sure'.

whereas the BBC has a higher proportion of coverage of government spending or cuts (13.3 per cent to 6.8 per cent). Housing and health issues appear on the BBC, while ITV includes news stories related to the armed forces, a feature noted above.

Adding subsidiary story topics into the mix only appears to reinforce the trends noted above. Crime still dominates for both channels, with the BBC balancing such coverage with cultural stories and ITV favouring accidents (coded under 'Other'). The BBC's focus on 'Government spending/Cuts' becomes even more pronounced as a disparity between the two broadcasters.

Radio coverage mirrors some of these patterns, with crime stories leading the way when we consider 'prominent story topics' only. Here the disparity in cultural coverage is not so apparent between the stations (see Figure 2.2). Differences in story topic are much more marginal, with the BBC still favouring 'Government cuts/Spending' and the independent Radio Aire showing more interest in the 'Armed forces'. However, 'hard news' issues such as health, education and housing are covered by both stations, albeit relatively rarely.

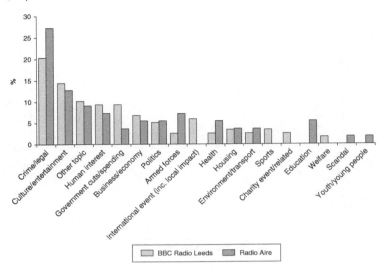

2.2 Radio: prominent story topic (as a percentage of all stories)

Note: No stories coded for 'National event' or 'Community relations'.

Including 'subsidiary story topics' in the mix for radio does not greatly alter the impression already presented. Certain trends are re-emphasized; the coverage of armed forces on Radio Aire, and economic and housing coverage is further emphasized in BBC coverage. One notable absence is 'International events' for Radio Aire, which is surprising given the 'Lockerbie bomber' story mentioned above. This reflects the different treatment the story garnered on Radio Aire, where this was coded as a 'human interest' story. Rather than quoting politicians or focusing on the war, the report noted how al-Megrahi was slipping in and out of a coma.

It appears, then, that crime, accidents and cultural events form the majority of stories that dominate local news coverage. Such a news agenda favours the topics generally considered to be 'tabloid' in nature (e.g. see Barnett et al. 2012), although the broadcast news bulletins appear to be resisting the all-out promotional copy that is common in local newspapers (as noted in the 'story type' results). It might be overstating it to say that the results indicate a tendency towards trivia or sensationalism, but these findings do raise the question of whether broadcast local news is providing adequate coverage of political and economic information pertinent to Leeds citizens. The recorded story topics also start to reveal different types of treatment from news providers towards similar or identical local and national events: the favouring of a human-interest angle (Radio Aire), or the economic and social consequences from government and local council spending decisions (Radio Leeds). Our results indicate that the BBC news, across television and radio, is more likely than that of its competitors to report on the consequences of economic policies, while also balancing its celebratory coverage of cultural events with the 'bad news' of crime and accidents.

Who gets to speak?

What do the different approaches to sources or 'voices' add to this recipe? Next we turn to the types of actors who appear as quoted sources within the news, whether representing themselves as a 'person from the street' or as someone with a publicly defined role, such as a representative of an institution or cause. The right to speak, give an opinion or even help define events in news stories is often studied as a key journalistic practice within wider debates on news production and power relationships (Tuchman 1978; Schlesinger 1990; Couldry 2010). To be given 'voice' in the news space is usually considered a 'good thing', and it is the access granted to an audience indicating a valuable, credible or useful point of view. Past research has tended to emphasize the preponderance of elite sources in news, a hierarchy of political and business actors in which the humble member of the public generally comes low down on the list (Gans 1979; Bennett 1990). Such studies sometimes have a particular type of coverage in mind (elections, live events, war) and do not tend to favour local news reporting, although there are notable exceptions (see Ross 2006). It is intriguing, then, that our study indicates a high proportion of news space allocated to the 'ordinary person' (see Table 2.4).

Our results for 'Actors quoted' indicate that *Calendar* is more likely to have no direct quotations from sources (44.1 per cent of stories), compared to *Look North* (32.7 per cent). Where they do appear, both channels rely on 'ordinary people' more than any other type; however, this could arguably cover a wider range of speaker types than other categories, not only street-based 'vox pops' but also family members or neighbours in the frequent crime-related stories. Each 'actor type' is counted only once per news item – that is, no repeated occurrences within a news item. In other words, we code

TABLE 2.4 Television: number/proportion of news items including direct quotations from each actor type

Media outlet/actors quoted	BBC Look North		ITV Calendar	
Not applicable/no quotes	32	32.7%	26	44.1%
Ordinary people: adults	29	29.6%	26	44.1%
Reps of other causes	11	11.2%	5	8.5%
Experts/academics	13	13.3%	2	3.4%
Private sector/business	11	11.2%	3	5.1%
Council workers/public officials	7	7.1%	3	5.1%
Community representatives	6	6.1%	3	5.1%
Politicians/elected councillors	6	6.1%	3	5.1%
Ordinary people: youth	5	5.1%	3	5.1%
Police	4	4.1%	3	5.1%
Trade unions/federations	5	5.1%	2	3.4%
Celebrity	3	3.1%	3	5.1%
Other	4	4.1%	2	3.4%
Public sector (medics, teachers)	1	1.0%	4	6.8%
Media workers	0	0.0%	0	0.0%
Total no. of source types	137		88	
Total no. of news items	98	100.0%	59	100.0%

for the *presence* of a certain type of actor for each news item, rather than the frequency or length of time given to multiple speakers of the same type. While *Calendar* is particularly reliant on contributions from 'ordinary people' (present in 44.1 per cent of news items, compared to 29.6 per cent for *Look North*), other notable differences are found in appearances by experts or academics – these are much more likely on BBC1 news (13.3 per cent against 3.4 per cent). When it comes to types of actors who are only cited (but not quoted directly in the same item), the numbers are relatively low: 74.5 per cent of *Look North* and 81.4 per cent of *Calendar* items have no additional cited sources. For the BBC, police spokespeople gain the highest number for this kind of reference (10.2 per cent) followed by public sector workers (6.1 per cent), while for *Calendar* it is business-related or private sector speakers (5.1 per cent). The private/public sector contributions merely rebalance the figures above for direct quotations, meaning that, taken together, a similar pattern emerges for those sources given access to speak on both channels.

Local radio news bulletins similarly rely on members of the public to speak on issues (see Table 2.5). For the commercial station Radio Aire, 60.0 per cent of their news items include no other voices apart from their own radio presenters and reporters, with 'ordinary people' given access in 16.4 per cent of news items. Radio Leeds also has numerous items with no outside speakers (42.4 per cent), with 'ordinary people' as the most likely contributors again (30.5 per cent). Unlike with Radio Aire, we do at least see a wide range of different types of sources drawn upon in the BBC reporting. For

TABLE 2.5 Radio: number/proportion of news items including direct quotations from each actor type

Media outlet/actors quoted	Radio Leeds		Radio Aire	
Not applicable/no quotes	50	42.4%	33	60.0%
Ordinary people: adults	36	30.5%	9	16.4%
Politicians/elected councillors	12	10.2%	4	7.3%
Reps of other causes	10	8.5%	2	3.6%
Experts/academics	7	5.9%	3	5.5%
Private sector/business	8	6.8%	2	3.6%
Council workers/public officials	5	4.2%	0	0.0%
Community representatives	3	2.5%	0	0.0%
Media workers	3	2.5%	0	0.0%
Ordinary people: youth	3	2.5%	0	0.0%
Other	3	2.5%	0	0.0%
Public sector (medics, teachers)	2	1.7%	1	1.8%
Police	2	1.7%	0	0.0%
Celebrity	0	0.0%	1	1.8%
Total no. of source types	144		55	
Total no. of news items	118	100%	55	100%

both stations, political actors (politicians and councillors) achieve a relatively high proportion of access (10.2 per cent for Radio Leeds; 7.3 per cent for Radio Aire). We should also note at this point the recurrence of invitations for viewers and listeners to text-message or email, or to comment via Twitter or Facebook, across our broadcast media. Tweets and Facebook comments are then integrated into the news items, whether pertaining to the announced Ministry of Defence cuts or the breakdown of the East Coast train.

For radio, there are few noteworthy findings to add from looking at citations rather than direct quotations, with no actor type cited in more than 6 per cent of news items. As with BBC television, police representatives are cited (but not necessarily directly quoted) on both radio stations and contributions are likely to relate to crime stories, but also to stories more directly involving the police as the focus (e.g. cuts to pay and pensions).

Overall, the figures for broadcast media appear to challenge the traditional notion that the voices of 'unknowns' are generally absent from news coverage. This is also being challenged in other surveys. In her study of Canadian television news coverage during a 2001 provincial election, Kathleen A. Cross (2010) noted unknown 'individuals' appearing almost as frequently as political leaders, suggesting a significant profile. In addition to an appeal to voter populism, Cross suggests the lack of expense and ease of access to such people could start to explain this finding: often it 'requires only that the reporter walk out onto a street or into a restaurant to mingle with the public' (ibid.: 419). However, once Cross analysed the length of quotations, the average soundbite was around six seconds as opposed to eleven seconds for elites, suggesting that 'they are, in fact, used as populace "fillers" of an already constructed news story' (ibid.: 424), rather than part of the debate. Election news has quite specific functions and its own formulas, of course, and the predominance of the 'ordinary person' is notable in our results as it relates to a variety of news stories, although admittedly we do not measure length of quotations. The ease of access and low cost for reporters are certainly credible factors in explaining their attraction to such sources, but it could also be a marker for what has been termed the 'demotic turn' across media genres and content, with increased visibility for 'ordinary people', signalling a wider shift in mediated discourse. It has also been noted that politicians appear to be citing the 'man of the street' rather than experts and statistical figures in their own speeches, in an effort to connect with voters through anecdote and folksy accounts, which act as a form of 'argumentative proof' through the elevation of 'everyday' experiences (Atkins and Finlayson 2013). Whether the noted shifts indicate a truly democratizing, pluralistic or creative turn in (local) news production, or in the public–media–politician power dynamics, would require further research beyond the present study; although this preference for 'real people' is also emphasized in our interviews with editorial news staff (see Chapter 6).

Reporting the political

As mentioned above, and related to the democratic functions of local media, we are particularly interested in the reporting of political stories – here categorized as those stories featuring a political representatives (MPs, councillors, parties) or political activities. We also included reports on government spending or cuts as politically themed, so that any story with a 'Politics' or 'Government spending/ Cuts' code (prominent or subsidiary) prompted the coder to record the nature of the political story. As noted above in 'story topics', we found that the BBC broadcasts were more likely to include stories of such a nature, especially in reporting of government cuts. Within this smaller corpus of politically themed stories, we can note the type of political activity reported. In Table 2.6, percentages represent the share within the smaller number of political stories only.

This measure is designed to capture the reported nature of grievances, claims-making on behalf of public officials and representatives, or other political controversies. We can note that stories dealing with these kinds of issues in which grievances, policy changes and consultations are expressly mentioned are relatively uncommon in local news, albeit more likely to be covered on BBC outlets: with twenty-five such stories (25.5 per cent) on television and twenty on radio (16.9 per cent); *Calendar* and Radio Aire presented eight each with 13.6 and 14.5 per cent of the total news stories, respectively. The story dominating the week, in political terms at least, was the announcement on 30 August of care home closures by Leeds City Council (discussed further in Chapter 8). We garnered most items on this announcement from Radio Leeds, usually covered as a 'Report of problems in service provision'. However, even this story was reported through various lenses, affecting the kind of

TABLE 2.6 Television and radio: political story type

Type of political story	Television		Radio	
	BBC Look North	ITV Calendar	Radio Leeds	Radio Aire
Ordinary person with grievance/demand/issue	6	0	1	1
	24.0%	0.0%	5.0%	12.5%
Campaigner with grievance/demand/issue	5	4	1	3
	20.0%	50.0%	5.0%	37.5%
Report of improved development in service provision	6	0	0	0
	24.0%	0.0%	0.0%	0.0%
Report of problems in service provision	0	1	6	0
	0.0%	12.5%	30.0%	0.0%
Policy considered/ consultation by political authority	3	1	5	0
	12.0%	12.5%	25.0%	0.0%
Confrontations of reporters and political decision-makers	0	0	0	0
	0.0%	0.0%	0.0%	0.0%
Other debates/controversy	5	2	7	4
	20.0%	2%	35.0%	50.0%
Total of political stories only	25	8	20	8
	100%	100%	100%	100%

political story it became throughout the few days of coverage. For example, it was reported that originally six care homes had been earmarked for closure, so that the final announcement that only *three* would close was framed as a 'reprieve' in some reports. Likewise, one item emphasized that the running of a care home in Leeds 'may be handed to the people who use it', emphasizing a sense of an empowered local community rather than cuts in funding. A number of reports focused on the 'human cost' and the reactions of individuals affected, while others heard from campaigners, who were said to 'welcome' the report (although this could be welcoming the *fact* of its publication rather than its message). Other political items reported redundancies in civilian police staff and armed forces, closures of fire stations and a school in Doncaster, and protests against NHS reforms. On a human-interest level, and again featuring the armed forces, *Look North* reported on the mother of an injured Doncaster soldier who was told she would receive only half the compensation she had expected from the Ministry of Defence (4 September, BBC *Look North*). Perhaps not surprisingly, given the greater tendency to report on such politically themed stories, the BBC's news bulletins, and particularly television news, were more likely to feature reporter analysis, or explanation from another source, in their reports of this nature. Given the conflict-driven tendency of news more generally, the overriding impression is that politically themed grievances remain relatively low down on the local broadcast news agenda.

The results detailed so far have covered only mainstream broadcast media, and not all of the measures have yet been reported. The database allows for near-endless possibilities for the collation and display of the data, while interrogation of certain themes or treatments and cross-tabulations can produce further results. We do not have space here to report on each and every measure for our entire local media sample, but we felt that the most consulted media for local news – television and radio – warranted this more detailed reporting of results. In turning to the local and hyperlocal press, we take a more selective approach and start to make cross-media references, thus returning to a number of the news stories mentioned briefly above.

Local print media analysis: 'At the heart of Leeds'

How, then, do local print media differ in their reporting of news? Our sample includes one daily Leeds-based newspaper, the *Yorkshire Evening Post*, supported by four weekly titles (*Morley Observer and Advertiser*, *Weekly News Leeds*, *Wharfedale Observer*, *Wharfe Valley Times*) and a newsletter produced by volunteers (*Kirkstall Matters*). Contrasting with its sister publication, the *Yorkshire Post* which promotes itself as 'Yorkshire's National Newspaper', the *Yorkshire Evening Post* (YEP) with its tagline 'At the heart of Leeds: your city your paper', focuses on local news and is therefore considered the most appropriate title for our study. It is worth noting that two of the weeklies, *Wharfe Valley Times* and *Weekly News Leeds*, are free-sheets, while the *Wharfedale Observer* and *Morley Observer and Advertiser* have cover prices of 75p and 50p respectively (at the time of the study). The *Wharfe Valley Times* and *Morley Observer and Advertiser* are both owned by the same company as YEP, the Scottish company Johnston Publishing Ltd. We noted a number of stories appearing in both *Wharfe Valley Times* and YEP in near, if not entirely, identical form (e.g. 'Irene's salute to heroes'). This could be a long-standing practice or possibly a sign of cutbacks in local media due to increased economic pressures. We also note that our daily paper (YEP) is not entirely comparable (in format or frequency) with other print media in our sample, especially given the one-week study period, hence we do not necessarily present all findings together here, but we can note thematic or formal patterns of diversity and similarity.

Representing a sense of local community

In this section, we begin from what we might call the peripheral and our most infrequently produced and hyperlocal example and work towards the mainstream in our discussion. The hyperlocal nature suggested by the title *Kirkstall Matters* is affirmed in the coding of its content. (See Radcliffe 2012 for a definition of hyperlocal media.) Like most current media titles, *Kirkstall Matters* has a presence both online and offline, with more regular updates on its website than its four-monthly publication can accommodate. Produced by volunteers from the Kirkstall Valley Community Association and delivered to members in paper copy, each issue is also available to download. However, unlike many online hyperlocal ventures, *Kirkstall Matters* retained its print primacy in 2011; its content is readable and downloadable as a PDF-style document, but not necessarily formatted as searchable web content. An active blog attached to the publication serves as the home page for its online manifestation (with a Twitter stream and links), but this remained supplementary to, and as a commentary on, the writing undertaken for each issue of *Kirkstall Matters*. By February 2012, six months after our study period, the imperatives of continuing to produce a print version were reassessed by volunteers, in light of the benefits offered by digital communication technologies:

> We sometimes find that with KIRKSTALL MATTERS only being produced every 4 months it can sometimes be too late to react to an issue or article raised within it. Our most successful attempts at raising volunteer interest has [sic] been gained

through electronic communication. By publishing local news, events, opportunities to get involved and articles to our website, everyone in our community can become a contributor, everyone can respond to what others say and everyone can become part of making Kirkstall a more active community.

Of course, not all our members have the internet, and we will need to look at how we can continue to engage with those that do not. However, for the majority this will be a more informative, timely and interactive way of communicating and the effort involved would be spread evenly throughout the year. (Dawson 2012)

This being a community-produced magazine, it is expressly shaped to represent local interests and encourage participation, and is sensitive to possible exclusion of some members in its shift towards online communication. Timeliness and success in 'raising volunteer interest' pull the volunteers towards digital communications, while retaining awareness of the possible exclusion of existing members without internet access. The community association newsletter can thus become more responsive to *current* local news, still focused on its hyperlocal community, but looking and feeling more like other local news sources in its online manifestation. However, as seen in the quotation above, its deliberation about its own place and role within the local community is overt and expressed as part of a dialogue with readers.

It is not surprising, given the above, that the vast majority of *Kirkstall Matters'* stories are coded as 'hyperlocal' in geographical focus (89.2 per cent). In contrast to the local broadcast news, its articles stay away from reporting crime or accidents, and instead favour cultural events, gardens, school or church events, competitions and local business concerns. In the summer 2011 issue (107), *Kirkstall Matters* includes a story on the proposals to build a new Tesco store in Kirkstall. The Kirkstall website archive reveals that this is a local issue they have covered regularly over the past two years. We note this here because this *type* of story appears more than once in our sample – it is not the proposed store in Kirkstall which is reported elsewhere, but similar stories of local concern appear around the same period.

During this period proposals for new Tesco stores can be considered emblematic of local campaigning news stories. 'Beyond

Guardian Leeds' (*beyondgdnleeds*), a curatorial blog collating stories from various media sources, reported on the approval of a proposed Tesco store in Harrogate; apparently the only mainland UK postcode ('HG') without a full-sized Tesco at the time (according to hyperlinked 'The Northerner Blog' on the *Guardian* website, 7 September). 'Theleedscitizen' and 'southleeds' blogs report on a proposed Tesco in Beeston, in Leeds, on 1 and 2 September. The Beeston and Kirkstall Tesco proposals do not appear to merit attention in our other local media: however, the Harrogate store attracts attention on BBC *Look North* on 31 August, and again on 5 September; its more newsworthy status guaranteed by its 'last-town-standing' significance and the area's upmarket retail reputation. Although falling just outside our core sample period, the 5 September *Look North* report, in particular, is indicative of this recurrent form of local story, one that is repeated throughout the UK during this time. The different voices heard in support of and in opposition to the approved Tesco store (councillors, business interests, campaigners, local residents) offer a configuration of interests and issues with symbolic resonances. A sense of the community, and who has a right to represent that community and its various interests and concerns (job creation, urban aesthetics, survival of small shops against 'giant retailers', impacts on traffic levels), are at the heart of such debates.

Similarly to *Kirkstall Matters*, our copies of the weekly newspapers indicated an emphasis on 'hyperlocal' stories, or at least news items, which reported on events affecting an area within Leeds, rather than promoted as a Leeds-wide or regional news event. Only the *Wharfedale Observer* bucks this trend (see Table 2.7). The news stories tend to be short descriptive pieces, or promotional items, previewing a local cultural event (bridge clubs, society meetings, work by local artists, walks, baking competitions, charity events), or alternatively local crime. In terms of 'story topic', then, the focus is generally on culture and entertainment, charity events and human-interest stories. For most titles, our numbers are too small to discuss in detail, although we do recognize a number of stories already mentioned, and which could be deemed more controversial in nature, such as the closure of fire stations and the petitioning of a local MP on NHS reforms (both – perhaps not surprisingly – in the *Wharfedale Observer*, 1 September).

TABLE 2.7 Print media: number of news items by geographic focus

Geographic location	Kirkstall Matters	Wharfedale Observer	Wharfe Valley Times	Weekly News Leeds	Morley Observer	YEP
Hyperlocal (within Leeds wards)	33	40	9	7	20	153
Leeds city	0	0	0	6	2	44
Regional (Yorkshire)	2	62	0	2	4	114
National	1	2	1	1	1	49
International	1	1	0	0	0	12
N/A/Not sure	0	0	0	0	2	13
Total number of news items	37	105	10	16	29	385

It is only really the *Yorkshire Evening Post* (YEP) that offers an equivalent to our mainstream broadcast news, given its daily publication, and circulation of just under 35,000 at the time (Sweney 2012). Indeed, its size, with an average of sixteen pages, allows for a greater number of news stories to be published each day than could possibly be covered in short broadcast news bulletins: on average we coded seventy-seven items each weekday with a total of 385. Many of these were 'news in brief' (37.4 per cent), items with fewer than sixty words devoted to them. Considering both brief and longer items together, the majority tended to be descriptive (68.8 per cent in total) rather than providing analysis or explanation, supplemented with a large amount of promotional material, such as reviews and previews (24.4 per cent). Just over half of YEP's news items related to Leeds or wards within Leeds (51.2 per cent), with a further 29.6 per cent coded as regionally focused. Stories were less likely than in the broadcast media to be coded as celebratory or disorder-focused with thirty-five reports (9.1 per cent) and forty (10.4 per cent) respectively, albeit with a similar city-based focus for such items. This was more so the case for 'celebratory stories', with 80 per cent of the thirty-five 'celebratory' items coded as Leeds-specific, compared to 48 per cent of the forty items coded for 'disorder'. Front-page stories throughout the week recall those already mentioned in the chapter: care home closures and the Chapeltown carnival (30 August); jobs threatened by fire station closures (31 August); the deaths of two people falling from a tower block (1 September); and the police murder investigation (2 September).

Figure 2.3 summarizes the 'prominent story topics' for YEP in order of prominence. We can note a similar focus to that of broadcast media on cultural events and entertainment (24.7 per cent), with 'charity events' also bolstering this kind of coverage (a further 11.7 per cent). In contrast to the television and radio bulletins, then, it is not crime which generates the greatest number of reports here (with only 9.9 per cent), and we can also note an increased focus on business or economic matters (14.0 per cent). Stories in this category cover job creation (and some losses), investment in the area and contracts gained. In addition to the large amount of cultural reporting, many of these stories promote a sense of vibrancy (e.g. 'Contracts delight for specialist scaffolding firm', 29 August; 'Guests praise apartments for their first class service', 1 September), although a smaller number of pieces lament closures ('Two hundred years of drinking history to go',

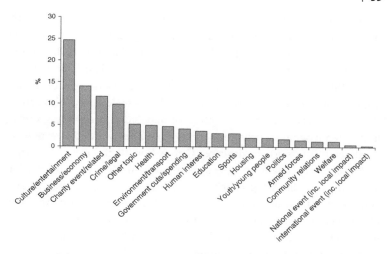

2.3 *Yorkshire Evening Post*: prominent story topics (as a percentage of all stories)

29 August). It is perhaps not surprising, then, that our results for news sources in YEP reveal a different pattern to that of the mainstream broadcast media: while 60 per cent of stories have no direct quotations, the most frequent type of actor quoted is 'business/private sector' (15.6 per cent of stories), with 'ordinary people' coming second (9.6 per cent). News of government spending or cuts receives less attention (4.2 per cent), compared to broadcast news. As noted above, we do not find as high a proportion of 'celebratory' stories in YEP, compared to television news, despite the strong cultural focus and tendency to promote Leeds-based activities over more negative features, such as crime. So while the newspaper's headlines promote a culturally and economically active city, the articles themselves tend to be more descriptive or informative in nature. With the lack of accompanying photographic images in the majority of cases, it is possible that such text-based media is often restricted to delivering its news in black-and-white tones, both literally and figuratively speaking.

Campaigning against NHS reforms

We have already indicated how certain stories attract coverage and travel across media outlets. With this is mind, we briefly consider the reporting of the campaign against NHS reforms across broadcast, print and web-based news providers in our sample. With 'health' being one of our highest-occurring issue-specific story topics, we were interested in tracking NHS-related stories across media outlets during the week. On 7 September 2011, the Health and Social Care Bill was due for its third reading in the House of Commons, containing controversial proposals for large-scale reorganization of the patient service and the creation of new 'commissioning groups', largely led by general practitioners (GPs), to be awarded new powers to allocate funds for healthcare. Opposition to the radical reforms had caused the coalition government to 'pause' in its introduction and launch a 'listening exercise' in April 2011 (see Coleman and Blumler 2011), which appeared to delay proceedings around the time of the May local elections, and saw the legislative process resuming in September. Our study period consequently coincided with the week leading up to the Commons vote.

Significantly, for the purposes of local media, this is a story initiated by local campaigners and concerned citizens, rather than politicians or institutional actors. Although they are *reacting* to reforms on the national level, the reporting of the events is driven clearly by the efforts of local people. This can first be noted in the *Wharfedale Observer* article on 1 September: 'Event to urge MP to reject NHS changes' (page 4, no byline). The short article reports on an event yet to take place, a meeting outside the Morrisons supermarket in Horsforth on Saturday to warn people about the Bill, and to call on the town's Conservative MP, Stuart Andrew, to vote against it. The campaigners' aims are expressed as 'hoping to persuade an MP to vote against proposed changes to the National Health Service this weekend', which they claim 'will put the future of the NHS under threat'. The nature of the actual reform is left relatively unexplained; the language of the organizers conveys anger at plans they believe will 'destroy' the health service: the 'NHS is not safe in David Cameron's hands and nobody should be fooled by the superficial changes announced after the so-called listening exercise'. The only organizer quoted is James Hanley, and he uses passionate language about the dangers faced by 'our NHS', with 'wasteful reorganisation' a 'recipe for chaos'. The event is named as part of the 'We love our NHS' campaign – a phrase adopted by the Labour Party and spawning various Twitter hashtags in recent years (#lovetheNHS; #welovetheNHS; #loveourNHS), among others which are used to highlight examples of outstanding NHS care and lament its precarious future (#saveNHS). Almost half the article is devoted to Hanley's quotations, and his reported message is one of impending disaster, but there is little information about the detailed shape of the reforms.

We can note an altogether different mode of address in *Kirkstall Matters* (2011: 17). Here the writer, Beatrice Rogers, directly addresses the reader as a member of the same community, with implied shared concerns. The headline is conventional, 'Fears rise of government health reforms', but the article combines the urgent horror noted in Hanley's quotations above with informative content regarding the reforms. Nonetheless, there is a clearly persuasive intention, and no attempt at balance. The article outlines 'four main things which you as a NHS patient should be concerned about'. In brief, these 'things' are the speed of the untested reorganization; growth and cost of bureaucracy; the change in the doctor–patient relationship; and the marketization of the NHS. The article warns of 'very little time' before the government ruins 'our NHS for good', urging readers to write to their MP, or fight the changes by getting in touch with Leeds Hospital Alert via email. In this hyperlocal space, the campaigners can represent themselves and make their appeal directly. Such direct advocacy is also displayed in the 'Beyond Guardian Leeds' blog, in its news round-up on 6 September. We have already noted that this blog is 'curatorial' in nature, a news aggregation site 'filling a gap after Guardian Leeds closed', run by volunteers and dependent on readers sending in links to news articles about the city (Beyond Guardian Leeds 2015). In other culturally focused stories, the blog notes the reporting of NHS protests in the *Yorkshire Evening Post*, providing a (now-broken) link to the newspaper's website.[1] The second link is to a petition, embedded in the paragraph:

> BGL [Beyond Guardian Leeds] recommends that anyone who gives a stuff about the NHS and its founding principle of care for all, start doing something about it! You can sign this petition here which argues that 'The Secretary of State should keep the duty to "secure and provide comprehensive health care for all"' – yes indeed! Tell your friends, family, anyone.

1 beyondgdnleeds.wordpress.com/2011/09/06/leeds-today-wuthering-heights-zombies-bridges-and-the-nhs/.

The blogpost goes on the implore readers to contact Unison about the latest protests or gather stories of 'how the NHS has helped you or your family'. This is evidently not a neutral news aggregation site, or certainly not when the subject of the NHS arises. The initial news story is merely a starting point for the blog's writers to advocate collective action, in both online and offline variations, appealing to those who 'give a stuff' in colloquial terms. The hyperlinked e-petition attracts 11,552 signatures before being closed, although it was likely to be in competition with other campaign groups promoting similar concerns.

Returning to the central news day of 3 September, the campaign attracts coverage across television and radio, with a series of protests and door-to-door petitioning taking place in Horsforth, in addition to the Morrisons event mentioned above.[2] On the morning news Radio Aire gives the story third billing, noting the door-to-door petitioning and citing David Cameron on greater powers for GPs, before giving 'Jamie' Hanley a direct quotation lasting thirteen seconds and focusing on the £1.4 billion cost and increased waiting lists. In the Radio Leeds report there is more precise detail; the campaign group is named as 'NHS Alert' and it is identified as part of a wider national campaign against NHS 'cuts' rather than 'reforms'. The group is cited as concerned about the funds being diverted to private interests and longer waiting times; then Jamie Hanley again provides a direct quote of around ten seconds, focusing on the 'top-down' reorganization costs of £1.4 billion, 'which they'd promised they would never do'. Unlike the Radio Aire report, this is balanced with a quote from Colne Valley MP Jason McCartney, arguing that, as we are all living longer, the reforms are 'vital' to give the necessary strength to the NHS while maintaining the 'free to everybody' principle. The short headline report is also immediately followed by an item on cuts affecting travel for disabled people. In this way, the BBC positions the reforms as part of the programme of government *cuts*, but with the opponents' concerns balanced with a rationale for the reforms from a local MP.

On *Calendar*, the story of NHS protests is the fifth news item in the early evening news. Three short 'anchor-only' items are followed by

---

2 Unfortunately, we are missing the editions of the *Yorkshire Evening Post* and BBC *Look North* for this day, so our mapping of the reporting is not complete, but indicative.

a report from Mansfield, where a 'parade for heroes' had taken place to raise funds for the charity Help for Heroes, with serving troops and veterans marching through the town and with a particular focus on injured soldier Alexander Brewer, who lost his leg in Afghanistan. This report is directly followed by the item on NHS campaigners' protests against 'controversial NHS reforms'. David Hurst reports, immediately drawing attention to the small nature of the protest in Horsforth: 'hardly the NHS big weekend promised by the organisers, though one of 60 protests around the country'. Campaigners named as Labour peer Baroness Glenys Thornton and mental health nurse Charlie Place give quotes, with a focus on cuts, pay freezes and lack of jobs for newly trained staff. The story is linked to 'uncertainty' over the closure of the Leeds children's heart unit,[3] and while the reporter mentions the government's insistence that the NHS will remain free at the point of use, available for all, he asks, 'But are the public convinced?' The two 'vox pops' that follow in the report certainly are not, voicing support for the NHS service in the past ('if it goes to pot, I can blame nobody else but the Conservatives'), and with any 'cuts' being 'bad news', albeit with the second speaker admitting to a lack of knowledge about the reforms. The report then moves to Bradford's doorstep campaign, and Unison spokesperson Pam Johnson saying 'it's going to take the N out of the NHS', breaking up the NHS into compartments. Finally, the news report mentions that the proposed reforms will go before the Commons again next week, but are likely to face opposition before becoming law. Interestingly, the reforms themselves are not detailed, possibly assuming a level of audience familiarity. The report links various uncertainties, threats and concerns (NHS jobs, Leeds heart unit, cuts), but its register is one of conveying local residents' affiliation with the NHS and their unspecified worries about it 'going to pot', rather than setting out what the reforms consist of, and their possible consequences for the health service. The sense of political balance identified in the Radio

---

3 This aspect of the 'uncertainty' of local NHS services continued to attract controversy and became an explosive national news story in March/April 2013 after NHS England's medical director, Sir Bruce Keogh, suspended procedures at Leeds over mortality rate concerns, just days after campaigners thought they'd saved the unit from closure in a High Court ruling. 'Child heart surgery at Leeds had to stop, says NHS boss', *BBC News*, online, 29 March 2013, www.bbc.co.uk/news/health-21974053.

Leeds report is less in evidence here, while the merging of reforms with cuts is again apparent.

Different news providers therefore offer a variety of treatments of the NHS campaign. However, differing modes of address, on a spectrum of strong advocacy to impartiality, do not necessarily correlate with efforts to provide high levels of informative content. In other words, the mainstream broadcast news providers often appear to assume a level of familiarity, rather than provide detailed explication of the 'reforms' or 'cuts' facing local opposition. Even quoted campaigners tend to provide emotive soundbites rather than facts about the reforms (albeit subject to editing by the media outlet). Of the sample we collected that day, Radio Leeds makes the greatest effort to balance its reporting, while the hyperlocal *Kirkstall Matters* provides the most information about the proposed reforms, notwithstanding its clearly persuasive intent. Apparent in each news item is the intensity of emotion, and of belonging, associated with the NHS and the related (national and local) values perceived to be under threat.

Concluding observations

Aggregate figures from a week's coverage can reveal only an incomplete or opaque picture of the kinds of stories emerging and fading throughout the week. Here, we have presented the content analysis results as one foundational element, beyond which we can further examine the kinds of concerns and ideals found within the Leeds news ecology. In Irene Costera Meijer's study of local news in Amsterdam (2010), she considered expectations that citizens of that city had regarding the social role of local television: 'Critical, honest, truthful and independent journalism is still valued highly, but today it should be wrapped, so to speak, in a more open, curious, compassionate and "good-humoured" professional attitude and tone of voice' (ibid.: 338). This is not just achieved through representing the city to residents, but by representing local residents to the city: 'In other words, media will have to find out how they can serve democratic society better by becoming more democratic themselves' (ibid.: 339). It would appear in our analysis that local news in Leeds could be giving 'voice' and visibility to its local residents. It is also worth keeping in mind that the celebratory, 'good-humoured' or conversational tone should not necessarily be viewed as a trend towards tabloid values, but as encouraging dialogue, a shared sense of belonging and recognition, and therefore maintaining an appeal to publics. We have already raised the question of whether broadcast local news is providing adequate coverage of political and economic information pertinent to Leeds citizens, and it will be intriguing to explore further how local journalists and their publics evaluate the performance of the local news providers and the *particular attributes* they reference in making such value judgements.[4]

---

4 The authors would like to thank the coders, Joseph Dempsey and Josh Herbert.

3 | HOW CITIZENS RECEIVE THE NEWS

Imagine a city in which there was only one source of news, accessible via a vast screen in the middle of the main shopping centre. People wanting to hear about local news would have to travel to this screen and take their place before it, as part of a collective audience. This would be a very inconvenient way of delivering and accessing news, but it would have one advantage. Anyone wanting to know what sort of news content, formats or perspectives were the most popular with the audience could simply visit the screen and observe how many people were attracted to watch particular features; whether certain features attracted certain types of people; and even, by walking among the audience and asking people, what sort of reactions and intended actions different features stimulated.

Imagining a city and its news in this way reminds us how very different from this reality cities are. In real cities like Leeds, there are hundreds of thousands of people who live and work in different areas from one another; they attend to and make news in many different ways. They possess a range of interests, needs, values, hopes, anxieties and personal histories. They are more or less culturally integrated and are connected to multifaceted networks of people who can be addressed as 'us'. In short, cities are characterized by their uncoordinated interdependence: interdependent, because they can function only on the basis of a minimal set of shared norms and rules, but uncoordinated in that the city is a messy amalgam of hundreds of thousands of autonomous lives and actions.

So, when we speak of news, we are referring to the multiple ways in which individual citizens make sense of their collective experience. When we speak of accessing news, we need to acknowledge that people will do this in countless ways, sometimes using several media sources and platforms to piece together a version of local reality. They sometimes trust some sources or platforms more than others. They sometimes look for different emphases and perspectives to the ones on offer. They sometimes regard the news as a kind of background white noise that assures them that nothing too awful is about to disrupt their lives; and they sometimes use the news as a basis for personal action, such as talking to others, challenging media accounts, protesting or engaging in the formal political process. It is this diverse, fragmented and dynamic approach to local news which leads us to refer to a *local news ecology*. What we mean by this is that both the media themselves and the audiences to whom they speak are both interdependent, but uncoordinated. How they relate to one another depends upon a complex set of actions that are best studied in close empirical detail and then joined together to create a picture of a news ecology that is greater than any of its units.

As much as we are interested in the uncoordinated nature of news ecology, and will explore in this chapter how a vast number of individual actions and attitudes can be read as a meaningful set of responses by Leeds citizens to the news, we should say a little more about why interdependence is also a very important characteristic of the news ecology. As we have already stated in Chapter 1, news matters because it provides common knowledge and stimulates a shared reflection, which makes it possible for strangers to coexist as mutually dependent citizens. The normative value of news is its civic capacity to point people towards aspects of their interdependence; to generate social solidarity, not as a romantic gesture, but in order to create the most elementary foundation for collective understanding and potential cooperation around issues that cannot be resolved individually. Several scholars have attempted to outline the terms upon which the media could, and should, serve democratic citizenship. For example Gurevitch and Blumler (1990: 25) say that democratic media should provide the following:

1. Surveillance of the socio-political environment, reporting developments likely to impinge, positively or negatively, on the welfare of citizens;
2. Meaningful agenda-setting, identifying the key issues of the day, including the forces that have formed and may resolve them;
3. Platforms for an intelligible and illuminating advocacy by politicians and spokespersons of other causes and interest groups;
4. Dialogue across a diverse range of views, as well as between power holders (actual and prospective) and mass publics;
5. Mechanisms for holding officials to account for how they have exercised power;

6. Incentives for citizens to learn, choose and become involved, rather than merely to follow and kibitz over the political process;
7. A principled resistance to forces outside of the media to subvert their independence, integrity and ability to serve the audience;
8. A sense of respect for the audience member, as potentially concerned and able to make sense of his or her personal environment.

Taken together, these characteristics of effective democratic media contribute in important ways to the sense of social interdependence that is necessary if citizenship is to emerge out of the manifold uncoordinated actions and perspectives of the mass public. With a view to understanding the complex relationships between media provision and audience reception, audience behaviour and audience reactions, as well as the local media's contribution to both civic interdependence and uncoordinated personal autonomy, we devised a survey which Leeds City Council invited the members of its Citizens' Panel to complete.[1] The twenty-three questions in the survey were devised as a means of finding out:

1. How often respondents accessed various media, such as local and national newspapers, radio, television, blogs, etc., and whether they ever listened to any of the city's non-mainstream local radio stations;
2. The sources to which respondents would be most likely to turn, in order to find out more information about a local issue that concerned them – and which sources they trust most, nationally and locally;
3. The main reasons why respondents looked regularly at news in general and local news specifically – for example, catching the headlines of what's going on; being reminded of local characters and places; finding out about weather and traffic conditions; having something to talk about with others; following the pros and cons of local issues; keeping up with local sports; following the

---

1 The Leeds Citizens Panel consists of around two thousand volunteers selected by the Leeds City Council from a pool of applicants, to provide the right balance of people from different age groups, backgrounds and neighbourhoods in order to get a good representation of views.

dramas, tragedies, problems and triumphs of local people's lives; keeping up to date with recent crimes, accidents and scandals; learning about developments that might affect the respondent or the city; keeping up with Leeds City Council decisions;

4. Features of local life that respondents thought local media *should* cover and *did* cover well or badly;

5. Whether respondents had encountered the media or local government in the past six months by, for example, being asked for their views by a media organization; contacting a local councillor, official or MP; becoming involved in some form of community action; or writing a comment about local news in a blog, web forum, email list, on Twitter or Facebook;

6. Which local media respondents thought represented the city of Leeds best and which represented them best, as individual citizens;

7. Whether respondents had come across recent local headline news stories; from which media they had heard about them first; and whether coverage of these stories was informative/balanced/, unfair/confusing/, relevant to the respondent's own life, too brief/ too detailed or a stimulus to action.

In addition to these questions, respondents were asked about themselves: how interested in politics they were, how often had they talked to someone else in the past month about global, national or local news; and, of course, a series of questions identifying their age, gender, ethnic background and socio-economic status.

Surveys can never tell the full story of how people think and act, but they can provide some valuable clues by pointing to trends in behaviour or attitude, either across an entire population or within a subgroup of the population. They can enable researchers to correlate responses, so that we might tell, for example, whether people accessing a particular local news source are more or less likely to talk about news stories with others, or whether people who are more interested in politics are more or less likely to express their views online. Taken together with the qualitative account of audience responses to local media presented in the next chapter, where we analyse our focus group discussions, we hope to offer some meaningful findings that will cast light on how people in Leeds access and consume news, how they evaluate local news and what they do with the news that they receive. In some cases how they contribute to making the news. Returning to our original statement about the news ecology, we might hope that these findings can offer us some illuminating insights into the dynamic relationship between complex patterns and practices of uncoordinated public attention to the media and the realisation of interdependent citizenship.

News consumption

As the results presented show, there are clear patterns of consumption and clear trends of preference among news consumers in Leeds, with some media forms more prevalent and others, including those often cited as transformative in modern developed society being pushed to the margins (see Figure 3.1). Our survey gives us a picture of a news ecology in Leeds that, in terms of consumption, seems to be dominated by the traditional broadcasters – TV and radio – and by national news providers rather than local. Sixty-seven per cent of our survey respondents stated that they access national TV news every day and 60 per cent accessed local news

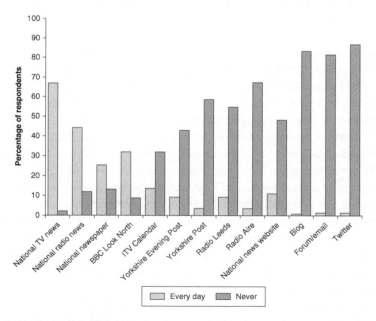

3.1 The number of survey respondents stating that they access a news channel either every day, or never

provided by national TV channels at least five days a week; either the *Calendar* news bulletin on ITV or the *Look North* local news show on the BBC. Forty-four per cent accessed national radio news and 36 per cent accessed national newspapers five or more days per week. In contrast, fewer than 21 per cent accessed one of the main local newspapers on five or more days of the week and news access via the internet was not shown to be significant among the general population. Only 11 per cent accessed national news websites daily and 63 per cent said that they accessed these sites less than one day a week, or never. Alternative online news sources were accessed by an even more marginal audience; 87 per cent claimed to access blogs for news less than once per week, or never, and the figures for forums or email groups and Twitter were similar, at 85 and 88 per cent respectively.

Though patronized less often than national news, local news outlets were still a significant source for many Leeds respondents. Of the several local outlets, *Look North* was accessed most often by the respondents (by some margin), followed by *Calendar*, local newspaper the *Yorkshire Evening Post* (YEP), and Radio Leeds. The same order applied when respondents were asked where, if anywhere, they recollected the reporting of five recent local news stories, except that YEP and *Calendar* changed places over those items. When asked about their agreement with several statements about local news outlets, respondents endorsed *Look North* much more frequently than other local news sources on two very positive statements: 'represents the city really well' and 'stands up well for you and people like you'. Clearly, there is a strong and continuing regard among our respondents for the city's main public service provider. As detailed in Chapter 2 of this book, our content analysis of local news showed that there were marked differences in content between *Look North* and *Calendar*, with the BBC programme featuring more stories about government, which is indicative perhaps of a stronger public service orientation.

As Figure 3.1 shows very clearly, there was little endorsement of new media news outlets as a source of choice for local news. While a number of scholars have observed a shift from offline to online news consumption, this pattern has tended to be localized or found only within younger age groups (Diddi and LaRose 2006), and our figures do not show any significant shift in overall access rates from traditional sources of local news to online sources. The question specifically asked about accessing local news from online sources, rather than accessing news more generally online. So could this lack of regular access of online local news be a function of its local nature? Perhaps national news is more prevalent in online sources than local news owing to the power laws of online attention: greater audiences, greater presence in search engines and news recommendation engines (Thorson 2008), and greater numbers of sharers. Any prevalence of national news may provide a positive feedback mechanism that encourages active news seekers to follow up on national news stories, rather than the less well represented local news stories, maximizing readership of the bigger national news stories and thus, for local news stories, minimizing the sharing activities that fuel online and social news readership (Diddi and LaRose 2006). Additionally, online news consumers are influenced by previous consumption habits (Mitchelstein and Boczkowski 2010), and may therefore be predisposed to access mainstream news sources, where local news is less prevalent. Whatever the reason, our figures suggest that online sources of local news do not seem to have had a significant displacement effect on the more commonly accessed traditional news media channels in Leeds.

However, more than half the sample specified the internet as the place to which they would turn to seek further information about something happening locally that was of interest to them (as shown in Figure 3.2). Fifty-six per cent said they would go online to find more information, the greatest number for any source, suggesting that there is an important place for this new source of local information in the contemporary news ecology. Several previous studies have suggested that consumption of news online can in fact be complementary to the consumption from offline sources (Chan and Leung 2005), and our figures suggest that while traditional news media may be those identified most often by the people of Leeds as sources of news, the internet is certainly being used to supplement knowledge of local issues. Furthermore, there is no distinct group of internet users in Leeds who choose to access this supplemental online source of local information, such as those who identified a preference for online local news sources; in fact, a broad range of respondents reported this preference. It is true that the majority (69 per cent) of those who view local news on national news websites on five or more days

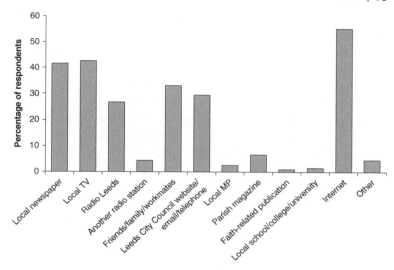

3.2 Sources of further information about something of interest happening in Leeds

per week also chose the internet as the preferred source for further information, but so did the majority of respondents in almost all the other categories of national news website access. Indeed, even of those who stated that they never accessed national news websites for local news, 46 per cent chose the internet as a preferred source of further information. This suggests, therefore, that our picture of online news being dominated by the national news providers may not show the whole story. The internet plays a more popular role as a tool for finding further information, and user-initiated searches in response to local events and issues follow the main trends of online access, governed by search engines as well as influential hubs, to direct the user to sources of relevant local content that were not categorized by our respondents as a sources of news.

So while the traditional broadcasters were identified by our respondents as the dominant sources for news consumption, the search-driven online resources seem to provide an important addition which people can use to enhance their understanding of local stories and events and delve deeper into issues that they may have initially been made aware of by the national or local TV news. Interestingly, though, of the few respondents who said they would access the local section of a national news website, more than a third of them

(36 per cent) said that they would do so on a daily basis. This regular usage of the newer medium may suggest that a potential new community of online news consumers is developing. Unsurprisingly, as observed in previous studies (Diddi and LaRose 2006), this community is relatively young, with 70 per cent of the youngest sample members (25–44) having endorsed the internet as a source of choice compared with only 32 per cent of those aged 65 or older.

The survey asked how often each respondent accessed each news source, and the responses from those who stated that they used the internet to seek further information provided interesting insight into how this might affect TV news access rates, in specific temporal ways. Only 61 per cent of those who indicated a preference for the internet as a source of further local information also indicated that they watch local TV news every day, compared to 76 per cent of those who do not use the internet to find local information. However, 13 per cent of those who indicated the online preference claimed to watch TV news five days per week (rather than every day), compared with only 3 per cent of those who did not indicate the online preference, and these figures were more pronounced for local news programmes *Look North* and *Calendar*. Perhaps this variation in access rates between online/TV access and five/seven days per week constitutes evidence of patterns of news source usage that are related to the Monday–Friday working week and the widespread reach of internet access throughout the Leeds area, which allows easy access to the internet at home. This effect is not confined to TV news access; a significantly smaller proportion of those who access online local information sources accessed newspapers daily than of those who do not (27 per cent versus 49 per cent accessed five days per week or more) and far fewer accessed local newspapers daily (8 per cent versus 29 per cent accessed the *Yorkshire Post* six or seven days per week). So one hypothesis that could be drawn from the data is that Leeds residents who choose to seek local information from online sources do so instead of accessing other local news sources, but do not do this uniformly through the week; the difference in behaviour perhaps being confined to weekends or days off, potentially when time is available for internet browsing. This change in behaviour may be a similar phenomenon to the negative association demonstrated by Flavian and Gurrea (2007), between searching online for specific, up-to-date news and reading newspapers at leisure. In this case, the difference is between keeping up to date through news bulletins during the week, and seeking further detail about local issues when time permits at the weekend.

However, this group of internet users seemed different in other possibly significant ways. In responses to several questions, they came across as less 'local minded' than the other respondents. For example, they endorsed each of the reasons suggested in our survey for using local media less frequently, including civic reasons such as 'keeping up with Leeds City Council decisions', which was endorsed by 16 per cent of this group, compared with 27 per cent of the rest of the sample. They talked with others about local news less often (71 per cent talked to others about local news once or more per week compared to 78 per cent of the rest of the sample), even though their involvement in conversations about national and international news was higher (89 per cent talked to others about national news once or more per week, compared to 79 per cent in the rest of the sample, and 86 per cent talked to others about international news once or more per week, compared to 77 per cent in the rest of the sample); and fewer remembered hearing about the five local stories that were described in the questionnaire (63 per cent of the group recalled coverage of the Chapeltown Carnival compared to 68 per cent of the others; 68 per cent of the group recalled coverage of a story about the closing of a care home compared to 77 per cent of the others; 37 per cent of the group recalled coverage of a report about first-time house buyers compared to 38 per cent of the others; 44 per cent of the group recalled coverage of the management of Leeds United football club compared to 51 per cent of the others; 10 per cent of the group recalled coverage of a story about the Holbeck viaduct compared to 19 per cent of the others). Perhaps the relationship between local news access and internet preference is more complex and the causal links are not one-way.

Preferences and evaluations: topics of coverage

The different topics covered by local news media featured in the survey in several ways: as reasons identified by respondents for following local news media, as topics identified by respondents as preferred subjects (subjects that *should* be covered by local news media), as subjects that respondents identified as currently being covered well by local news media, and as subjects identified by respondents as currently being covered badly by local news media. The questions that focused on these points suggested a range of topics to respondents, including headline news, traffic and weather, entertainment, celebrity and local characters, but also topics that had more of a strictly civic purpose, which may help to characterize the local media sources as civic actors, in the way that Gurevitch and Blumler (1990) defined.

Respondents accessed local news primarily to catch headlines and find out about weather and traffic, but a large proportion also wanted to learn about topics of a more 'civic' nature, particularly 'developments that could affect them or the city' but also 'City Council decisions' and 'the pros and cons of local issues' (see Figure 3.3). When asked what they thought was covered well by local news media, what was covered badly and what they thought should be covered, respondents chose local sports and big local events as the topics that were covered well, but most thought that these were not the most important topics that should be covered, instead stating

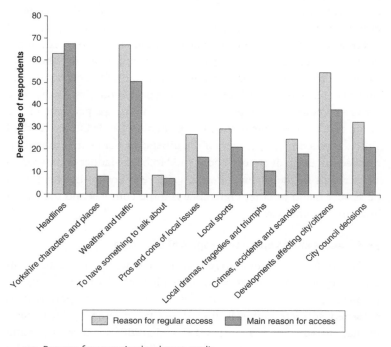

3.3 Reasons for accessing local news media

a preference for news about policies and developments that might affect them or their neighbourhoods. This strong preference for coverage of a key civic issue was accompanied by mixed feelings about how well this issue was covered, with negative feeling about coverage slightly outweighing positive feeling (see Figure 3.4). While seen as much less of a priority, most respondents did report that items on council services and facilities were also covered poorly.

These figures clearly show a preference for civic topics to be covered by local news media and a feeling that this demand is not currently being met well. However, this opinion is not uniform across our sample. Respondents were also asked to rate their own level of interest in politics and the level of interest reported seemed to correlate with differences in the type of content that respondents chose as reasons for accessing local news media and their opinions about the quality of, and priorities for, coverage of the different categories of content. This is particularly interesting when looking at reasons that are related to 'civic affairs', such as 'following the pros and cons of local issues', 'finding out about developments that might affect them or the city' or 'keeping up with Leeds City Council decisions'. Respondents who were very interested in politics were more likely to use local news media to follow the pros and cons of local issues than the other respondents, with 42 per cent of those very interested or

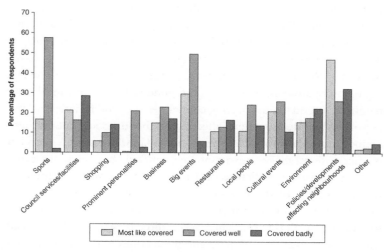

3.4 Features of Leeds life covered by local news media

interested in politics versus 27 per cent of those somewhat interested or not at all interested, to find out about developments that might affect them or the city (64 per cent versus 52 per cent) and to keep up with Leeds City Council decisions (50 per cent versus 32 per cent).

Drilling down farther, this pattern is more obvious: 20 per cent of respondents listed keeping up with council decisions as a main reason for following local news, but among those 'very interested' in politics the figure was 32 per cent, whereas it was only 8 per cent among those not at all interested in politics. When asked about what they thought local news media should cover, those with a high level of political interest were more likely to say that local news media should cover business, industry and jobs than other groups (23 per cent versus 15 per cent), and also policies and developments affecting neighbourhoods (52 per cent versus 47 per cent), council services and facilities (24 per cent versus 21 per cent) and cultural events (25 per cent versus 19 per cent). Respondents who reported no interest in politics were unsurprisingly the opposite of the above, being far less likely to use the local news media to follow the pros and cons of local issues than the other respondents (27 per cent versus 42 per cent) to find out about developments that might affect them or the city (37 per cent versus 52 per cent) and to keep up with Leeds City Council decisions (12 per cent versus 32 per cent). Twelve per cent of this latter group thought that local news media should cover shops and shopping, which was double the rate of those with more interest in politics; and they were also more likely to think that local events and festivals should be covered (38 per cent versus 31 per cent), as well as restaurants, clubs and entertainment (18 per cent versus 12 per cent). Respondents reporting that they were very interested in politics were more likely than other respondents to say that local news media do a good job of covering council services and facilities, as well as policies and developments affecting neighbourhoods, but they also seemed more likely to say that they do a bad job. Perhaps their level of political interest makes them more opinionated about civic affairs?

Overall, we see a picture of a local populace which recognizes the importance of the coverage of civic affairs by the local news media, but which does not perceive this function to be carried out to a high enough degree. When asked directly whether they agreed with the statement 'Local news and media does not provide enough detail about council decisions', 34 per cent agreed while 28 per cent disagreed, an effect magnified by increasing interest in politics, with 42 per cent of those interested or very interested in politics agreeing compared to 24 per cent who disagreed. With the statement 'Local news and media does not do enough to hold powerful people to account', 53 per cent agreed while only 15 per cent disagreed; among those who were very interested in politics 61 per cent agreed. Clearly the demand for civic content is strongest among local people who have an interest in politics, while those less interested in politics like to see alternative topics covered, but even in the groups with least political interest the reporting of policies and developments that might affect them and their neighbourhoods appears to be the top preference for local news coverage.

It is interesting to note that despite this demand for information of a civic nature, these civic actions are not the main reasons why local people access media. The reasons for this are unknown. Perhaps people recognize the importance of the local media for civic purposes, but are not actually that interested in it themselves, or they are too busy in their everyday lives to interact with these topics, choosing instead to access the headlines, traffic and weather; things that they perceive to have an instant effect on their day-to-day routines. Alternatively, maybe people do not look for civic information in local news because they do not think that they will find it there. Indeed, our content analysis of the news created by local news outlets (covered in Chapter 2) shows that the greatest amount of coverage was given to stories about crime and culture and that political stories are relatively uncommon in local news, posing the question of whether we are now seeing coverage of local policy-making further displaced by other types of news. Whatever the reason there seems to be a perceived mismatch between what is deemed important and what is delivered by local news media in Leeds.

Evaluation and appreciation

Despite less exposure to local rather than national news sources, a very large majority of the respondents agreed with the statement that 'Local news is as important as national news'. A surprisingly decided endorsement was given to local news when the respondents were asked to say which in a number of respects they would expect national or local news to be better, if they both ran the same story (as seen in Figure 3.5). They said that they would expect, by large margins,

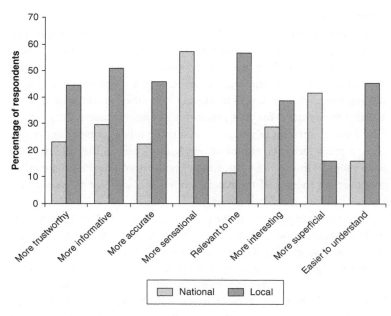

3.5 Opinions of national versus local news media

the local version to be more relevant, but also more informative, more accurate, more trustworthy and easier to understand; and to a somewhat lesser degree more interesting. They would also expect the national story to be more sensational. Local news media were regarded less well than national media only for being more superficial.

As was seen earlier with the responses regarding reasons for accessing local media and topics covered, opinion of local media seems to be linked to levels of political interest. Respondents who reported being very interested in politics seemed to have less of a difference in trust between local and national news sources (30 per cent versus 35 per cent, rather than 20 per cent versus 39 per cent in the whole sample), whereas those who were not at all interested in politics were more likely to distrust both local and national news media. Those who were interested or very interested in politics conform in general to the overall trend in which local news was rated as more accurate and informative, but this group seemed more opinionated. They were also more likely than those with less political interest to rate national news media more highly in these regards, choosing 'neither' or giving no answer less often. The respondents who reported being very interested in politics bucked the trend on one point, being more likely to rate national news media as more interesting than local news media, in contrast to all of the other respondents, including those who were merely interested or somewhat interested in politics. In general, respondents rated national news media as more sensational than local, regardless of their reported level of political interest. However, respondents who reported being interested or very interested in politics were more likely than others to say the opposite, that local news media were more sensational. They were also more likely than the other groups to rate local news media as more superficial, though still attributing this to national news media most often. Only 10 per cent rated national news media as more relevant to their concerns, but those who were very interested in politics were nearly twice as likely to rate national news media as most relevant to their concerns, whereas those with no interest in politics were less than half as likely (18 per cent versus 4 per cent).

The survey also asked about the level of interpersonal talk about news that respondents engaged in, and such talk about local news seemed to be connected in some way to opinions about local news media. Respondents who talked about local news with others once a week or more were more likely than those who did not talk about local news to state that they trusted local news media more than national news media (45 per cent versus 27 per cent), that local news was more informative (52 per cent versus 32 per cent) and more accurate (47 per cent versus 28 per cent) than national news media, more relevant to their concerns than national news media (58 per cent versus 35 per cent) and easier to understand (43 per cent versus 31 per cent). Respondents in this group were also more likely to state that national news media were more sensational than local news media (57 per cent versus 42 per cent), that they were also more superficial (38 per cent versus 25 per cent), and that local news media were more interesting (41 per cent versus 24 per cent), with a much smaller effect found for the reverse (25 per cent versus 30 per cent).

Retrospective assessments

When the respondents were asked whether they thought that local media provision in Leeds had improved or worsened over the past five years, the sample of responses was about equally divided. Regardless of their opinion of relative improvement or worsening, respondents were equally sure that local news is as important as national news. However, those who perceived improvement said they accessed local news media for all the reasons specified earlier more than did those who discerned a worsening (see Figure 3.3). The former were also more inclined than the latter to say that the local media covered a range of specified topics well, and a greater number of them recalled each of the five stories that had been in the news in a recent week. Looking at the topics deemed to have 'civic' purpose, 22 per cent of those who perceived recent improvement in local news media said that it covered local council services and facilities well, compared with 14 per cent of those who perceived that the local news media had worsened. Sixty-nine per cent of the latter thought that the local media did not do enough to hold powerful people to account compared with 52 per cent of those in the 'improved' group. Thirty-eight per cent of those who considered that the local media had worsened over the years agreed with the statement that the local media provide insufficient information about local council decisions, in contrast to 29 per cent agreement among those for whom the local media had improved. It is perhaps not surprising that those who thought that the local news media had improved recently also thought that it performed these civic actions better than those who perceived that it had worsened recently. It is unclear what the link is here, but perhaps opinion is changed by specific stories that stick in the mind; perhaps those who notice specific examples of success in civic action see this as an improvement in the local news media, and vice versa.

After the news

As noted previously, the democratic communication system envisioned by Gurevitch and Blumler (1990) allows for more than just the reporting of information to the public. It supports dialogue within mass publics, enabling citizens to express and experience a wide range of views. It encourages citizens to seek further knowledge, to learn and participate in political processes. It provides citizens with mechanisms to hold those in power to account. All of these actions should be supported within a news ecology so that the citizen can be fully involved in the democratic shaping of society around them.

Our figures suggest that in Leeds following up a news story by some form of action was a minority pursuit, with only around a third of the survey respondents (32 per cent) stating that they had taken some sort of action following their access of local news. Contacting a local councillor was the most popular activity, followed closely by 'becoming involved in some form of community action', with somewhat fewer reporting other activities, such as contacting the local media. This rate of action was also influenced by people's level of political interest. Unsurprisingly, respondents who reported that they were interested or very interested in politics were much more likely to take action, whether that was contacting a councillor or MP, contacting local media or commenting on a forum or Twitter. Thus, contacting the local media was reported by 10 per cent of the sample but 24 per cent of those 'very interested' in politics and 2 per cent of the 'not at all interested'. Seventeen per cent of the sample had contacted a local councillor, official or MP; in the 'very interested' group 29 per cent had done so, but just 6 per cent of those from the not at all interested. Fourteen per cent had embarked on some form of community action (26 per cent versus 8 per cent for the 'very' and 'not at all' interested groups).

Political interest was not the only factor that emerged as an indicator of the rate of taking action. According to the survey results, people are also more likely to take action as they get older (with action rates of 5, 8 and 10 per cent in the respective age groups of 25–44, 44–64 and 65+), but less likely to take action in the form of contacting local media or contacting a local official, councillor or MP. Unsurprisingly, perhaps, the older age groups did not report any interaction with blogs or emails and the younger age groups were more active on Facebook. Twitter was not reportedly used much; only the 45–64 age group and a single respondent in the over-65 age group reported usage. The younger age group did not report Twitter usage in this way, perhaps preferring to use Twitter for non-news purposes. However, it did seem that the respondents who stated that they would use the internet as a preferred source of additional information about local events were more likely to follow up a news story with action in some way than the other sample members (14 per cent reported contacting local media, 18 per cent contacting a local councillor, and 10 per cent commented on Facebook, in contrast to 6, 15 and 3 per cent respectively among the rest of the sample). This is slight evidence, perhaps, of the increasing power of websites as a tool for lobbying and interest groups, or perhaps just a reflection of the internet being the preferred source of information for those who are more likely to take a form of political action.

For the sample members with an ethnic background, however, involvement in community action was the most often mentioned follow-up to a news story, while fewer reported using 'new media' (internet, blogs, online forums, email or Twitter), these being the options available on the survey for taking action. Classifying respondents by the National Readership Survey (NRS) social grade, the statistics showed that those respondents in category A were more likely to be involved in community action; respondents in categories A, B and C used new media to take action and were more likely to report contacting councillors, officials or MPs; those in the C1 and C2 groupings reported higher rates of action in the form of contacting the media; those in category D were more likely to report that they had been asked for their views by local media than respondents in other categories. Respondents in category E reported almost no action taken at all, with just a single respondent claiming to have contacted a local councillor, official or MP. This is perhaps surprising when it is taken into account that category E respondents were much more likely than other categories to choose keeping up with Leeds City Council decisions as their main reason for accessing local media. Perhaps this group is affected more severely by changes in policy; arguably the less well off are usually more dependent on local authority services. Similarly, category E respondents are most likely to choose council services, facilities, policies and developments that could affect them or their neighbourhoods as subjects that they would most like Leeds news media to cover, showing that, while they may not take action, they are still very interested in the political occurrences around them. They access local news media to keep in touch with these civic issues, but for whatever reason do not feel empowered enough to do anything about them.

Political dialogue and action extends, of course, beyond the formal practices of contacting MPs and media and the semi-formal actions of blogging and posting on social media. The democratic news ecology should also impact upon the informal and private spaces of the public, cultivating political discussion between friends, family members and colleagues. To investigate this, respondents were asked to report whether they had talked with others about items of international, national and local news in a recent period.

Although they reported somewhat less conversation about local news than about national and international news, it nevertheless seemed appreciable. Forty-three per cent said they had talked with others about something in local news twice a week or more often, compared with 61 per cent who had talked about national news and 55 per cent about international news.

The relationship of respondents' levels of political interest to these reported levels of interpersonal talk is intriguing. Whereas this variable greatly influenced conversations about international affairs (80 per cent of the 'very interested' having taken part in them twice a week or more, compared with 42 per cent of the not at all interested) and about national affairs (86 per cent for the 'very' interested and 47 per cent of those 'not at all' interested), political interest did not seem to have affected the readiness of Leeds people to talk to others about local news at all, with 46 per cent of both the 'very interested' and the 'not at all interested' having done so. Although fewer than half of the respondents had talked about local news, the presence of this conversation among people from across the spectrum of political interest is perhaps indicative of a distinctive way in which local news can do something for all members of the community. These conversations occurred despite a lack of interest in politics and despite all of the party affiliations and ideologies that exist among those with high levels of political interest. Local news seems to offer something that strikes against that grain of stratification that runs so often against many facets of political and communication organization.

Conclusion: a survey-based picture of the news ecology

Setting aside details, what broad features of the Leeds news ecology emerge from the testimony of those individuals who inhabited it as audience members, news consumers and citizens? First, the provision of local news mattered to many of them. It is true that overall they received more national than local news. But attention to local news was far more than an optional extra. Frequency of local news consumption was quite substantial, and in the case of the most popular news medium (television) it was almost as great as national viewing. Moreover, approximately three-quarters of the respondents agreed with the proposition that local news was as important as national news; even among those individuals who thought that the quality of local news had worsened over the previous five years. When asked which qualities they would expect to find in local or national news coverage of the same story, the former was rated more highly on all the specified desiderata except one: for relevance, informativeness, accuracy, trustworthiness, interest and not being sensational, though liable to be more superficial. Although respondents who described themselves as 'very interested' in politics were somewhat less critical of national news by some of the above criteria, they too tended to give the nod to local news. It is not possible to say whether these responses amount mainly to a vote of confidence in local news, a lack of confidence in national news or some of both. Whatever the explanation, local news did seem qualitatively superior in many respects to the national news with which people were familiar. Despite the difficulties with which all the local media had had to contend in recent times, it is not as if the sample as a whole considered that their news provision had gone downhill as a result. In fact, respondents who thought that Leeds' news services had improved over the previous five years roughly equalled those who declared that they had declined. Those who 'voted' for 'improvement' were also more positive about a number of specific features of local news.

Second, although all four of the city's mainstream outlets will have attracted significant audience numbers and presented local news in somewhat distinctive styles, one service seemed to stand out for its centrality to the Leeds news ecology, namely *Look North*. Its audience appeal was appreciably greater than that of the four other outlets. Asked where they had first heard about each of five recent news stories, the respondents again mentioned *Look North* most often (typically followed by around half the number for the *Yorkshire Evening Post*, and then in turn by *Calendar* and Radio Leeds). When evaluative statements comparing the four services were put to the respondents, *Look North* stood head and shoulders above the rest: 64 per cent agreed that *Look North* represented 'the city really well', compared with 39 per cent for the *Yorkshire Evening Post*, 36 per cent for *Calendar*, and 34 per cent for Radio Leeds; and for standing up 'well for you and people like you' *Look North* scored 45 per cent, compared with 31 per cent for the *Yorkshire Evening Post*, 26 per cent for *Calendar*, and 24 per cent for Radio Leeds. The fact that the city's main public service news provider is such an ecological epicentre is worthy of note. This suggests that policy-makers in government and industry should take care when considering measures for local media change that might disrupt the ecological balance for the worse.

Third, the survey has disclosed a striking mismatch in the sample members' orientations to new media. Although very few of them received news online, over half designated the internet as the source to which they would turn if they wanted more information about something happening in the city. Moreover, those would-be internet users were on average younger than were the other sample members and were less frequent patrons of mainstream-supplied local news. Naturally, this situation may be unstable and might eventually be resolved in favour of increasing online news consumption.

Fourth, the introduction to this chapter depicted a city such as Leeds in terms of an almost radical diversity – as comprising a range of different interests, needs, values, hopes and anxieties. On the whole, the spread of our sample members' responses to local news topics – as reasons for following local news, as ones they would like to be covered, and as ones that were covered well or poorly – do seem to reflect something like such diversity. Local news may differ from national news in aiming to provide a panorama of different kinds of city events in diverse situations, involving different kinds of people, rather than a more concentrated news focus on a given day. With sometimes up to ten items in a half-hour bulletin, it would be natural for the television news programmes especially to feature a range of topics, reflecting different aspects of city life at large. From this point of view, Leeds audience members and news producers may have been more or less in accord regarding how they considered that the city should be depicted.

Fifth, the same cannot be said about respondents' perspectives on local news treatment of the other main facet of urban life discussed in the chapter introduction: namely, a civic arena in which citywide issues and problems can be identified and aired, citizenship performed and democracy realized. It is not easy to give a precise estimate of people's levels of interest in such matters and in news coverage of them. Some individuals might overstate their degree of civic concern, though the anonymity of a survey questionnaire should be a safeguard against such exaggeration. The extent of professed civic awareness could also depend on how the question about it is posed; greater perhaps if developments affecting the fabric of the city or one's own neighbourhood are mooted than, say, for following the ins and outs of council discussions and decisions. It appears from responses to items in our questionnaire that segments of between approximately a fifth and a third of Leeds residents would welcome the provision in local news of material about some aspects of civic affairs. Their assessment of what was on offer in this sphere was at best lukewarm. In fact, more individuals reckoned that local news treatment of certain civic topics was poorly done than thought it was well done. Almost half the entire sample agreed or strongly agreed with a statement put to them that the local media do not 'do enough to hold powerful people to account', as opposed to only 15 per cent who disagreed.

Sixth, only a portion of sample members reported having been prompted by a local news story to contact an MP, a councillor or the media or to engage in some form of community action. Unsurprisingly, those individuals who described themselves as interested in politics were more likely to have taken such steps, perhaps being more knowledgeable about how to go about making the necessary contacts. The relative failure of the local media to cover civic developments substantially and well may also help to explain why not many individuals will have been moved to undertake some form of follow-up action. It is not implausible to maintain that a higher profile of civic news could result in a higher rate of citizen activity.

Seventh, local news does seem, however, to provide material for quite a lot of conversation and discussion among individuals afterwards, which is something that interviewed news producers actually said they hoped to achieve. It is true that the sample members talked about national and international news with other people somewhat more frequently than they did about local news stories. Interestingly, however, the respondents' levels of interest in politics had no effect at all on their involvement in local-news-stimulated talk. From this point of view, it is as if Leeds local news ties into a communication process which is less characterized by those differences, and gaps that can stem from socio-political stratification.

In summary, the Leeds news services do seem to bond well in many ways with their audience members. However, this is definitely not the case as far as the highly important civic domain is concerned. Nonetheless, precisely because of their other strengths, the Leeds news providers should be able to find ways of improving their civic performance and bringing it in line with what they claim they want to do.

4 | HOW PEOPLE MAKE SENSE OF THE CITY

The previous three chapters have taken an aerial view of the Leeds news ecology – almost as if they were flying above it and mapping a series of communicative practices, circulating messages, receptive attitudes and activities. They asked about the type of stories and perspectives that various local media organizations were offering for public consumption. They considered how particular news stories emerged and spread across the city. They examined the extent to which the diverse people of Leeds accessed different types of news from a range of media platforms. They asked people about how much they trusted the news, the extent to which they discussed it with others, and whether it satisfied their perceived information needs. These are very important aspects of understanding a local news ecology with a view to mapping relationships between news in circulation (and news absences) and news reception (or inattention). What such macro-analyses cannot tell us is how people in Leeds feel about their relationship to news. Is it something that is produced by others and either consumed or ignored by the public as an audience? Do people know what news looks like when they see it? Do different people have different conceptions of what constitutes news? Are there ways in which people interact with the news, without necessarily assuming the role of journalists? Do people have hopes about the kind of news ecology they would like to live in? Can they imagine news in new and different forms? More than just a set of questions about how it feels to live in a local world of news (paradox intended), we wanted to learn more about how people know what is going on in their local environment – the feeling of being locally connected. To live 'in' a city is to experience an attachment that cannot be reduced to the bureaucratic letters of a postcode or the random consequence of residing in the catchment area of particular media channels or local newspapers. The phenomenology of belonging arises from a sense, however tacit and unconscious, that what is going on can't be happening without you being there. To live in a city is a kind of cultural immersion that surveys are unlikely to capture or describe.

How best to tap into this sense of knowing what is going on? We organized a series of focus groups in which we attempted to probe participants' habits and strategies for apprehending the local. Focus groups are a form of group interview that capitalizes on communication between research participants in order to generate data. The method is particularly useful for exploring people's knowledge and experiences and can be used to examine not only what people think, but also how they think and why they think that way. Unlike the data on which our survey analysis is based, the focus group findings are not intended to be representative of the Leeds population or to carry any quantitative weight. Rather, the analysis presented in this chapter offers a qualitative insight into the mediated experience of feeling part of a major city.

Local news as word-of-mouth

Most studies of local news start with 'the media', and it is assumed that news is delivered to people through a process of journalistic transmission. As we shall see, people do receive some of their news in this way. When we asked focus group participants to tell us how they go about discovering local news, it turned out that word-of-mouth grapevines are paramount. They are crucial both for the acquisition of local information and as ways of establishing community connections. For most of our focus group participants, 'local' meant 'my street' or 'my neighbourhood'. It almost never meant the city of Leeds as reported in the daily local newspaper, the *Yorkshire Evening Post*, and certainly not the vast regions of Yorkshire and beyond, covered by TV news programmes such as the BBC's *Look North* or ITV's *Calendar*. Indeed, our participants frequently regarded news coverage of Yorkshire, and even Leeds, as unsatisfactory precisely because it was too distant from their immediate local experiences. Rather than turning first to these reports of media-constructed locality, they turned to people 'in the know':

> Local information. I would say 90 per cent comes from school when dropping off or picking up. Either actually speaking to people or just overhearing. (Female, Group 2)

> [N]ews, as in gossip ... my neighbour is the sort of person that knows everything about everybody, so I get it from her. (Female, Group 1)

Yes, she just about knows everybody. You can't die without her knowing. The amount of funerals she goes to is unbelievable. So we get a lot of information from her ... (Female, Group 5)

In informal discussions, definitions of news, gossip and information overlap. Such imbrication highlights the ways in which news is interwoven into everyday life; the extent to which it is not simply received, but practised. At the same time, these overlapping conceptions of what constitutes news can be troublesome, posing problems for the qualities of reliability and objectivity that have come to be associated with journalistic news production.

Do you trust word of mouth more than you trust the press?

No. It's like Chinese whispers, isn't it. (Female, Group 5)

How do you get to know what's going on?

Nosy neighbours, and—

How do you check out who the trustworthy neighbours are?

I've only lived here about eighteen months, but the next-door neighbour is part of the Neighbourhood Watch, I think she knows what's going on. (Female, Group 6)

Word-of-mouth news is paradoxical; it is highly unreliable in the sense that it is not subject to any form of professional rigour, of the kind that shapes the news outputs of traditional news institutions. People understand it precisely as gossip and chat, and yet, at the same time, word-of-mouth news is heavily relied upon as a trusted source of news because it comes from authentic experience rather than from the (frequently) distrusted news-producing media institutions.

Our research participants' emphasis on the hyperlocal as the proper site for 'local news' meant that word-of-mouth was appropriate to the scale of circulation – although this was often supplemented or replaced by online grapevines, sometimes separating news from its geographical constraints. Indeed, in speaking of local news travelling by word-of-mouth, our participants did not feel any need to distinguish between online and offline communication. In the contemporary news ecology, news travel through grapevines that are variously mediated – in person at the school gates, on a telephone, in an email, or on Facebook. Asked in general terms where they found out the most important things they needed to know about their locality, people automatically invoked the notion of a news ecology:

> Yes, there has just been a Neighbourhood Watch set up on the estate and the guy that is running that, he emails us the local police news and I suppose because it's new at the minute I do keep having a look to see what's happened. (Female, Group 1)

> My daughter wouldn't know anything about the news or anything in our village unless it was on Facebook or Twitter, she would never read a paper, and she is twenty-five – you are right what you said earlier, it's a good new ... like last night in our village there are people knocking on your door saying we are doing free heating assessments and they were burglars and they had done five in a street. Now she knew – that is the only way my daughter would find local news – she is twenty-five – she would find news on Facebook or Twitter. (Female, Group 5)

> Facebook is for younger people and most young people have Facebook or Twitter and that is where I hear things like that. (Male, Group 2)

> Grapevines, school, Facebook. (Female, Group 6)

Whether taking place online or offline, word-of-mouth news practices encompass both telling stories and seeking information, often at the same time. The concept of practice is important for understanding how these different kinds of news coexist in people's everyday experience.

News travelling by word-of-mouth is not limited to concerns about the local street or neighbourhood. In discussing how news travels through local communities, our participants made clear that *community* is not only geographic, but entails more complex ties of class and ethnicity. One participant from the Leeds Sikh community explained how its members see themselves as a specific community with its own information needs and how its news tends to travel via word-of-mouth and provide *different* news from the mainstream media:

Because the Sikh community is quite big in Leeds anyway basically, and then there's the media, I suppose you've got your radio and TV. (Female, Group 4)

For local grapevines to work, key people are crucial. These key people are not newsreaders or journalists. Instead, our participants spoke of policemen, firefighters, teachers, Neighbourhood Watch representatives, shopkeepers and 'nosy' neighbours. These are people of varying status, but all of whom are positioned in ways that enable them to receive and disseminate trusted forms of useful and desirable information. They are purveyors and distributors of local news. Key people were mentioned in every one of our focus group interviews. Sometimes our interviewees referred to other people playing this role and sometimes they claimed it for themselves:

One of the neighbours is very good at picking things up – she finds out all sorts of stuff. There is also a local parish newspaper that comes out quarterly.

That neighbour – does everyone tend to go to that neighbour's house?

No, she works in a local shop, so she chats to everybody and passes it on. She is very informative. (Male, Group 2)

Yes, through, like, antenatal groups we met up with girls and then, maybe, then again at nursery and preschool, I am also a primary school teacher as well, so little ... people will ask me about the local schools. (Female, Group 1)

Well, I've got local mates that are in various bits and bats, ex-coppers that seem to know everything before it's even happened. (Male, Group 6)

Yes, because I'm connected with the police and I am a Neighbourhood Watch coordinator and I work with Victim Support, so I know what's going on throughout the area. I also send out an email to all the residents that I work with in the Neighbourhood Watch with anything that's related to break-ins around the area, or to look out for a certain car or person, so I communicate regularly with the people. (Male, Group 5)

My mother-in-law lives next door to a woman who [is part of the Neighbourhood Watch scheme], so we do get it all passed to us. So yeah, we do get to know a little bit. (Male, Group 5)

Key people tell stories. They are not news sources whose facts are checked, nor are they journalists who are expected to provide reports, but they do seem to be widely trusted, partly because of their position in relation to local networks and partly precisely because they are not telling stories as a job. They are key because they have access to certain kinds of information straight from the source, as if it were unmediated. Again and again in our participants' references to key people as sources of local news, it was the rawness and authenticity of their accounts that made them seem credible. Of course, the stories told by key people *are* mediated – that is the nature of a story as opposed to direct experience; because it was initially experienced by a person who seems to live in the world of common experience, it feels unmediated.

Our participants seemed to respect key people because they possess direct *experience* of an aspect of local life. From such experience comes a range of contacts with others who can enrich the experiential texture. So police officers are assumed to be in the know not only because of what they are able to encounter in the course of their work, but because of the network of variously positioned local witnesses with whom they come into regular contact:

I think, because of what goes on in Leeds, and my job, people ask me what's going on. So with the recent riots in Chapeltown, people ask me about that and other things. I've got friends who work on the other side of Leeds and firefighters who work in Hunslet. (Male, Group 1)

Meanwhile, other people become important at particular moments. For example, one participant told us that her dad lived in the Leeds neighbourhood of Chapeltown, so she phoned him to find out what was going on there when so-called riots took place across the country. Of course, as with all storytelling, the stories that are told vary considerably and so, just as this participant gave her account of what sparked the disturbance in Chapeltown, another participant in the same focus group claimed she had heard a very different story:

Yes, it was the shooting. Two friends, one was an Asian guy and one was a black guy, and the black guy was going out with the Asian guy's sister, so the Asian guy went to go score a draw from the black guy, but thinking he didn't have to pay for it because he was going out with his sister, and the black guy said no, you need to pay for it, so apparently, all of a sudden, they had this little argument and the gun went off in his face. So this is the reason this is the first time I've not gone to the carnival up Chapeltown. I've been brought up ... I was in the carnival from such a young age. At one year I was the Queen in the carnival so I've always, always gone. But this year I was advised not because there was going to be some carrying on because that issue wasn't closed with the shooting ...

That story you just told, I've got a completely different one that was from a friend of the Asian guy ... (Females, Group 4)

As well as key people, participants referred repeatedly to key locations for *hearing* (and *overhearing*) the news. As in the market squares, salons and coffee houses of the early public sphere, news circulates more intensely in key places of social intercourse. For our participants, local news tended to emerge as that which is embedded in the locations of daily life where stories are overheard, misheard, adapted and passed on. The most common of these locations were the school gates, shop, pub and community centre:

I live in Rawdon and I've got two young children that go to the local school, so that's kind of my way of finding about what goes on locally.

How does that work?

It's just talking to the other mums. Obviously, if there are things going on at the school or church then you usually find out through school. We've got a cricket club and a donkey derby coming up and there was a leaflet about that in the school bags ... (Female, Group 3)

We are not part of any big community thing. We pick up a fair bit in terms of my daughter's school – that type of thing. (Male, Group 3)

Because we've got a community centre next door, we share information. (Female, Group 4)

While we should be suspicious of the conventional association between grapevines and gossip, rumour and myth, there can be no doubt that networks of local storytelling are not always sociable and benign. They can also facilitate the repetition of misinformation and negative stereotypes. Some stories are undoubtedly partial, biased and fanciful; not unlike much that journalists produce in the name of news. Storytelling through grapevines both fosters community and divides communities. People's communicative practices in the contemporary news ecology can work to shore up pre-existing divisions. An exchange between two of our focus group participants illustrates this point. One woman explained that attending the Chapeltown carnival did not appeal to her, but she did not say where that lack of appeal originated. A man responded that, despite positive mainstream news coverage of a jolly carnival, 'we all' know better. Knowledge garnered through grapevines framed the Chapeltown area as dangerous and unruly before any news was even circulated about the specific event. The result was a belief that the Chapeltown carnival is dangerous and for other (read not white) people, no matter what the local newspaper cover photo of a costumed dancer might suggest:

F: It's never really appealed to me to go [to Chapeltown carnival], and it's not that far away.
M: I think it's because you know exactly what goes on there. It's not all singing and dancing. (Female and male, Group 2)

At the same time, people's own practices enable them to reflect on the news they garner from across the news ecology. Thus, one woman shows just how complicated news can be. She explains that she knows about the carnival from her school pupils and that is enough to put her off attending. Mainstream news portrayal of the riots across the country further deterred her. And yet she was at pains to point out that she knew better than to accept the image of the carnival as a dangerous place of theft and riot. She knew better, from listening to people she knows personally. Finally, however, she ends her evaluation of the event in a divisive way: her use of the words 'down there' signified the imagined distance of Chapeltown from its adjacent neighbourhoods:

> I've been before, I've got pupils who have been part of the carnival and it's incredibly busy – that was why I didn't go. I have to be honest as well. I was reticent because of all the rioting, etc., etc. However, knowing some of the families that I do *down there*, I don't think it was perhaps fair of me to make that judgement. (Female, Group 1, emphasis added)

Another participant was one of many in our focus groups who began to reflect on news stories and how these intersected with their everyday lives, leading them to wonder about what they know and how they know it:

> I heard it [Chapeltown carnival] had gone well and been a positive and well attended event. Over years it's a big, positive thing for the Leeds community, so I don't understand why I haven't been because I know people who do go. (Male, Group 2)

> M: You shouldn't be frightened of Chapeltown. It's like any area. Just because in Chapeltown there is a high ethnic mix …
> M: Yes, but there were riots in the eighties …
> M: Yes, but … I like driving through it. I drove through it the night after the riots with my son and my wife said 'Put the buttons down' and there was nothing, but there is a legacy like there is with the Liverpool Toxteth riots and places have got tarnished from a long, long time ago. (Conversation, Group 6)

There is also a historical dimension to word-of-mouth news. Stories stick around. Old stories are solidified as The News, framing and defining an area and its population. When people do not have direct access to grapevines from an area such as Chapeltown, they resort to stories that have endured historically within their own grapevines:

When I moved to live from London to Leeds the first thing I was told was 'Don't go to Chapeltown'.

Wasn't it the same in London: Don't go to Brixton ...

Exactly, that's what I mean ... and it's like, no taxi is going to take you to Chapeltown. Well, actually, I got into a cab and he did take me to Chapeltown. But I think it's a perception. (Females, Group 4)

So, stories circulate; some clearly emanating from word-of-mouth, others from the local media and others still of no certain origin. In our focus groups, participants moved between these different types of narrative without feeling a need to acknowledge the difference between mediated and interpersonal sources.

The uses of local media

Previous studies of local news have put media organizations at the centre. Our study sees local news media as links in the chain of public communication – or, in line with our theory of news ecology, as significant nodes within networks of circulating information that comprise interpersonal as well as mass-mediated communication. Just as people 'pick up' local knowledge from their daily interactions and conversations with others, they pick up and put down, tune into and drift away from local media channels. A key message from our focus group participants was that attention to local news media tended to be fleeting and episodic. For example, speaking of the city's daily newspaper, the *Yorkshire Evening Post*, participants stated that:

I probably don't read all the articles. I will skim when it is something that is interesting. (Male, Group 1)

I don't get it delivered. My mum and dad get it delivered every single night. If I go round I will flick through it. I don't go to read it intentionally. (Male, Group 1)

Similarly, very few people spoke of listening to particular programmes on local radio. When asked whether they listened to BBC Radio Leeds, participants suggested that they turned to it in

moments of uncertainty (such as dangerous local weather conditions)
or as company when they drove through the city:

> It gives snippets of anything that's going on or if anything has
> happened or if there's a motorway or road blocked because
> there's been a big accident. You pick up on things like that.
> (Male, Group 1)

> Every week I have to go to my mother's, so every week when I
> set off I put the news on and I enjoy it, yes. (Female, Group 2)

> For severe weather, there's nowhere else to go. (Male, Group 3)

> Only when it is snowing, to see if school's shut. (Female, Group 1)

In reviewing these responses, we were struck by this image of
local radio as a sort of urban soundscape, guiding people through
the uncertainties of urban life rather than standing beyond it and
offering a remote journalistic commentary.

The two local television news programmes, *Look North* and
Calendar, were regarded as important local markers within the daily
television schedule. They served to remind people that they were not
only in Britain and the world, but in an area of the world with which
they might expect to have some familiarity; a way of speaking about
the world inflected by an accent and a set of common experiences that
warranted a particular kind of trust. As one focus group participant
put it, 'I trust hearing it from a local source rather than from like
London' (Female, Group 1). While the local news programmes were
certainly regarded as being somehow 'closer to home', they were
subjected to two common criticisms: first, that thirty minutes was too
short a time to provide more than superficial and fleeting snippets of
local news, and second that, as both programmes were charged with
providing news for regions far beyond the city of Leeds, much of the
'local news' was too geographically broad and journalistically limited
to offer a comprehensive account of life in Leeds. As one participant
explained:

> Locally, you get so many small, little issues that media groups
> have got to find the right one. And they've probably got so many

to choose from, but each only hits a small interested audience. If they tell a story about Horsforth ... St Margaret's School on the local news, my ears will pop up. If they start talking about some other locality that has nothing to do with my lifestyle, it's selfish, I know, but I switch off. (Male, Group 2)

A number of people said that they regularly watched both of the regional news programmes, but, in line with the survey data in Chapter 3, there was a broad consensus in favour of *Look North*, which was regarded as being better resourced and more likely to report stories in depth than *Calendar*:

F: You just feel that the BBC is going to be better news.
M: And there are no adverts. (Female and male, Group 3)
F: *BBC News*, it's more professional than ITV. They seem to
   be on the ball and it's always been. I think they've done it
   just right. *Calendar*'s too laid back. The presenters are too
   unprofessional at times.
F: I think it doesn't grab your attention as much.
F: To be honest, if I'm cleaning up and *Look North* comes on
   I'm straight on watching it, and I stop what I'm doing just to
   watch it. If it's *Calendar* you just carry on. Like you said, it's a
   bit laid back. (Females, Group 4)

A number of the participants were confused by the relationship between the nightly national news bulletins and local news. For some, the former was 'the main event':

I would say fifty per cent of the things that are on *Look North*
has already been reported on the BBC [national news]. Well,
surely, they would be better reporting on something else. (Male,
Group 5)

I watch *BBC News* first and then the other [local] one. I do it
that way every time. I like to find out about the main things.
What is going on in this country? (Male, Group 5)

For such people, the value of local news was that it could offer a local perspective on the vast, often abstract, national and global issues of the day:

F: How it is affecting people in Leeds?

F: Like the financial industry … when they were talking about fifty thousand job losses, it's going to affect Leeds at this stage because Lloyds employ two thousand eight hundred employees, so the high energy is going to come from Leeds and the surrounding areas … I know what you mean, that was what I was saying about getting it more local – how is it going to affect you? (Females, Group 2)

M: It's like a lot of the time, if you have a massive story like petrol, recession, jobs, community … the stuff that is happening in the national media doesn't tend to get reported on locally. And I think it should. And I think that is what I would like to see … (Male, Group 3)

M: We are talking about the recession and things like that. That is a national story. So, like, when it comes into local news … because it is dealt with nationally it doesn't have a local representation of that news. And what I would like is something like that, that is a national story – I would like a spin on it within Leeds. (Male, Group 5)

For others, the local programmes seemed to offer a retreat from hard news; a lighter, homelier perspective on the affairs of daily life, sometimes verging on celebratory parochialism and at other times tending towards folksy condescension:

F: I think they try to make it a little bit more relaxed, being a local news as opposed to *Six o'Clock News* where they are sat behind a desk and they are very straightforward … They try to put a bit more jollity in and try to be a bit more family orientated …

M: they try a bit too hard … I think that's the problem. (Female and male, Group 2)

I think the way local news is portrayed is small, like the little sister of the big news. And they don't want to do the main stories. They only want to do more light hearted, jovial stuff. It seems more like a cottage industry. (Male, Group 5)

They tend to have more happier stories than the doom and gloom you get on the national news ... It's more like 'It's not all that bad'. (Male, Group 2)

I think they treat you like you have either got senile dementia or you are about eight years old – both of them. (Male, Group 2)

What did our focus group participants want from the local news? Many wanted what they were never likely to be offered: a regular update on their own neighbourhoods, featuring people like themselves – probably people they actually knew:

If I knew somebody was going to be on it that I knew or a story that I knew about, then I would watch it to see what it was about and I think I would probably do the same if it was a major news feature. You wouldn't sit and watch it if you had something else to do I wouldn't have thought. (Female, Group 6)

I would like to see some proper news, like if something goes on at the airport or in the centre of Leeds. There was a rape recently – that was very poorly covered, I thought, down near the bus station. (Female, Group 5)

A common criticism of local news related to its negative tone. Several of our focus group participants were irritated by what seemed to be a focus upon crime, disorder and social incohesion to the exclusion of more positive accounts:

They all tell you the negative, bad things happening in communities, as opposed to the good things. So it forms your attitudes, even on a relaxed level like 'I don't like them because of this and this' ... There could be other things that happen that don't get focused on. (Female, Group 1)

This is, of course, a common public criticism of news, and some journalists have argued that it is disingenuous; that although people claim to want to know when their fellow citizens are doing good things and events take place successfully, it is the stories of antisocial actions and government incompetence that tend to attract audience attention. But we did not sense that people wanted to replace persistent negativity with anything like parochial complacency. Rather, they were suggesting that the local media fails to capture the richness of everyday communities across Leeds. One woman expressed this with particular force and clarity:

> I actually did Race for Life this year at Temple Newsom and I raised quite a bit of money, and there were five thousand women there. It was unbelievable, it was so heart-warming and emotional and everything, and I expected this massive media thing on *Look North* and *Calendar*, and nothing ... about a thirty-second slot. I thought, 'How disgraceful is that, that was for such a good cause, every one of us will know someone who's affected by it, and they let us down, and I'd still do it again.' But the media, they took loads of photographs, *Yorkshire Evening Post*, and *Look North*, were they involved? No, they weren't involved – because *Calendar* was there and one of the presenters was there and they still managed to show about thirty seconds in a slot. I thought that was so sad. Especially when it only happens once a year and it's for a good cause. (Female, Group 4)

Focus group participants who came from the city's mainly black and minority ethnic communities, whose members were specifically represented in one of our groups, were particularly concerned about what they saw as a double focus by the local media: most of the time, they were rendered invisible by journalists who simply did not understand or know about their news; and then, when there was negative news to report, these communities would be singled out for special attention. This left them doubting the extent to which the city's 'multicultural' claims were being mediated fairly:

> In forty years Leeds has become a multi-cultured city. I think really the onus is on the top end to show that it is multi-cultured. And they don't show the multi-cultured events. They only show certain events ... like I say, multi-cultured society is on the bottom. We are not on the top. (Male, Group 4)

> They should show it as a multicultural society in Leeds ... it's no good admitting it, but not showing it. And they have got to

show in the programme that Leeds is a multicultural society. When you can see it on the programmes they show you, they can say they are doing something. Up to now they haven't done that. If they do this, that will be a good start. (Female, Group 4)

People who don't know a lot about the culture wouldn't cover it enough. If I know something about Sikh, I would cover it more than maybe a white person would. I'm not being racist, but I think it's the knowledge of what you're doing and how you perceive things and you put it forward to everybody. (Male, Group 4)

But it was not only participants from ethnic minorities who complained about this failure to represent all of the city's communities. Several people recalled the aftermath of the 7/7 bombings in London when it became clear that the perpetrators were from Leeds. Suddenly the local media were rushing to the area of east Leeds from which they came to find out more about it. Why not before then? As one participant put it when asked whether the local media did a good job representing people like him:

To be absolutely honest, yes, because ... I'm a white, middle-aged, middle-class man, living in an affluent area. It ticks all the boxes for me, selfishly. (Male, Group 6)

We were struck by a set of broadly held assumptions running across all six of our focus groups. The first was that, despite media producers' emphasis upon recruiting 'ordinary voices' as contributors to and framers of the news, many of our participants seemed to regard 'local news' as something beyond them; above them; targeted at them. It was as if there was life in the city and then there was the news of the city. Sometimes the two coincided. Often there was a gulf between what people experienced as important local events and the local media's recognition of them. While several of our participants were able to provide examples of occasions when they had passed on news stories to local journalists, most of these accounts tended to be characterized by frustration and disappointment:

My husband works at the paper mill that's just celebrated
this summer 125 years, and he organized this big fun day for
everyone that works there, and it's a big thing: it's the last paper
mill that produces this certain paper. It's shipped all around the
world. And nobody was interested. They [local press and radio]
said, 'Oh, will you mail us some pictures?' so he did, and there
were over six hundred people.

*Why do you think that is? I mean what went through their minds that
stopped them from wanting to come?*

Well, this is local people that work there and have worked there
for generation after generation.

But why do you think the Yorkshire Evening Post *and Radio Leeds
and* Look North *didn't cover it?*

Maybe they didn't think it was of any interest to other people ...
(Female, Group 5)

A firefighter gave another example, albeit from a few years
earlier:

I can give you an example where something happened and it
was the *Yorkshire Evening Post* ... it was the *Yorkshire Evening
Post* and they never printed it. When we went on strike there
was a road crash on the ring road on the A64 where two people
were trapped and somebody came running up to Gipton fire
station and said. They actually broke the strike line, did the
lads. They went down and cut these people out and saved their
lives. *Yorkshire Evening Post* were told all about it ... that they
had done this and they said, 'Great, that will make a great story.'
And it never hit *Yorkshire Evening Post*. Nobody knew about it
at all.

Did Look North *or* Calendar *cover that?*

No, the news crews were there filming it all because they
followed the army. The army turned up as well. (Male, Group 3)

It is not for us to decide upon the editorial merits of reporting
these stories, or the several others like them that we were told about.

But we were struck by the sense of resignation with which people spoke about such failed attempts to make or influence the news. They spoke as if the idea of media accountability to the public had never been conceived. Occasionally such accounts of failed media contributions were followed up by semi-conspiratorial theories about who really controls the media agenda. But for most people it was not a case of the local media being either politically skewed or inherently untrustworthy. The assumption seemed to be that journalists would operate in accordance with a mysterious private logic – one that would often disappoint local expectations and against which there seemed to be no obvious channels of appeal.

Secondly, we noted the strong connection in people's minds between local news and interpersonal discussion. According to our survey (Chapter 3), approximately two-thirds of respondents talked about local news to other people at least once or twice a week. This continuation of the mediated news in more personal settings can be understood as a process of ecological circulation. As one participant put it:

> News tends to report things that are out of the norm and you go down the pub and the bartender will say, 'Did you see that on the news about ...?' Because, yes, it's unusual. It's not the norm. (Male/female, Group X)

This is how news travels ecologically. It is not simply transmitted and received, but passes through a range of social contexts, sticking in some and missing others. Furthermore, judgements about what constitutes local social norms are never wholly stable. Journalists offer stories about normative exceptions and affirmations, but it is in the living rooms, pubs, workplaces and other spaces of shared reception and reflection that norms are embedded, revised or rejected.

A third common assumption runs counter to the popular discourse within current North American studies of local news. The latter offer some suggestive accounts of the internet opening up new spaces for the circulation of local stories and perspectives, transcending traditional journalistic gatekeepers and equalizing power between citizens and elites. While there is some evidence of this happening in Leeds on a minor scale, such a rebalancing of media power was certainly not apparent from our focus groups. Even though one of the groups was recruited with a view to hearing from frequent users of online media, discussion of online communication across all the groups seemed to draw a sharp distinction between the mass media (offline and online) as a source of publicly relevant news and social media (including email, Facebook and Twitter) as a space for interpersonal socializing. The idea that the internet might be a space for the dissemination or reception of local news and views, beyond the online platforms of the mainstream media, hardly ever registered with our participants, although one woman reported that 'My daughter wouldn't know anything about the news or anything in our village unless it was on Facebook or Twitter; she would never read a paper, and she's twenty-five' (Female, Group 5). Nobody in any of our groups produced a blog or reported reading blogs produced by others. A few tweeted, but none reported following any of the city-related Twitter feeds. None of this necessarily means that local news is absent within the millions of online communications that pass around the city every day. Indeed, if, as we have suggested, grapevines are key sources of local news and information, we can suppose that the same is true of virtual grapevines. Digital communication is surely connecting the city in new and unexpected ways, but there remains considerable work to be done in analysing the flow of common and contested knowledge within spaces that are neither conventionally interpersonal nor centrally mediated.

We began this chapter by suggesting that living in a city involves a certain kind of relationship; a feel for place; a sense that one's presence matters. In our focus group discussions we heard accounts of how such relationships were both nurtured and let down at different times by various local media. Sometimes news stories hit the spot and served as powerful symbolic reminders of place and history. Sometimes local culture seemed to exceed the formulaic formats of local journalism. Perhaps the clearest picture of the relationship between people, the city and the mediated narratives that tie them together emerged not from reflections upon the quality of specific news stories, programmes or channels, but from occasional, seemingly throwaway comments about what it means to be spoken to – and sometimes for – by someone else. For local attachments are not simply founded upon an ongoing supply of the latest information. The experience of feeling part of a neighbourhood, city or community depends upon the confidence with which people feel able to use the words 'we' and 'us'.

Often, a mediated sense of place emerges through identification with voices that are attuned to local experience. For example, several participants in our focus groups identified less with the news per se than with its veteran Yorkshire presenter, Harry Gration, who has co-presented the *Look North* programme for many years. Gration seemed to personify a certain way of looking at and talking about the world which they understood as speaking to – and sometimes for – them. 'He's a presenter who's been there for years. He went to work for the Rugby League and then he came back,' explained one woman. 'I like Harry because he brightens you up a bit,' explained another. 'Yes,' said a third, 'I think it's because he's always been there' (Group 3). One participant explained how she had recently become a regular listener to Radio Asian Fever: 'They've got various different presenters and I am glad that they are not just one religion; they've got diverse unity in itself' (Female, Group 4). This notion of 'diverse unity' concisely summarizes the cultural heterogeneity of this late modern city. The voices that can address hundreds of millions of people in their pluralistic coexistence speak not only to the shared rhythms and idioms of the consolidated city, but to the latent anxieties and untranslated misapprehensions that blight mutual communication. It is as translators of experience between communities, grapevines and individual citizens that local news media need to show their worth. The evidence from our focus groups suggests that the construction of a mediated Leeds 'us' calls for a more nuanced approach than currently prevails.

5 | THE MAINSTREAM PROVIDERS OF LOCAL NEWS

The mainstream media form the perennials in the news ecology of Leeds and have the highest public profile. BBC and ITV regional television, BBC and commercial local radio, and city newspapers are the big plants in the media garden.

Our aim here is not so much to dwell on the content produced by the Leeds mainstream media, though inevitably some of the content considered in Chapter 2 is relevant and will be referred to throughout. Our aim is to attempt to access the local decision-makers working there and to find out what motivates them and informs their judgement. We wanted to discover how they see their roles vis-à-vis the communities they provide with local news every day and how they perceive challenges as local news providers. Inevitably the news agendas of local media are influenced by national and sometimes international news, so we also wanted to ascertain how national stories might translate locally.

We were able to conduct semi-structured interviews with editors and producers from four of the mainstream outlets based in Leeds, and we also followed a national-to-local story from its source to publication, interviewing representatives of the source institution as well as the media editors who considered the publicity material. We were given access to the newsrooms and personnel at BBC Radio Leeds, BBC *Look North*, and ITV's *Calendar*, where we were able to observe and record editorial meetings as well as conduct the interviews. The *Yorkshire Evening Post*'s editor and his principal online journalist spoke with us in their offices but did not want the conversations recorded. Later, they provided answers to our questions by email. Before outlining our findings, it is useful to set down for the purposes of context something of the history and background of the news outlets studied.

Who are the mainstream providers of local news?

Newspapers in Britain are privately owned and operate in a competitive market; their success depends on sales recorded in circulation figures and on the support of advertisers. In their editorial pages the national papers are proudly partisan, each of them openly supporting a political party, especially during election campaigns, and the red-top tabloids will seek the more sensational stories to maximize circulation and income. The local and regional press, on the other hand, is less brazen in its approach, because it depends on the respect and goodwill of local readerships too much to wear its politics on its sleeve, or compete for the most sensational of news stories. Nevertheless, local newspapers are businesses, so competition is directed at serving local people with news, sport and entertainment that matters in the places where readers live and work every day.

Decline in newspaper circulation is a nationwide phenomenon which has already been the subject of a fair amount of scholarly analysis. It is widely recognized that a concentration of ownership has reduced diversity. Subsequent changes in newsroom routines and practices have resulted in a homogenization of journalistic output. Both of these practices are related to the lack of advertising revenue because consumers and advertisers have moved online (Lee-Wright et al. 2011; Fenton 2009). Several studies of the regional press have shown the ownership move away from local proprietorship to large monopoly newspaper groups (Aldridge 2007; Franklin 2006; Greenslade 2004).

Yorkshire Post Newspapers (YPN) is a textbook example. Today the *Yorkshire Evening Post*'s (YEP) circulation is a mere 21,946. What was already a steep decline has gone into freefall more recently with a 16.5 per cent year on year drop in sales (ABC 2015). Franklin (2006: 8) points out that by the time Johnston Press took over, YPN had experienced four owners in ten years, whereas in the previous 240 years it had just one. Johnston Press achieved huge economies of scale because of the takeovers and amalgamations it engineered, making it one of the big four owners of the regional press. It has cut costs by shedding staff and sharing print plants (Yorkshire Post Newspapers are now printed in Sheffield and Sunderland, not Leeds), and realizing property assets. YPN's landmark building at the end of Wellington Street, which housed its printing press, was recently demolished to make way for some modern city apartments, restaurants and bars. The remaining YPN staff were moved to new, less prominent premises on Whitehall Road. This kind of radical restructuring matters because it has a significant impact on the news ecology of a city in two important respects. First, the main city paper is no longer a physical presence, a landmark that makes its doings accessible to a public that got used to calling in to order photos or place adverts in the classifieds. According to Franklin, 'a serious consequence here is the loss of routine contact with the local community where the paper circulates' (ibid.: xxi), and Aldridge wonders to what extent decline in sales for city evening papers has been accelerated 'by a loss of literal visibility and thus identification with "our" paper, whether loved or hated' (2007: 43). Second, restructuring matters in that it is more likely to produce a homogenization of content because the economies of scale thus achieved enable the centralization of services, including news services. The payroll at YPN has gone from 1,300 to 400, and that cannot happen without operational consequences that include 'intensified working practices, passive newsgathering and the sharing of generic content' (ibid.). In the case of YPN it has also meant a sharing of editorial responsibility in-house as well, since the role of editor was rationalized and the YPN and YEP came under the same editorship at the beginning of 2012.

Yorkshire Post Newspapers has a growing online presence and has adopted a 'digital first' policy so that its online product takes priority. Though the web browsing figures look robust enough with a 38 per cent increase over the last five years, monetizing that increase is a conundrum yet to be fathomed. Though both titles are relevant to the Leeds media, this study will confine itself to the Leeds evening paper, the *Yorkshire Evening Post*, which reports news from and about the city; the *Yorkshire Post* is a self-styled national daily with a much wider brief.

In contrast, the entirety of British broadcasting was assumed to be guided by public service principles. The BBC, financed by a licence fee levied on all television set owners, had been founded in the 1920s in accordance with such principles, and when Independent Television was introduced in 1955 to offer competitive and complementary programming, its regulation was designed to ensure that it too would form a public broadcasting system, albeit financed by the sale of advertising. On both sides informational news and current affairs programming were at the heart of the public service idea. For their part, the ethos and output of British regional and local television and radio stations were also guided by this public service heritage.

Radio Leeds was one of the first BBC local radio stations to be born from a particular recommendation of the Pilkington Committee in 1962, that the Corporation extend its reach to encompass local radio. An initial two-year pilot of eight stations, including Leeds, worked well enough to roll out the service across the nation. They operated on a shoestring budget and the money was to be found by the stations in the locality; it was not to come from the licence fee or the rates, though local authorities did foot much of the bill; what little funding that was available made no provision for news because the BBC had assumed that local newspapers and news agencies would supply the stations with copy, seemingly oblivious to the fact that a BBC local station would be regarded as a competitor in the news market. The local papers jealously guarded their stories and the news agencies wanted payment at the market rate. Somehow only Radio Leeds managed to prise the money from the BBC for three news reporters and so for a period became the only one of the eight to broadcast hourly news bulletins. Then, having no money for publicity and very little for staff and programming, station manager Phil Sidey came up with some novel ideas to make ends meet. He bought a greyhound he called 'Radio Leeds' just to get the station's name in the sports pages of the local papers. He saved on the programming budget by getting listeners to bring in their own favourite music and talk about it. For a week he gave the station over to Leeds teenagers, who were not paid for their efforts but enthusiastically took the opportunity to broadcast their own material (Sidey 1994).

His determination to fight for the Radio Leeds corner paid handsome dividends when Sidey penned an influential article in the *New Statesman* which, according to Frank Gillard, the former managing director of BBC Radio, 'convinced the entire Labour hierarchy of the success of the BBC's local radio experiment' (The Independent 1995).

It was the arrival of commercial radio in the early 1970s and extended further in the 1980s that brought the BBC intense competition that was initially hard to overcome. Licences with public service remits were granted to enthusiastic local broadcasters to deliver local news and programming alongside chart music. In Leeds, Radio Aire was a palpable success, breathing new life into what by then looked like a moribund formula from the BBC. Even some of the BBC's own audience research suggested the output was becoming 'trivial, parochial and inward-looking'. The newsroom at Radio Aire, in the purpose-built studios next to Yorkshire Television on Kirkstall Road, was populated with young, aspiring journalists, typified by Mark Mardell and Mark Easton, now national and international BBC news correspondents. Its music emanated from the personal choices of brash, innovative disc jockeys like Andy and Liz Kershaw and Chris Moyles.

The 1990s saw an exponential growth in commercial radio stations as a new, deregulatory climate took hold. Following legislation from both Conservative and Labour governments engineered to take down regulatory barriers so that commercial competition could thrive in the sector, the early years of the twenty-first century were characterized by corporate takeovers and the expulsion of much of the local news and factual output. The new regulator for commercial broadcasting, Ofcom, was explicitly tasked with delivering a 'light touch' regulation when it was set up in 2002. In 1995 Radio Aire became part of the colossal EMAP group, which was in turn bought by the German multinational Bauer Radio. The station is now a host to the kind of generic branding that means agency news and formulaic music is in the ascendancy. Though it still retains a handful of local news reporters and producers and insists it is still committed to local news reporting, it is a mainstream music station nevertheless, with its two-minute news bulletins read speedily on the hour, over a music bed. The Ofcom requirement for commercial stations is that they 'broadcast local news at least hourly throughout peak time', though it does not stipulate how long the bulletin should be. Hargreaves and Thomas (2002: 62) found that 'news agendas have moved towards being dominated by entertainment and sports news', while Aldridge (2007: 113) comments, 'in most cases local radio's commercial provision of regional news is vestigial'.

Despite its solid anchor in public service, for a while the BBC felt forced to respond to the challenge of commercial competition and, according to critics, made a significant mistake by using specifically commercial radio marketing techniques to create typical local radio 'personas' which had been used since 2000. A senior presenter at Radio Leeds says that the autonomy of BBC local radio stations was chipped away, 'the fatal blow being struck during what local radio folk know of as the Dave and Sue era when BBC Nations and Regions invented a mythical couple, a fifty-five-year-old plumber and his second wife, to whom all our programmes were to be addressed' (Radio Today 2011). As part of its 'Project Bullseye', a target audience was identified and then personified. 'Dave and Sue' were presented to all eighty-seven BBC local radio stations as the listeners of choice, to challenge the shrinking market reach. 'Dave' the plumber was self-employed and his partner 'Sue' was a school secretary; they came with full character profiles, wardrobes and shopping habits. The employment of corporate marketing techniques such as these to attract a specific market sector at the expense of the general listener never appeared to be an unalloyed success for the BBC. David Self in the *New Statesman* complained, 'Dave and Sue don't want arts or political coverage, controversy or even reality. In fact they don't want public service broadcasting – which is why it is no longer on offer' (Self 2005: 33).

The experiment was jettisoned in 2010 when local radio became part of the News Division of the BBC and its remit was to put news and journalism first once again. Each station is required to act as a conduit for local news but also as a source of national and international news and debate, a kind of one-stop shop for listeners to hear news and views from home and abroad. It is characterized by a strong civic purpose and is dominated by speech rather than music, constantly encouraging public participation.

The BBC was the first to bring television to Leeds in the 1950s from its regional studios in Manchester. Local camera crews, working with celluloid film stock, would traverse the Pennines with undeveloped footage of local Yorkshire stories, to be processed and presented from Manchester, until new transmitters enabled Yorkshire to develop its own television services in 1968. Later the same year, Yorkshire Television (YTV), one of the strongest and most productive of the new independent regional television companies collectively known as ITV, began transmitting from Leeds. It was better known for its original comedies and dramas, but it also established regional news and current affairs programmes, including the nightly news magazine *Calendar*. From the start, YTV was altogether richer and more glamorous than its BBC counterpart because it was commercial – funded by wealthy regional backers and by the advertising revenue, which simply poured into independent television companies in those early days, so much so that the media mogul Lord Thomson, then chairman of Scottish Television and owner of Times Newspapers, said a regional TV franchise was 'a license to print money' (Seymour-Ure 2003: 100). Yorkshire Television was broadcast from a purpose-built multimillion-pound studio complex on Kirkstall Road. These were said to be the biggest and most up-to-date studios in Europe. In contrast, the BBC had to make do with the ground floor of some rather dilapidated rooms in All Soul's Church on the other side of town, where, according to its first Head of Centre, Bill Greaves, the news magazine programme *Look North* was broadcast without sufficient soundproofing and staff could hear the clattering feet of the local tap dance troop, practising on the floor immediately above the studio (BBC 2003). Greaves was also in charge of feature programming and his idea was to develop an artistic hub in Leeds which would put the city on television's cultural map. Following a move to new premises on Woodhouse Lane, he succeeded in attracting gifted writers and cinematographers who brought international awards to Leeds.

Regional television had its flippant side in the 1970s and 1980s, encouraged by *Nationwide*, the BBC's networked early evening news magazine programme that made household names of regional reporters and presenters by asking them to do humorous stunts for the nation's amusement, or film animals in anthropomorphic mode, epitomized by the infamous skateboarding duck from *Midlands Today* in 1978. *Look North* and *Calendar* had their fair share of presenter stunts and talking animals during those years too, though frivolity took a break at the BBC in Woodhouse Lane, as it did in all BBC regional news outlets, after the appointment of John Birt to the News Directorate in 1987. Successive regional editors were encouraged to 'value the significant and the serious above the sensational and merely curious'. Serious public service journalism had returned to BBC regional television, which enjoyed some of its most successful years in terms of both quality news reporting and public appreciation. *Look North* and *Calendar* have both been subject to the vicissitudes of government policy-makers, centralized management and the commercial media market, but deregulation of the British media in the 1990s severely affected Yorkshire Television, much more than it affected the BBC regions.

The Thatcher government intended to wake up commercial television and encourage more aggressive competition, which it predicted would curtail a perceived endemic complacency. Some scholars and broadcasters have suggested the Conservatives were irritated by some of the critical documentaries emanating from the large and wealthy independent television companies like Granada, Yorkshire and Thames. It seemed the 'licence to print money' privilege they enjoyed was interpreted in Downing Street as a licence to make programmes critical of the Tories (McNair 1996; Crisell 2002; Goodwin 1998). So, the 1990 Broadcasting Act obliged each commercial company in the ITV stable to rebid for its own franchise to broadcast, against any other company in that transmission area wishing to challenge it – a process very quickly dubbed a 'franchise auction'. It appeared that the winning bidder would get a licence, depending on the amount of money it was prepared to hand over. In the Yorkshire case, though YTV was awarded the franchise, its management and shareholders had agreed to an overpriced bid in order to secure the company's survival. They paid more than £37 million, which they could not recover. Though YTV continued for some years to produce popular and influential factual strands such as *Jimmy's*, a reality TV version of daily life at St James hospital in Leeds, serious documentary-making was over after a decade with the end of the *First Tuesday* series in 1993. When the inevitable takeovers and mergers of ITV companies took place, resulting in just one ITV company by 2003, Yorkshire Television – now ITV Yorkshire – began its swift decline. In 2009 came the announcement of the closure of the main Kirkstall Road studios with the loss of 192 jobs. All that remained was the soap *Emmerdale*, which was shot on location anyway, and the news programme *Calendar*, which moved into an adjacent, smaller studio complex. The news studios in Sheffield were also shut.

From November 2014, Leeds began providing one of the fourteen local television services so far established across the country, after the Coalition Government brought in legislation to add another tier of local media provision, sidestepping perhaps the greater challenge of funding ITV regional television news, which was agreed to be in a parlous state. Plans for it to share BBC facilities or top-slice BBC funding were shelved, though Ofcom was unequivocal about the consequences if government did not intervene. Its research has shown that audiences value their regional news provision and that they expect to be given a choice of specifically public service provision 'beyond the BBC', and that 'whether or not ITV chooses to remain a public service broadcaster' or to 'give up its public service licenses, the current ITV networking model looks increasingly unsustainable' (Ofcom 2009: 1.63).

Since then ITV has been awarded a further ten-year licence and has been granted its wish to reduce regional news programming by a third. When Ofcom returned in 2014 to re-examine public service broadcasting, it found that the viewing of regional television news in England 'has declined by over four hours since 2008 to 24 hours per person per year' and that the majority of the decline had been in ITV regional news viewing (Ofcom 2015). This latest report has been rather overshadowed by headlines proclaiming the biggest overhaul of the BBC's remit since its inception, planned by the new government as part of the charter renewal negotiations. So contextually, this study was carried out at an interesting juncture in the history of public service broadcasting in the UK.

Finally, it is also important to point out that the regional television news programmes viewed by the citizens of Leeds have always enjoyed a much wider audience, not only in the sizeable county of Yorkshire but also across much of the north of England and east of the Pennines.

At the chalkface: the editorial interviews

Our aim was to explore how the editorial decision-makers in the Leeds mainstream media outlets perceive their roles and to discover what informs their judgement. We conducted unstructured but pre-planned and broadly comparable interviews with leading personnel from four of the mainstream local news media in Leeds (*Look North*, *Calendar*, Radio Leeds and the *Yorkshire Evening Post*). *Look North* and *Calendar*, both regional half-hour television news magazine programmes, are aired respectively at 6.00 and 6.30 p.m. each weekday evening. Radio Leeds is on air in West Yorkshire from 6.30 in the morning to 7.00 in the evening; before and after those times listeners join either pan-regional broadcasts or the national station Radio 5 Live. The *Yorkshire Evening Post* is a daily newspaper for the city of Leeds whose first edition is distributed at lunchtime every day, and it also has an online edition.

Averaging approximately an hour in length, these interviews covered the informants' perspectives on their work in respect of: recent developments in their outlets' situations, including the main sources of change; the outlets' overall roles and purposes, actual and preferred, and forms of public service envisaged if any; most satisfying types of stories to present (and least); local story priorities, preferences and related perceptions of a Yorkshire character; relations to available national stories and how the latter might be localized; types of 'voices' or actors preferred and to be avoided; perceptions of relations to their audiences; uses of social media; and any lines of self-criticism. The interviews were recorded, transcribed and then analysed in detail in matrices under headings that represent the key concerns and preoccupations that emerged: public purposes; preferred stories; preferred 'voice'; sense of the audience; and new media. It was recognized that the interviewees' statements might not correspond in all respects with the kinds of news the services actually produce. To some extent that can be checked, however, by the results of a content analysis of one week of their output that formed a complementary part of the project's work and was described in Chapter 2.

Preferred stories

To some extent the news values of our respondents resembled those that guide provision in many other journalistic enterprises: importance, relevance, interest, novelty, breadth of impact, originality (including exclusives where possible), conflict and controversy, and human interest. As an editor summed it up, 'we want to be seen to be relevant, interesting and at times entertaining and informative'. Having a strong emotive impact, 'a wow factor', as another editor put it, was also thought to be desirable at times, especially for first stories. Something which may be more characteristic of local journalism in general emerged when we asked our interviewees to talk about the stories that they most liked to cover. Often mentioned was a concern to imagine what their audiences as local people were like and would therefore appreciate in their output. According to the editor of the *Yorkshire Evening Post*, it is 'hugely important to take on board the issues your readership is interested in. We are both a friend and an advocate on their behalf'; examples are the newspaper's campaigns criticizing the private bus operators in the city, or supporting the Leeds Children's Heart Unit in its fight against closure. The friend-of-the-people orientation was presented in its strongest form by a *Calendar* producer who simply declared that it was a '*people programme*'. *Calendar*'s editor chose as an example their continuing coverage of the disappearance in 1991 of the Sheffield child Ben Needham on a family holiday on the Greek island of Kos. He was especially proud of the relationship his reporter developed with the family. It enabled the programme to take Ben's grandmother back to the island on the anniversary of the boy's disappearance to gauge her thoughts and feelings twenty years on. 'We've come up with something staggering ... which is fantastic journalism,' he told us, because it was an exclusive which also chimed with the human-interest stories his audience loved. Producers of local media are aware that crime stories like those concerning missing children or infamous killers affect the local community in a materially different way to their impact on national audiences, because it is personal and it is about identity. *Look North*'s editor mentioned the disappearance and subsequent discovery of Shannon Matthews, the child kidnapped by her own family in South Yorkshire, and the Bradford killer known as the Crossbow Cannibal – both crimes reported nationally – as examples of stories that are top of his news priorities, along with the effects of the recession and freak weather conditions. They are 'the big stories' and they are 'the stories people judge you on and that people remember you by'. He professed to be guided by two golden rules – 'one, you need pictures' but 'two, you need your human story in there'. He believes that sometimes populist stories mean more to audiences than a serious and exclusive piece of journalism. He told us that he had put up two stories that *Look North* intended to cover that week on the programme's Facebook site. One was an extended report of exclusive access to Moorland prison near Doncaster, following riots there which had caused extensive damage. The other was a report from a video journalist who had been with police arresting people using their mobile phones when driving and had got 'great footage of people being arrested, basically'. The public response to the prison exclusive was virtually non-existent, but the *Look North* page was inundated with comments about the mobile phone item. According to the news editor:

> The prison thing is arguably important and I'm not saying I'm going down a completely populist agenda but it does give you a guide as to when you might be a bit sort of traditionalist; thinking these are exclusive pictures [of the prison] and they [the audience] are really going to be interested in this, when maybe

actually what really bothers them is some idiot using a mobile while he's driving.

The BBC editors in particular made the point several times that they were intent on covering the effects of the recession and the subsequent austerity programme or 'cuts' thoroughly and in a variety of ways. It was our impression, though, that this could seem a bit of a chore at times unless they had a strong human-interest story to tell. The two television outlets felt obliged to report on cuts in local services but were intimidated by the task of covering the whole region so, on occasion, instead of looking at individual areas where news of specific cuts in services had taken place, they preferred to take a service that was being reduced across the country and see how cuts in that service affected different parts of their patch in Yorkshire. While this might have the advantage of economies of scale, it is clearly in danger of missing an important development in one area while possibly exaggerating something in another. *Calendar* said their cameras were at virtually every city and large town in the region for the Trade Union Congress day of action in March 2011; *Look North* 'did nearly half the programme on libraries' reporting on library closures in Leeds, North Yorkshire and Doncaster, but admitted that in the end if viewers wanted the specific details for their area it was best to go online. It is hard to argue with that, given the size of the transmission areas for these regional television programmes: 'if you want a list of the thirteen that are going to close [in Leeds] we're not going to tell you actually because we have better things to do with our time, we've only got half an hour, you need to go online and that is where online is brilliant'.

Yet the same logic does not seem to apply to all types of story. Human-interest stories and entertainment-led features, on both channels, whether grave or amusing, are often exceptionally local.

Public purposes

The personnel of the studied outlets shared a similar sense of themselves as working professional journalists. Equally, they shared a sense of public purpose, though perhaps unsurprisingly this was articulated with more certainty by the BBC outlets. The editor of *Look North* was very clear that 'BBC impartiality matters more than anything else. If the audience don't trust us, we've lost it.' He was also open about the differences between the BBC and ITV regional output in respect of an obligation to avoid daily reporting that fails to contextualize and explain: 'If we just did stories on the day there is a danger you do too much crime and you make people feel bad, and actually by doing things that just happen on the day you end up doing not very much of consequence.'

He said people tended to have heard the headline news anyway, during the day, 'and arguably what they want is a bit more explanation, a bit more analysis'. After listing a range of different types of reporters and correspondents the BBC employs, he pointed out that a similar investment in expertise was not an option for their ITV counterparts but that *Look North* was bound to invest in specialism, 'otherwise how can we justify the licence fee?'

Editorial staff at *Calendar* identified the same differences of both style and purpose, pointing out that in their view BBC news programmes spent too much time on laboured explanation, usually in front of a video wall with charts and graphs, whereas *Calendar* 'is a people programme' and they 'are not fans of figures on the back wall, because it's not very visual and doesn't have a resonance with people watching it'. Instead, with a story about inflation, for example, *Calendar* would talk to people about what their daily spending is and the difference it would make to them, 'because we try to be people focused'.

Like her television counterpart, the assistant editor at Radio Leeds is sure of the BBC's public role. She argues that the audience wants more than the facts:

> ... they want to hear why and they want answers about what is going on and they want to be able to call people to account and they want to feel that local radio is fighting their corner. I think some of the BBC's public purpose is to community and citizenship and that local radio has a really important role to play and I suppose that's what I mean by fighting their corner.

This political objective was frequently and emphatically voiced by almost all our respondents; they felt their duty was to hold local/regional authorities to account. As one interviewee put it, 'via a sit-down grilling or by tenaciously pursuing a story until one gets answers'. The Radio Leeds editor felt public purpose would be the remit of BBC local radio if it was the only news service left standing and asked rhetorically: 'Where is the place for local accountability? Who is going to challenge the council leader over roads and schools, for example? We feel very strongly that our strategy and our public purpose means that in the BBC landscape we [in local radio] have a very distinctive place because nowhere else within the BBC is doing that.'

The editor of Yorkshire Post Newspapers also strongly asserted this role, claiming that: 'We call those in authority, such as the council, the police force, the health authority to account [as well as] supporting them as appropriate when they lobby central government or national decision-makers.'

Indeed, all our respondents made strong representations about the sense of public purpose in their journalism and editorial decision-making, which did seem to us occasionally at odds with some of their views expressed later on other topics and also, sometimes, with the resulting output.

The other frequently mentioned aims in this category concerned the diversity, especially the ethnic diversity, of the local population. Spokespeople from all our outlets considered that they were under an obligation to reflect in their output the various issues and peoples of the area. As one respondent said: 'On covering ethnic communities, I think we should really, genuinely be trying to reflect the audience out there. So that means in terms of age, of our demographic ethnic mix, we should be representing what's out there, on the screen.' We return to this question of ethnic representation below and, later, in Chapter 8, when discussing how our outlets view their audiences.

The preferred voice

Representation is an important theme of this book, in part because cities are 'products of communication'; they are 'not simply uncovered or exposed' by it (Anderson et al. 2015: 74), so an essential requirement of a city's media on the part of its audiences is that they represent them as they are. This is manifested in two different and distinct ways. First they require political representation and feel strongly that their media should, but on the whole do not, hold their political representatives to account on their behalf. Almost half the sample in our focus groups (see Chapter 4) agreed with the statement that the local media 'do not do enough to hold powerful people to account' as opposed to just 15 per cent who disagreed. Yet the mainstream media in Leeds, according to our interviewees whose responses are detailed above, overwhelmingly believe they are assiduously carrying out this job of political representation, the prerogative of traditional media in liberal democracies.

Subsequently, there is the way the community itself is represented on air and the choices journalists make in selecting which 'voices' are heard and which are set aside.

All of our outlets were unanimous in their quest for what they described as 'real people' or 'normal people' to be the voices and faces of their output, as opposed to 'men in suits'. As far as the editor of the *Yorkshire Evening Post* is concerned, 'in all stories we would prefer to quote real people and provide real-life examples'.

'We don't want the suits,' said a BBC producer, 'we would rather hear from real people who are affected.' The editor of *Calendar* used remarkably similar language: 'I don't want too many suits on the programme; I think you need [them], but it's hugely important that we reflect the views of normal people.' Radio Leeds also employed similar words and phrases to insist on the kind of voices preferred; their producer is worth quoting here at length:

> There can be too much reliance on that white middle-class voice when it comes to explaining stories and not enough real people and the more real people we can find the better ... There has been a growing emphasis on real people and hearing real people's voices and real people's experiences and I think it's becoming even more important now; real people are almost making the media themselves ... I think in my early days it would have been more about the suits and more about official voices.

One of the obvious reasons for this change in emphasis is the internet and the rise of social media platforms, hence the reference to people who 'are almost making the media themselves', but we also found in our interviews a certain disconnect between the traditional, official sources of news like politicians, police or public service mandarins and the news producers. Often official sources prove elusive, and according to the *Calendar* editor, 'It's very rare that we get the chance to put these people on the spot and give them a hard time, all we often get is a statement ... Please, I don't want an official statement, I want somebody who was involved in making the decision to speak to us ... I'm a bit fed up with this blocking action.'

A *Look North* producer describes the same experience: 'We don't have the voices to be able to put things to all the time – and it's just statements [instead].' They suggest the preferred voice is that of the 'real' or 'normal' or 'ordinary' person and that officialdom is less welcome. On the other hand they also seem to suggest that often there is no choice, because the official voice of authority is often not available or refuses to take part, and that has become a norm. Instead, press releases or the ubiquitous 'statement' are offered. The editor of YPN explains:

> My pet hate is having to deal with press officers who issue press releases on behalf of a council or an authority but are not sufficiently knowledgeable about a particular story, so it limits the type of information provided. We would rather talk to a Director of Education, or chief executive, rather than some council PR official that operates a virtual newsroom.

It is hard to determine whether officialdom went into hiding first or whether it was the media that stopped featuring the 'suits' quite so much and began to rely on the 'real people'. One BBC producer who wanted the public officials to 'put up a more robust defence' by agreeing to meet journalists and answer 'the hard questions' told us, 'It's just thinking about how we use these people. Do we need men in suits to explain something? Well, probably not, we should have our own reporting teams who have the ability to explain the complicated issues.'

What our respondents called the 'real' people were often valued as representatives, to give voice to the feelings of the listeners. When the City Council announced the closure of care homes in Leeds, for example, Radio Leeds, like most of the other outlets that covered the story, were not always entirely clear how many care homes were being closed and how many reprieved. The assistant editor did not seem worried at all about this; she felt the station's coverage

> ... got real people talking about the issues in a way they wouldn't get the chance to anywhere else. So within minutes of it being

announced that five, possibly three care homes were going to be closed by the council we had very angry families of residents talking about what it would mean to their families. Actually hearing those voices and giving them a place to publicly vent was the most important thing yesterday and not necessarily getting the facts a hundred per cent straight.

This latter admission seems strange indeed coming from the editorial voice of the BBC, but even allowing that it may be a slip or an unguarded comment or even a remark in the context of simply enthusing over the joys of local radio access, it does suggest that the priorities have moved away from the perhaps rather stiffly bland, objective, factual reporting of the pre-recorded radio 'package' to a point where broadcasters actively encourage candid emotion and instant opinion from their listeners, allowing this to be the central message of the story. Previously, where an emotional reaction might have been a welcome add-on to give perspective to a factual report, it is often now considered enough to stand on its own – in this case perhaps regardless of the facts.

When questioned about their role, all the senior journalists we interviewed expressly highlighted their duty to ensure politicians are accountable to their citizens; yet when they move on to discuss the kinds of stories they wish to tell and the people they would ideally include to tell them, the official spokesperson, pictured in a suit, is shunned in favour of someone 'real'; assumed to be representative of their own audiences.

Look North screened two stories one after the other, featuring mothers who were blaming authorities – a council and a Church of England diocese respectively – for failing the memory of their dead children. In the first case the mother wanted a fence or barrier put up around the area of the canal where her son had drowned; in the second the mother of a girl who had died in a car crash was prevented from erecting her chosen headstone by the diocese, because the very distinctive features were not in keeping with church policy for that graveyard. The deputy editor explained they were there at the top of the programme because they were good examples of the 'stories of the heart' that chimed with his teatime audience; they had related the stories on Facebook during the day and 'got a lot of reaction; we could tell the audience was engaged by both of these stories'.

He mentions 'an outpouring in terms of the drowning story ... the death of a young child does touch people', and comments that the gravestone story was helped by good pictures: 'for us, the pictures are important and the pictures we saw reinforced the story we felt we were telling'. Again, what struck us about this was the lack of any kind of counter-view expressed by the council in the first case or the diocese in the other. Viewers saw two mothers, emotionally distressed and complaining, but with apparently no redress from the authorities; the impression was enforced by the juxtaposition of the two items, both placed at the top of the programme.

At the other end of the spectrum, an item on the Radio Leeds breakfast show featuring someone described by the assistant editor as 'the winner of the bog snorkelling championships, which is hardly the most significant thing ... ticks the boxes of being interesting and tells us something fun about local people in the local area, reflecting local character'.

We are in the realm of representation once again. It is tempting to query this view of 'local character' and ask, if it 'ticks the boxes', where do these boxes come from? Just as there is a disconnect between the apparent absence of *political representation* as perceived by our focus groups and the keen sense of a public purpose, political in its nature, in the automatic responses of the journalists, evidence suggests local people are not always enamoured by the *social and cultural representation* of their area in local and regional media either. The impression is sometimes created that they are occasionally seen as providing amusement because of some idiosyncratic 'local character' common to all. In its latest research Ofcom found that it has become increasingly important to people that their region is portrayed fairly, 'but there remains a large gap between the importance the audience places on their portrayal and their satisfaction with its delivery' (Ofcom 2015).

Audience

'We are trying to reflect the audience' was a commonly expressed aspiration. A *Look North* producer said that editorial decisions were often made 'in respect of where the audience are on stories' and that 'it's a family audience, a slightly more down-market audience'. The editor is conscious that Yorkshire has a definite identity but he is keen to avoid the stereotype and wants to present 'a dynamic, diverse community' and not 'something which is … preserved in aspic'. The Radio Leeds editor makes a distinction between Leeds and the rest of the West Yorkshire audience: 'I think of our audience as hard on the outside and soft in the middle. It's a Yorkshire thing. The Leeds lot are intelligent, they're savvy.' *Calendar*, like *Look North*, has a much wider geographical reach, but can still distinguish its Leeds city audience from the rest: 'The audience in Leeds is different. Leeds people and the Leeds commutation is more media savvy because it has the media within it,' while the editor at the *Evening Post* knows the habits and tastes of his 'traditional yet aspirational' city readership. He knows they follow Leeds United or Leeds Rhinos, and very definitely look to the city for their 'entertainment, housing and employment needs' and that 'it is hugely important to take on board the issues your readership is interested in'.

The main reason for reflecting the audience, and attempting to cater to their tastes directly, appears to be the changing nature of news consumption. According to the *Look North* news editor, more of the audience is fickle now; they 'nibble' on news from different sources on different platforms. He told us that weekly BBC audience research tries to gauge the kinds of stories audiences appreciate by asking 'Do you relate to this story?' Radio Leeds says its audience 'isn't very loyal' and consists of 'more utility than emotional listeners' who 'just dip in and out', while *Calendar* also sees its audience as 'fragmented' and prone to choose other things to do with their time. The *Calendar* editor is aware that his viewers' use of media is changing 'absolutely enormously' and that 'they all use social media but not to catch up with daily news'. It means the audience is not just fickle but diminishing, and he says they don't watch *Calendar* every night now as they used to because 'people have got busy lives; they have other things to do'. So, according to one editor, 'We can no longer ignore the audience. We can no longer say this is what we're giving you because we think it's good for you.'

It is notable, though not unexpected, that the audience for these traditional media outlets is ageing, and though it varies in terms of media type and location, the age demographic is generally over forty-five and largely over fifty-five; they 'are not middle-class' and are not nearly diverse enough ethnically, according to the editors and producers we spoke to. This latter point concerns them a great deal, especially the representatives of BBC outlets, who seemed concerned they were not representing some ethnic communities enough in their reporting. 'We need to do more to reflect that, we're not always good at that,' admitted the *Look North* editor. The editor of Radio Leeds told us that the station is entering into a partnership with a community station in Bradford in an attempt to engage with 'an audience that traditionally is difficult for us and remains frustrating because after forty years of broadcasting in West Yorkshire, we still haven't nailed a particular city or community and it isn't good enough'. She thinks there are some people in Bradford's Pakistani community and some people in the African-Caribbean community in Chapeltown who would never dream of listening to the BBC.

We examine the representation of this community more thoroughly in Chapter 7, but it is interesting to note here the desire by the BBC to forge official links with community radio in order to communicate more effectively with the Asian community in Bradford; and also to highlight an observation of one of the *Look North* producers who sees the answer in striving for a more diverse newsroom. Once more he uses the language of representation: 'I suspect we pretty much reflect the newsroom quite well and we probably don't reflect what's outside the newsroom half as well [...] I think we are probably not representative of the city and we probably reflect that in our storytelling to a degree.'

New media

There seems little doubt that new media in the shape of weblogs, community websites and, most of all perhaps, the prevalence of social media has changed the way newsrooms operate around the world (Fenton 2009; McChesney 2012; Curran 2012; Pavlik 2004; Dahlgren 2009), and regional newsrooms in Britain are no exception. The internet is quicker and more comprehensive than the earlier method of mining facts from a variety of disparate sources, and social media puts journalists in direct, interactive contact with large swathes of their audiences.

The way in which Leeds citizens and their various media outlets across the city communicate via new media will be examined in more detail in the following chapter. We felt it of interest here to reflect briefly on the attitudes of the interviewees from the mainstream outlets, because we see their use of new media as an important part of their outlook on their professional lives.

Our editors and producers use new media in their journalism in the following specific ways:

1. *To access the audience online and find out their tastes and preferences.* They are aware that their audiences are already spending considerable amounts of their time in cyberspace and therefore chasing them is a matter of survival. They know those audiences are 'fragmented' and no longer loyal. So they perceive that finding and tapping into popular stories and talking points will help them target readers, listeners and viewers in a shrinking market.

2. *To help with news gathering; finding, creating and sourcing stories.* Increasingly journalists use social networking sites to find stories, until it has almost become the primary tool of use. Instead of 'pounding the streets and knocking on doors', they 'follow' what they consider to be significant people and organizations on Twitter, 'catching breaking news'. This has the clear advantage of saving money when budgets are squeezed, but by its very nature the information is already in the public domain and there is no option but to reprocess it, presumably reducing the opportunity for original reporting and investigation.

3. *Crowd sourcing – largely to trawl for people to appear or take part in their programmes.* Our outlets cast around on social networking sites for people who have a story to tell, or strong feelings to share, usually connected with an item the station is already committed to covering. 'We put a line on our Facebook page' and 'We got a lot of reaction on social media' were frequent comments from producers.

4. *To promote or advertise themselves.* 'Selling what we do better' is clearly something all of our respondents see as an instant benefit of new media, from the overtly commercial point of view of the *Yorkshire Evening Post* selling browsers to advertisers, to the perspective of the BBC, taking every opportunity to cross-promote its programmes and services on social networking sites and across its own burgeoning websites.

We felt there was a sense of anxiety in much of what our interviewees said, particularly BBC personnel, expressed in urgent terms as though time and audiences were slipping away from them: 'if someone spends a minute on the BBC website, they spend eleven minutes on Facebook. End of argument. We've got to get those people,' and 'some people say that at some point in the next generation people may decide to get all their information from social media and may not engage with the BBC'.

We also detected a tension between a lack of funding and an evidently thwarted desire to engage in resource-heavy, traditional reporting and investigating. Using social networking sites to access people and their stories was seen as a cheaper, quicker and fashionable alternative; though perhaps not a substitute. Our outlets tended to use social media to enhance many of the things they were doing anyway. They were keen to be a conduit, '*giving people a voice*' but somehow still determining the agenda.

For all the undoubted enthusiasm expressed by our interviewees for engaging with audiences in cyberspace, it seemed to us that at this stage they were not exploring its potential for including people in a more creative, deliberative discourse. It was our impression that somehow they were missing a trick in not regarding the use of new media in more transforming terms.

From source to mainstream

In questioning whether 'the contemporary ecology of UK local news' could be said to constitute a local public sphere, Aldridge asserts: 'If we value democracy, news must be more than a list of events enlivened by gossip, however interactive' (2007: 25). It is also clear that news coming in from outside the environs of the parish pump or the city hall inevitably impacts locally and that impact can be very specific. So news ecologies are cross-fertilized from farther afield, from the sometimes rather more exotic flora of national and international news, much of which has a discrete and specific significance for the locality and also has the capacity to enliven debate.

From the outset, we wanted to follow the 'national to local' progression in our monitoring of mainstream news, to establish and even interrogate the sources of stories and examine the journey of those stories through the Leeds mainstream outlets. It would, we felt, be interesting to see which stories from the national agenda would be picked up locally and how those stories would be adapted by Leeds media organizations to serve the needs of the local population. Would stories be framed differently when they moved around the

Leeds news ecology? Would they communicate the messages their sources intended? Would they be taken up by almost every outlet or appear in a haphazard fashion and lose momentum? In other words, would they flourish or wither?

Genuinely new stories emanating from national establishments that made their way into the Leeds media and that were also covered by all of the mainstream networks based in Leeds were relatively few during the week recorded and monitored by this study. If we exclude the events, entertainment and crime stories, we are left with just three: a report published by the National Housing Federation about what they described as an increasing housing crisis in the UK; an announcement by the Ministry of Defence that 2,000 jobs were being cut in the armed services; and word from the Royal British Legion that the repatriation of soldiers killed in Afghanistan would no longer be routed through the village of Wootton Bassett, where they had provoked spontaneous emotional support in the past. Radio Leeds covered all three stories, unsurprisingly since its remit is to report national and international as well as local news; the *Yorkshire Evening Post* only briefly included the housing and defence cuts stories on its national news round-up page; *Calendar* covered the defence cuts story as its lead item on the day of the announcement but did not feature the housing crisis or the Wootton Bassett repatriations, and *Look North* reported on none of these stories at all in its main 6.30 p.m. news magazine programme. It seemed to us that the report from the National Housing Federation would be the most appropriate to examine because it was clearly a national story that had an equal resonance across the country and because the Yorkshire area was deemed by the authors to have one of the highest number of people waiting for social housing.

We interviewed representatives of the NHF, the 'source' responsible for generating the story; and we asked our Leeds media interviewees responsible for covering it – or deciding not to cover it – about the processes they used to determine whether or not to include the story and how they tackled it.

On 30 August 2011 the National Housing Federation (NHF) published the findings of a report, 'Housing market economics', which it had commissioned from Oxford Economics, originally an arm of Oxford University's business school but now an independent economic forecasting organization. The original report is a detailed, analytical affair that monitors trends, details statistics and is substantial in terms of both description and policy recommendations. It uses the word 'crisis' to describe housing in England and its short-term projections for mortgage lending are poor. It goes on to suggest this has an immediate impact on the rented sector, causing rents to rise, and says that the public rented sector – council homes and housing association properties – is suffering because the building of new social housing has ground to a halt. The NHF distributed press releases based on this report and customized the information for each geographical area. One of the worst-affected areas in all of this was Yorkshire and the Humber; the Oxford Economics report (2011) pointed out that Leeds had 'cut their future housing allocations by a total of 88,000 according to the Home Building Federation' and that 'it will take until 2020 or beyond for new starts to reach pre-crisis levels'.

The problematic outcome for the NHF in commissioning a report about the housing market in general – when its own clients were the housing associations responsible for social housing, many of whom had long waiting lists – was that media attention immediately picked up on the story about mortgages, which somehow evolved into a story about first-time buyers. Their own press releases and pamphlets called 'Home truths', aimed at Yorkshire, declared immediately, 'Homelessness rose in 2010/11 for the first time in seven years and the region has one of the highest proportions of households waiting for a social housing home in England.' Homelessness had risen by 14 per cent, above the national average, and the strain on social housing was acute; the media outlets, however, were firmly focused on homeowners or on the plight of first-time buyers, whose difficulties were also outlined in the original Oxford Economics report.

Our data, matched with data we obtained from the NHF, shows that Radio Leeds and the *Yorkshire Evening Post* were the only mainstream outlets based in Leeds to cover the story at all and that it was framed consistently by both as either a private sector housing crisis in general, or a first-time buyers' crisis in particular. The YEP confined its coverage to a short, factual report on the inside pages and a 'news in brief' paragraph. Radio Leeds gave the story extensive coverage throughout the day on 30 August, making it an interactive discussion point on its breakfast programme and letting it run on to a second day when the *Drive* programme on the 31st featured it again, asking whether 'a generation of young people' would be excluded from the housing market, becoming 'the lost generation'. It is also indicative that in the NHF list of all media outlets across the north of England, there was just one television report about the housing story, and that came from ITV's Tyne Tees & Border television area. Every BBC local radio station aired a report, as did the vast majority of local and regional newspapers from Merseyside to Tyneside, but just one of the eight regional television programmes covered the story, a point we will return to later. From this it is possible to conclude that this story from the NHF, describing a housing crisis in England and highlighting the North as having particular difficulties, did not appeal to television news outlets in the area while appearing very popular with newspapers, some commercial radio stations and all of the BBC's local radio stations. BBC Radio Manchester ran ten feature items about this story on the day it was announced; Radio Leeds ran five, which is still considerable. As far as the Leeds-based media that chose to run the story were concerned, the focus was not on homelessness or on social housing but on house prices, mortgages and first-time buyers, contrary to the aspirations of the source, the National Housing Federation, whose clients, the Leeds housing associations, were experiencing exceptionally harsh conditions. According to an editor at Radio Leeds:

> We had a good and instantly accessible headline with the housing story so we were able to look at potentially an entire generation being locked out of the housing market and something's there that is emotional and connecting me [as a listener] with family matters with things that, even if it's different from my life, it's my children's lives [...] your children won't be able to buy a house in the same way that you could buy a house.

She said it was an important story to cover because 'that was a local and a national story at the same time almost' and 'we would be looking, every time we did a story like that, for the local story within the national story, if there is one to tell'.

Yet it seems Radio Leeds did not pick up on the factor in the story that did distinguish Leeds, and Yorkshire, from much of the rest of the north of England: the rise in homelessness and the squeeze on the housing associations at the same time as the local authority, according to the NHF report, was 'cut[ting] their future housing allocations by a total of 88,000'. When we asked what the rationale was for using and handling national stories like this, the Radio Leeds editor said it depended on the story; that there was not a formula:

> The difference with the housing story is that it is a national story but it is different locally so what we will be doing with a story like that is going 'oh well, that is interesting but it's coming out of London, but what does it mean in West Yorkshire?' So we would end up with a local headline through our research and through talking to kind of local important people and guests.

The National Housing Federation has its headquarters in Holborn, London, but administratively is divided into ten regions across England. It represents all of England's housing associations, and because 30 per cent of housing associations are based in the North, there is a larger administrative office in Manchester with responsibility for the North as a whole. The three northern regions – the north-west, north-east and Yorkshire and the Humber – report to the Manchester office. The administration team there is built round a policy officer, a communications officer and an events officer. We interviewed the policy and communications officers about their 'Home truths' report, released on 30 August 2011 and based on the Oxford Economics study.

Right at the start they were keen to point out that their own publicity had an incorrect emphasis; the policy officer told us that although headlining the crisis in social housing and homelessness they also focused on house prices, pointing out that they had commissioned the report before the last election and its publication came 'in a very different political environment'. He said the previous government's priorities were about growth in the housing sector: 'it was all about new towns, building in the south-east, about eco towns', and one of the publicity drives from the NHF at the time was 'all about how we make sure that social housing gets its fair share of that growth'. The focus of the Coalition Government, he believed, was 'about how to get people onto the housing ladder' and 'not people who have not got housing. So although this was a very successful campaign and we still got a lot of headlines out of it, the social housing message got lost.'

The second problem identified was a restructuring of their

organization, which was not completed until the report had been published. A new director of communication and head of media has been installed in the London headquarters and that emphasis seems to be reflected now across the regional offices. The communications manager in Manchester told us she was also new in the post with a background in regional newspaper journalism. She says she gets the impression that the new head of communications in Holborn is setting about changing the way they operate and indeed the kind of reports they commission to 'directly address the changing policy agenda', which means communicating directly their policy priorities, namely pushing social housing farther up the media agenda.

Her strategy is to provide local and regional media outlets with what she knows they like, and she adopts a mediatized discourse: 'the more local your statistics are, the more you can drill down and find good, human-interest case studies, the more appetite there is, I'd say'. The 'good, human-interest case study' is nourishment to local media. She wants to work with her policy manager to ascertain 'what chimes with Federation policy, what we want to pull out of it and then ... to use my own kind of news sense, because the things they pull out may be of no interest to the media at all'. She is acutely aware of why media outlets do not always leap at the chance to highlight the problems of housing associations: 'there's a general preconception about social housing tenants and the sort of people that live in our properties ... it's the scally ... the view of our tenants is that they're all on social welfare and they're the undeserving. Social benefit scroungers they call them.'

This new and proactive communications manager says she is already building up a good relationship with Leeds journalists; she mentions the *Yorkshire Post* and *Evening Post* and also Radio Leeds. 'So yeah, I'm getting there but maybe because the flow of stories hasn't been as strong [in the past] there's not always the collateral to push out to.' It is a relatively simple formula.

> Just by calling them up, offering them stories, trying to cherry-pick. If I see something that's coming up, you know, like a positive case study or even a terrible case study of a family who are waiting for social housing, I think, you know, how can I package that to the media. Which media outlet would that be perfect for, and then approaching them.

She was not especially disappointed that *Look North* and *Calendar*, or indeed most television programmes, did not pick up on the 'Home truths' report and said it was necessary to 'box cleverer' with television. 'A lot of regional newspapers, you know, they're short on resources and if you've written something, sometimes they'll just put in your press release as it is,' confirming the conclusions of relevant studies (Davies 2008; Fenton 2009; Lewis et al. 2008), 'whereas with television in particular, you need a case study, you need something to bring it to life'. There is clearly some degree of success with ITV Tyne Tees & Border, the only company which produced a filmed piece about the 'Home truths' report for television during our monitoring week. The communications manager had arranged another story to be filmed by them in the week we interviewed her. 'I found out there's this girl who's training to be a plumber and she's sort of very glamorous with sort of nails and make-up and stuff, so we use that as the hook and as a result ITV [Tyne Tees & Border] are using it.'

Another reflection on the way the housing story travelled from Oxford to Manchester via Holborn and then on to Leeds, undergoing subtle changes as it went, concerns the intervention of the Press Association, the UK's principal domestic news agency. The press release designed for the Yorkshire media, which came from the National Housing Federation in Manchester, highlighted four things from the Oxford report: a growing 'strain across the region's housing markets'; rising house prices; a dearth of new building; and the resultant problems of the housing associations and the homeless. It did not mention first-time buyers – the focus of the story on Radio Leeds and in the *Yorkshire Evening Post*. The NHF communications manager confirmed that when they send out publicity to the media, it also goes to the Press Association, which picks it up, 'does its own take on it', and some of the media rely on that rather than looking at the material from the source, the National Housing Federation. She said: '… because it's easy. I know since when I worked at the *Sheffield Star*, six years ago now, there's maybe half the number of journalists, and circulation had gone down by about twenty thousand.' She believes papers like this depend on Press Association copy rather than the material that comes to them directly from sources: 'it's just an easy way to fill the space'. It is somewhat reminiscent of the 'internal mechanics of an industry that has been deeply damaged'

(Davies, quoted in Street 2011: 192). The original source, the Oxford Economics report, does mention the problems of first-time buyers, so media outlets could certainly have found the information by consulting the original document; it devotes just a paragraph on page twelve of an eighteen-page report to the plight of first-time buyers. Under the heading '5:2 Burden of deposits for first time buyers', it uses seventeen lines to say mortgage availability will ease over the next three years but that lending will improve only gradually, and that means 'that first time buyers are likely to face increasing difficulty getting on the ladder in many parts of the country', and briefly discusses saving capacity. The paragraph's conclusion is that first-time buyers in London and the South-East will suffer most, 'while in the North, the burden falls slightly, as house prices soften over the coming couple of years' (Oxford Economics 2011). It does not suggest there will be a 'lost generation' of young people in Yorkshire because of the difficulty of buying a first home and concludes that the first-time buyer in the North is, relatively speaking, in a better position than those in other parts of the country.

This paragraph is relatively difficult to find, or at least it is not immediately accessible and would take time to locate. Press Association reports, on the other hand, are ubiquitous across newsrooms and are readily accessible at the click of a mouse.

The role of economic forecasters like Oxford Economics is to use their data, crunch the numbers and project what is likely to be the case in two to three years' time. They produced a report, 'UK housing market', in 2009 (not on this occasion for the NHF), which said that mortgage lending was depressed, that 'first time buyers are being hit particularly hard by this', and went into some detail concerning the hardship first-time buyers will continue to encounter for some time. Their forecast was accurate. In the ensuing two years, the UK media often ran stories about the plight of first-time buyers, and by August 2011 it was clear that mortgage lending had almost ground to a halt. Journalists and their news editors knew that the mortgage market was depressed and that first-time buyers were hardest hit. When the new report from Oxford Economics in 2011 was précised by the National Housing Federation and sent to newsrooms across England, they already had the frame. The report itself was projecting to 2014, rather than describing the current situation. John Street, discussing the reporting of political news, cites journalist Sarah

Benton, who argues 'the plot is always the same' for journalists who generally like to slot news into preconceived storylines: 'there are only old stories which we know already ... we know it all already because information about politics only becomes news when it can be fitted into a story that we know already' (Street 2011: 57). Gans famously describes the traditional symbiotic relationship between journalists and their news sources as a 'a dance' in which 'sources seek access to journalists and journalists seek access to sources', but that 'more often than not, sources do the leading' (Gans 1999: 116). The sources he describes, people he calls 'Knowns', are invariably institutional figures of authority, usually politicians. Later studies taking data from Britain, Europe and the USA (Manning 2001; Lewis et al. 2008; Strömbäck and Nord 2006) have confirmed these findings, that professional bodies and political actors are journalists' principal sources. However, in our examination of the mainstream media in one city in the UK, the principal media actors were united in their desire to avoid official sources, 'the suits', as much as possible and to give much more space and airtime to 'real people', often from the ranks of their own readers, viewers and listeners. In contrast, in this instance, the media source was a formal and authoritative institution, the National Housing Federation; nevertheless, we found that attempts were made to foreground the 'real' or 'ordinary' voices into the report, but they were the voices of homeowners and first-time buyers, not those of housing association tenants or the homeless – regarded as 'undeserving social benefit scroungers', according to our NHF interviewee.

It seems at least very likely from the interviews we conducted that the NHF was very surprised, if not seriously disappointed, that their report had been framed in a way that distorted the message they wished to convey. It is interesting in the first place to note how few of the mainstream media outlets took up this story and that the BBC radio station that did cover the news took an entirely different approach. However, in their work examining the news coverage of Swedish elections, Strömbäck and Nord (2006) contend that in the power struggle between journalists and official sources, politicians have the power over the news-making and the news agenda, but 'it is the journalists who have the ultimate power over the framing and the content of the news stories'. So in the Leeds example, the official source had the news and set the agenda – a housing crisis in the

UK – but the radio journalists had the power of framing the news and the content of the story, turning it from a shortage of social housing and a dilemma of homelessness into a problem for first-time buyers.

Conclusion

Our research suggests that the individuals we talked to – the editors and producers – and the people working with them are caught up in, and are wrestling with, several tensions: tensions seemingly brought about by a severe constraint on resources as they try to engage with their audiences more directly in an exhaustingly competitive market. In their role of communication and disseminating information the tensions are between: the viability of their operation, simply keeping afloat, and their ambitions for their news services; the clear sense of public purpose and what they perceive to be the audience response. In their role of *representation* the tensions are between the desire to be the instruments of political accountability and the rather slanted selection of 'voices' chosen to access the public debate; the clear identification of a lack of ethnic diversity evident in the output and the seeming inability to find the means of achieving it.

Information and communication According to Peter Dahlgren, 'Journalism's position within people's ensemble of information sources has been downsized. What the public knows is to a declining degree a result of traditional journalism; this trend is of global proportions. From these developments, its role in democracy is thus being altered, decreased' (2009: 42). He cites a number of scholars to conclude that what he describes as the 'classical paradigm' of journalism is 'waning' (ibid.: 42).

As far as this study is concerned, the mainstream news organizations based in Leeds clearly represent what would have been described as traditional journalism, albeit of the local variety, and would once have been expected to conform to Dahlgren's notion of traditional journalism, 'providing reports and analyses of real events and processes' and laying claim to 'accurate and impartial renderings of a reality that exists independently of its telling and which is external to the institutions of journalism'. From our observations, these outlets also seem to be conforming to his notion that this form of journalism is on the wane and that another manifestation, a 'difficult transition to a new media alignment', is under way (ibid.: 43).

The job of communicating with citizens to provide them with trusted information so that they might be better equipped to make rational choices is a long-established role of journalism in Western democracies; albeit an ideal role and sometimes seen 'more in the breach than the observance'. The postmodern challenge for journalism, nevertheless, is to negotiate the still-problematic and often confusingly contradictory nature of new information technologies in an attempt to perform this ideal public duty in radically new ways. From our observations of the Leeds media outlets we conclude that, though they are appreciative of the scale of the challenge, they are less sure of its nature and have not yet arrived at innovative ways of allowing it to emancipate local people and communities.

Of course, they are hidebound by the lack of resources that would enable an ongoing physical engagement with the various communities they serve and that would allow enough time for the tasks of thorough research, investigation and verification of information coming from a myriad of official and non-official sources. A competitive media market barely allows thinking time. So trawling social media sites seemed to us to be regarded as an alternative to both the physical presence of reporters on beats and a thorough oversight of source material. In truth they should be loath to discard these traditional professional skills but keen to play more of an enabling rather than a controlling role when it comes to communication with individuals and communities on social media. We believe an imaginative use of the internet could challenge the atomizing imperative of audience-chasing and indeed the very commercialization that so evidently deadens journalistic enterprise. What may be required is what Martin Conboy (2009: 225) has labelled 'a set of dynamic responses from journalism which involve audiences in the social aspects of its core practices'. In the Leeds case, for example, harnessing the ideas of community leaders, social and civic groups and their members and providing some facilities and expertise to enable them to spread their disparate voices across the full spectrum of Leeds programming could have that emancipating effect. The key may well be in allowing citizens to use the internet to make and produce their own material, to act as agenda-setters and editors as well as contributors. They would be enabled to achieve basic production values and legal compliance through the expert advice and guidance of professional editors and producers.

As things stand, our mainstream outlets clearly want to utilize social media in the way they are used to dealing with all their sources and resources, by top-down control, by a kind of centralized orchestration whereby they call the tune. We would query whether they will get the best out of the new information technologies by attempting to fit them into the old news production templates. Of course, handing over the editorial agenda is problematic if not nigh on impossible for centralized media leviathans like Britain's main broadcasting companies, as they are currently structured; nevertheless, a degree of devolution, to grant local outlets more autonomy, would give journalists the opportunity to enable local communities take the initiative in new and imaginative ways. The old media model was predicated on analogue technology, dependent on spectrums and bandwidths. Companies with defined geographical premises where product is made and protected by the scarcity of the means of communication are attempting to accommodate the internet within the confines of the old, centralized model because it is a model they have held to for sixty years. Now the internet has opened up communication so that information can travel irrespective of ownership and often without protection or sanction or any other inhibitor.

Yet there is a perceptible fear of the digital superhighway and what it might do to the broadcasting model, or at least a fear that if they do not get to grips with it, it might overwhelm them and even destroy them. Our respondents often exuded the air of desperately trying to find and engage with the audience online before it was too late; hauling them in with tempting offers, to have their say. Whether by putting out messages on Facebook or trying to coax people into an opinionated discourse on air, it seemed to encourage the 'public venting' described earlier. Here we found it was sometimes in danger of falsifying information as well. Clearly the outlets have been told by their head offices to go online and bring in the audiences, as a matter of survival; but programme structures, staffing and resources are built around the same or similar formats as those in place many years ago, even though financial pressures have reduced the number of journalists available.

Communicating to provide trusted information may not be the chief role of journalism in the future when information is readily accessible from original sources online, but for those of us who believe nevertheless that 'journalism is necessary for a broadly informed public able to critically engage with the contemporary world' (Conboy 2009: 225), some serious stab at accommodating the overwhelming strength and creativity of online communication is overdue.

Representation Our research also indicates broader concerns about the way people and communities are represented politically and culturally; indeed, that the political and cultural are linked. All of our respondents were very clear about their public purpose, expressed in terms of the ideal role of journalism in democratic societies. The broadcasters highlighted their own independence, as a guarantee that they were organizations sufficiently trustworthy to be charged with holding elected representatives to account. The BBC respondents were very aware of the Corporation's public voice as authoritative, even instructive; unapologetically arguing that the 'analysis' often embodied in electronic charts and graphs and dismissed by their ITV rivals is an essential part of the BBC's remit, and is alive and well at BBC Yorkshire.

Yet this often seemed at odds with much of the programming we examined and indeed with many other things our respondents revealed. They appeared to be well aware, for example, that their readers, viewers and listeners no longer have much interest in hearing the voice of authority and officialdom, and have clearly made a decision to ban 'the suits' whenever possible. The tendency to promote 'real people' as sources certainly serves a laudable public purpose, but if it is done at the expense of any official sources on the scene, it could possibly lead to a feeling of discomfort and uncertainty in the minds of viewers and listeners, if problems seem to have no possible solution and no one is seen to be on hand to redress the balance or provide perspective. The city burghers might be pardoned for feeling impotent in the face of people 'venting' opinion, concern and even anger. As Harju (2007: 101) puts it rhetorically, 'Is the ideal citizen of journalism, thus, a loud and angry person who rises up against the ones in power and so provides material for colourful stories and dramatic pictures?'

Equally, producers and editors were keen to point out that they avoid cultural stereotypes like the plague, yet they appear to seek out regional characters to season their output which often fit them.

This chimes with Ofcom's recent findings that people are generally dissatisfied with the way their area is portrayed by local media.

Finally, our outlets are clearly failing to represent the people who read, listen to and view the media output from Leeds. When he was the BBC Director General, Greg Dyke made the point that his organization was 'hideously white', yet fourteen years later editors and producers in the BBC Leeds newsrooms consider that their output reflects the newsrooms rather than the communities they serve. They are genuinely angst-ridden about their inability to properly engage the Asian and African-Caribbean communities. Local broadcast journalists, especially reporters, tend to be predominantly young as well as white, and more often than not are middle-class graduates as well.

Behind these changes in practice and in emphasis there are obvious economic, social and technical forces at play. News is chronically underfunded and our Leeds outlets are as overstretched as any for reasons outlined earlier in the chapter. Lack of resources can be a significant determinant. A more imaginative and citizen-focused use of the internet and social networks, though no substitute for a physical presence in some of the less accessible communities, should be an opportunity to give citizens access to political debate and decision-making, which, as research has shown (Bennett 2008; Carpentier and Cammaerts 2007; Couldry et al. 2010), could be transformative. It is unfair to suggest this is in a static state, of course; journalism is in transition and journalists, editors and owners are being forced to change their thinking and their practices constantly and, in terms of the news ecology analogy, they are on new and still rather alien terrain.

6 | CITIZEN NEWS-MAKERS AND NEWS PRACTICES

This chapter looks beyond the traditional news providers discussed in the last chapter to examine how citizens themselves contribute to making local news in Leeds. What roles do citizen news media play in the news ecology at the local level and how do citizen news-makers understand their practices? What is the nature of the relationship between citizen news practices and the mainstream news media?

According to some commentators, journalism is undergoing a process of transformation and democratization, as citizens, aided by new media, become increasingly involved in producing and circulating news themselves rather than simply consuming the products of professional journalists (Benkler 2006; Shirky 2009). Shirky (2009) suggests that we think of journalism today as akin to driving, with some paid professionals, but many more non-professionals. 'Like driving, journalism is not a profession,' he writes, 'and it is increasingly being transformed into an open activity, open to all' (ibid.). Along similar lines, Benkler (2006) argues that there has been a shift away from a mass-mediated public sphere, dominated by a small number of commercial media organizations, towards a decentralized 'networked public sphere', where numerous ordinary citizens may contribute. 'We are witnessing a fundamental change in how individuals can interact with their democracy and experience their role as citizens,' he suggests, where citizens 'are no longer constrained to occupy the role of mere readers, viewers, and listeners', but 'can be, instead, participants in a conversation' (ibid.: 272). Most ambitiously, Benkler (ibid.: 264–5) argues that the networked public sphere is able through 'peer production' to perform the democratic roles usually limited to professional journalists, not only contributing to news but also acting as a watchdog that can monitor and hold the powerful to account.

Other writers cast a more critical and sceptical light on recent developments in journalism, questioning whether citizen volunteers are able to take over the labour of professional journalists and so compensate for job losses and financial pressures in mainstream news media (Fenton 2009, 2011). Research that has examined the issue empirically supports this view, finding that much of what might be thought to be 'citizen journalism' does not involve original news or investigations and is in fact reliant upon the news that professional journalists produce (Pew Research Center 2010). Furthermore, the majority of citizen news sites lack visibility, attracting only small and specialized audiences, while people's attention online still tends to be focused overwhelmingly on professional news providers (Curran 2010; Hindman 2008). For these reasons, citizen media appear unlikely to be able to plug the growing gaps that are emerging as a result of the decline in traditional news media. As Curran (2010: 471) concludes, 'the Web cavalry riding to the rescue is too small and without sufficient firepower to offset the decline of traditional journalism'.

While reaching divergent conclusions, both the celebratory and more critical accounts of citizen news media have tended to pitch citizen news-makers and professional journalists against one another, viewing one as a more or less effective substitute for the other. We argue that this view is mistaken. From an ecological perspective, it is better to think of professional news media and citizen news practices as making distinct and potentially complementary contributions to local news (Anderson 2010; Goode 2009). In our research, we found no credible evidence to suggest that 'citizen journalists' could replace the work performed by professional journalists, or that they would want to. Nonetheless, there are examples of where citizen news-makers are producing valuable forms of news at local level, especially so-called 'hyperlocal' news and news stories connected with communities of identity and interest, which can supplement the news stories typically circulated by mainstream journalists. In addition, the contribution of citizens to local news is not limited to the production of original stories. Adopting a news ecology perspective, we argue here that citizen news practices also play a role in translating and making sense of news stories, broadening the range of interpretation and discussion around news and building different types of social relationships, around and through news.

We begin this chapter by mapping out citizen news practices in

Leeds. These range from quotidian and difficult-to-capture public conversations to more organized forms of citizen news-making. Focusing on the latter, we then ask what those involved in citizen news media aim to achieve through their contribution to local news and how their practices fit into the broader news ecology. Based on ten interviews with those involved in citizen news media in Leeds, this chapter attempts to explore the complex ways in which people neither simply consume nor produce news, but engage with news as a social practice.

Mapping citizen news-makers

Once we move beyond traditional news providers, the practices of which are clearly institutionalized and defined, it becomes difficult to know what to include and what not to include under the category of 'news'. If we understand local news in the broadest terms, as involving accounts of what is happening or has recently happened at the local level, then a potentially large range of citizen practices could be involved in making and circulating news. These practices range from everyday public conversations, where local news is shared, circulated and discussed among people as one topic among others, to more organized and focused efforts by citizens to produce and contribute to local news.

Our research suggested that public conversation plays an important role in circulating local news in Leeds. As noted in Chapter 4, respondents in our focus groups talked about how interpersonal conversations helped them keep up with local news and referred to the importance of gossip and a 'local grapevine'. Local news circulates in key locations in the city, at places like the school gates, shops, pubs and community centres, and is also mediated digitally through social media platforms such as Facebook and Twitter, email lists and web forums. Of course, we can expect that the various news grapevines and networks that operate in the city are diverse. In our research interviews, for example, participants described how those working in community development, the cultural sector and local government use social media for city-related discussions, but then these networks and the conversations that characterized them appear different from the local grapevines talked about by our focus group participants. Although this is not something we were able to explore in the context of our study, one important question is the extent to which different networks in the city intersect with and are open to one another.

There are specific online groups in Leeds that have been set up to foster broader discussions of local news and issues among citizens. A prominent example is a Facebook group called Leeds Online, set up by a local marketing company, Hebe Media. The aim of the group, as the company describes it, is to 'create the Facebook version of the "chat down the pub"' (Hebe Media 2011). As such, the group began by posing general questions about Leeds to its followers, such as 'What a nice sunny day, what is everyone up to?', and it soon grew to attract an impressive 50,000 followers. After our initial data-gathering period had come to an end, the company started to distribute news online and started a local newspaper under the name of *The City Talking*. It has now established a partnership with the *Yorkshire Evening Post* in order to ensure wider distribution for the newspaper. There are various other forums and discussion spaces in the city, including Leeds Forum. This forum was set up in 2010 and was established by the founder of another successful forum set up in a neighbouring city. The aim of Leeds Forum is to provide a space for citizens to discuss issues and news in and from Leeds.

Public conversation about local news is of course informed by consumption of mainstream news media. Indeed, while it is not possible to give precise figures, we can assume that a significant amount of conversation about local news relates to things people see, read or hear from traditional news providers. Yet it would be mistaken to dismiss such practices as being of no value to the local news ecology. As we noted in the last chapter, originality and in particular finding 'exclusives' are important news values for professional journalists. Likewise, there is a tendency for academic research on news and journalism to focus on the production of original news stories. However, the interpretation and circulation of news also can play an important role in defining and constituting what local news is (Anderson 2010; Goode 2009). Indeed, Luke Goode (2009) argues that this is where new media's 'democratizing effects' are most likely to be found. He notes that 'There might be a temptation to dismiss the "metajournalism" of rating, commenting, tagging and reposting as considerably less significant than "real" citizen journalism which heralds an apparently more radical mode of public engagement' (ibid.: 1290). However, 'what blogging, citizen journalism and social news sites yield are new possibilities for citizen participation at various points along those chains of sense-making that shape news – not only new possibilities for citizens to "break" news' (ibid.: 1291).

In addition to the circulation of news through public conversations, there are also more clearly structured and focused attempts by citizens to produce local news and contribute to the news ecology. The practices and actors involved are again disparate and difficult to define precisely. A broad distinction can be drawn between practices organized around communities of place and those focused on identity and interest. In our research, we encountered a number of local blogs, print publications and community radio stations dedicated to serving particular neighbourhoods or areas of the city; what have been called 'hyperlocal' news media (Williams et al. 2014). We also found examples of citizen media that served particular cultural and religious groups that are not well catered for by mainstream local media. Finally, we also came across citizen media based on particular communities of interests, from media organized around local sports teams and music groups to political campaigns.

The analysis that follows focuses on ten examples of citizen news media, which we selected as broadly indicative of citizen news media in Leeds at the time of our study in 2011. The sample is made up of seven websites or blogs, two community radio stations and one print publication and website (see Box 6.1). We conducted semi-structured interviews with people centrally involved in eight of these citizen news media (About My Area, Culture Vulture, Friends of Leeds Kirkgate Market, Holt Park Today, *Kirkstall Matters*, South Leeds Life Blog, Radio Asian Fever and South Leeds Community Radio), while the Leeds Citizen blog agreed to respond to a set of questions via email. We did not contact anyone involved in Beyond Guardian Leeds in our study, but we did interview the journalist involved in Guardian Leeds, which preceded Beyond Guardian Leeds and was related to it. The aim of our interviews was to try to understand the purposes of the actors involved in citizen news media and how they perceive their roles and contribution to the local news ecology.

Box 6.1 Citizen news media

About My Area (LS7)

About My Area is a national network of local sites, one of which serves the local area in Leeds and is run primarily by one person. The network describes itself as follows: 'AboutMyArea has a national network of over 2,000 community websites, each sharing the common goal of keeping their community informed with relevant local information'.

Beyond Guardian Leeds

Beyond Guardian Leeds is a blog where writers collate and aggregate stories from various local news sources in a regular blog post. The blog is written by various contributors. Beyond Guardian Leeds was set up following the closure of the Guardian Leeds blog (hence the name) in order to try to continue the work the Guardian Leeds blog had begun in curating content from local blogs and sites.

Culture Vulture

The Culture Vulture is a multi-author blog with a number of contributors, which is dedicated primarily to discussing cultural issues and events in the city. The site was set up and is run by a local resident. When asking for new writers, the site asks: 'Are you an industry insider with behind the scenes access? Do you know about everything before it happens? Do you have a show/exhibition/book launch etc that you would like to document for us?'

Friends of Leeds Kirkgate Market

This blog was set up in connection with a local campaign to support Leeds Kirkgate Market, a large covered market in the centre of the city. As the blog describes: 'Friends of Leeds Kirkgate Market is a new group for everyone – customers, traders, citizens and visitors – who love Kirkgate Market and want it to survive and flourish in its present form and not become yet another bland and soulless shopping centre.'

Holt Park Today

Holt Park Today is a hyperlocal news blog, serving a particular area in the north of the city. While the blog invites contributions from others, the site is updated and run primarily by one individual. The blog describes itself as an 'independent community driven website that provides very local information that is not readily available elsewhere' and which focuses on 'news, events and other useful information on the things that matter to those that live, work and socialise in Holt Park and the immediate locality'.

Kirsktall Matters

Kirsktall Matters is a hyperlocal newsletter, which is produced every four months by volunteers of the Kirkstall Valley Community Association and delivered to members in paper copy. Each issue is also available for download online. The content is readable and downloadable as a PDF-style document, but not necessarily formatted as searchable web content. An active blog attached to the publication serves as the home page for its online manifestation (with a Twitter stream and links), but this remains supplementary to, and as a commentary on, the writing undertaken for each issue of *Kirkstall Matters*.

Leeds Citizen

Set up in July 2011, Leeds Citizen is a local blog which focuses on local news in the city and in particular the activities of the local council and partner organizations. The person who runs the blog worked in the past for the BBC's monitoring service and so has been involved in professional journalism previously (Harcup 2015: 6). The blog describes itself as 'A minor irritant on the flesh of the body politic of Leeds'.

Radio Asian Fever

Radio Asian Fever is a community radio station, licensed by Ofcom, which caters specifically for the South Asian community in Leeds. The station describes itself as follows: 'The station serves all South Asian communities in the city, combating under-representation and exclusion from mainstream media. The station works across the cultures, faith groups and their many denominations. It aims to bring the whole community together and has notable achievements in fostering cooperation between groups across the city.'

South Leeds Community Radio

South Leeds Community Radio is a community radio station set up in 2006. It aims, as its website describes, 'to give local people a voice and encourage people to get together and show the world how much talent and activity there is in the area' and to 'produce quality programmes, made by and for the people of South Leeds'. The station 'involves local people in media, making their own programmes about issues that concern and ideas that inspire, and playing music for everyone in the community'.

South Leeds Life

South Leeds Life is a hyperlocal news blog, which covers a number of local areas in South Leeds. A small group of bloggers manage the site and contribute regularly, but the blog also invites contributions from others. The blog explains that: 'We aim to tell you about events and stories going on in South Leeds – Holbeck, Beeston, Cottingley, Hunslet, Belle Isle & Middleton.'

By highlighting specific examples we do not want to exaggerate the extent or prominence of citizen news media in Leeds. Certainly, citizen news-makers are less widespread and visible than celebratory accounts of new media suggest. The volume of news produced by citizen news-makers is also typically low compared to traditional news providers. For example, while only a selection of our citizen news media sites were included in our content analysis, those that were included produced a comparatively small number of stories: Holt Park Today published nine posts in our extended three-week period and one post in our core week; South Leeds Life posted twelve altogether and three in our core week, while Leeds Citizen posted thirteen altogether and four posts during our core week. Culture

Vulture was the most active blog, posting sixty posts altogether and twenty-one during the core week. Citizen media also do not appear to figure highly in people's news consumption. Our survey does not ask about all the citizen media we discuss in this chapter, but it indicates that only 4 per cent of respondents reported using blogs and Twitter weekly for local news, 6 per cent used forums or emails weekly for this purpose, and 5 per cent reported listening to a community radio station within the last month. By comparison, mainstream media still command comparatively high audiences: 60 per cent of respondents reported accessing local news provided by national TV channels (either the ITV *Calendar* news or BBC *Look North*) at least five days a week, while over 20 per cent accessed one of the main local newspapers on five or more days of the week. For these reasons, there are no grounds to think that citizen news-makers can step in and replace full-time professional journalists in Leeds. However, as we describe below, this is not to say that citizen news media do not make an important contribution to the news ecology. Furthermore, we suggest that citizen news practices could also be harnessed more effectively than they currently are, through more productive relationships with traditional news media.

Newsworthiness

The citizen news-makers we interviewed did not see themselves as performing the same work as professional journalists or as being in competition with them. Given their central position within the news ecology, professional journalists have better access to powerful organizations and individuals and to other sources and flows of local information. Because of the resources they have access to, professional journalists can also react more quickly to news events and cover a greater range of stories across the city. By comparison, citizen news media are at a smaller scale and are specialized around particular communities of place, interest and identity. As such, citizen news-makers may cover content that is not likely to be deemed 'newsworthy' by mainstream news providers. Although we did not investigate this systematically in our study, our impression was that citizen news media did produce qualitatively different types of content that did not simply replicate stories produced in mainstream news media.

One possible 'gap' in the existing provision of news which citizen news media can help to fill is content relating to small geographical areas or neighbourhoods. As we noted in Chapter 4, for most of our focus group participants 'local' meant 'my street' or 'my neighbourhood' and news coverage of Leeds, let alone Yorkshire, was viewed as distant from their immediate local experience. Although there are local newspapers operating below city and regional levels in Leeds, commercial pressures have challenged the viability of more local news (Williams et al. 2014). Of course, news about particular areas of the city may be still be covered within city-wide or regional media, but then the emphasis here may be on appealing to or maintaining the attention of a broader audience, rather than catering for residents of a particular area, which can lead to the prevalence of certain types of story and a particular type of coverage. When covering public sector cuts, as we noted in Chapter 5, regional news broadcasters may opt to select cuts that affect all parts of the region, with the result that they overlook important stories in specific areas. By comparison, hyperlocal citizen news media can be more sensitive to what is happening in particular neighbourhoods or areas of the city.

Hyperlocal news is not the only possible 'gap' in news provision that citizen news-makers may fill. As described in Chapters 4 and 7, focus group participants who came from the city's mainly black and other minority ethnic communities were critical of some mainstream news coverage. Citizen news media organized around communities not adequately catered for and represented by mainstream media play a crucial role here. One prominent example is Radio Asian Fever, a community radio station for the South Asian community. An interviewee from Radio Asian Fever explained that the radio station contributed something different to traditional news providers: 'the South Asian community is the biggest community after the white community, yet we've got no provision for it here'. Traditional news providers, she says, 'don't understand the communities so how can they provide for it and that's what it is and they don't provide, they haven't got provisions for the South Asian community'.

Not surprisingly, there is also a range of other citizen media in the city connected with particular communities of interest, ranging from sports and music groups to political sites and groupings. A prominent example is the collaboratively produced blog Culture Vulture, which involves in-depth coverage and discussion of cultural events and issues in the city. While this is a Leeds-wide blog, it addresses

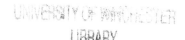

content for a particular community interested in the cultural life of
the city and again picks up content and stories that are not likely to
be deemed 'newsworthy' by mainstream news providers. As noted
above, Culture Vulture has a range of different contributors and it
produced the largest volume of stories out of the blogs included in
our content analysis.

Citizen news-makers may also supplement professional news
media by pursuing and exploring topics and stories in greater
depth. One example is the Leeds Citizen blog, which describes
itself as 'a minor irritant on the flesh of the body politic of Leeds'
(the leeds citizen 2015; for a more in-depth analysis of the blog,
see Harcup 2015). Leeds Citizen produces stories about the city as
a whole, often focusing on the local council and its activities and
other powerful organizations in the city. In our email interview with
the Leeds Citizen blogger, he described how he feels that coverage
of the council by mainstream media is inadequate. Asked how well
local media report the council and its decision-making process, he
responded:

> Badly [local papers]. Very badly [local radio]. Since they've
> all stopped having a local council reporter who would trawl
> agendas and go to meetings and badger councillors, they've lost
> it. Their council news agenda is now more likely to be governed
> by council press releases or high-profile public campaigns rather
> than investigation.

Harcup's (ibid.) more extended study of the Leeds Citizen
blog suggests that it plays an important role in monitoring local
government. He concludes that: 'Four years of the site's existence
have demonstrated over a sustained period what even a lone but
motivated individual citizen can achieve: critical yet evidence-based
reporting that scrutinises the actions of the powerful in a specific
locality' (ibid.: 16). More generally, a recent study by Williams et
al. (2014) found that the reporting of local politics and government
is quite widespread among hyperlocal blogs in the UK. They report
that, 'We have seen clearly from the data on story topics that readers
of hyperlocal news are getting a large amount of information about
politics, particularly the politics of local government, which relates to
the news' ability to foster informed citizenship' (ibid.: 10).

The Friends of Leeds Kirkgate Market blog is another example of a citizen media site focusing on a particular topic of local interest. There have been significant concerns among some Leeds residents about the future of the Kirkgate Market, which is a large covered market in the centre of the city. The Friends of Leeds Kirkgate Market blog was set to provide news about the market and updates relating to the campaign to maintain the market in its present form. Mainstream news media, such as the *Yorkshire Evening Post*, have picked up the story of the Kirkgate Market on occasion. Not surprisingly, though, the coverage is less frequent and comprehensive than that of the blog. As one of our interviewees described in relation to this story, 'I think that what tends to happen with mainstream media is that they've only got so many column inches', and so they tend to 'dip into an issue, once every six months', when there is something 'newsworthy' about it. Not constrained by the same commercial imperatives and sense of what is or is not newsworthy, blogs like Friends of Leeds Kirkgate Market can provide more depth and context for a local issue, not replacing but rather supplementing and extending the coverage of mainstream providers.

Another example relates to the local campaign against reforms or cuts in the National Health Service, which has already been discussed in relation to our content analysis in Chapter 2. Whereas mainstream media picked up on stories about cuts in the National Health Service, less information was given about the nature of the reform: the coverage appears to assume some familiarity with the story and does not provide detailed explication of the changes. Even quoted campaigners tend to provide emotive soundbites rather than factual accounts of the reforms. Despite eschewing impartiality and taking a clearer political position, citizen news-makers may provide more background and informative content. For example, our content analysis indicated that the hyperlocal *Kirkstall Matters* provided the most information about the proposed reforms, notwithstanding its clearly persuasive intent.

Citizen news practices

When they reflected on how they may differ from professional journalists, the citizen news-makers we interviewed did not just talk about the different types of content or stories they covered. They also described the different nature of their news practices and in particular the different types of social relations their practices enact. As noted previously, mainstream news media may be attempting to appear more popular and informal by drawing more on the voices of 'ordinary people' and less on official sources (the 'men in suits'). We have suggested in the previous chapter that mainstream local news media may to some extent be moving away from Dahlgren's (2009: 43) description of 'traditional journalism' as 'providing reports and analyses of real events and processes' that seek to produce 'accurate and impartial renderings of a reality that exists independently of its telling and which is external to the institutions of journalism'. And yet, as noted in Chapter 4, many of the participants in our focus groups still seemed to regard 'local news' as something that stood apart from and above particular communities in the city. By comparison with mainstream news media, citizen media is seen as more immersed within and part of particular communities (of place, interest or identity). It takes the perspective of a community member, who is part of and invested in a community, not that of an external and disinterested reporter.

In Chapter 2, in relation to the story about the National Health Service, we noted how the mode of address used by the citizen-produced *Kirkstall Matters* (2011: 17) was different to that adopted by mainstream news media. The writer of the story made their appeal directly to the reader as a member of the same community, with implied shared interests and concerns. The mode of address adopted by citizen news media may also be more informal than that typically adopted by professional news media.

As people rooted in their localities, citizen news-makers are invested in the community and its future. This is clearly the case with local campaigns such as the Friends of Leeds Kirkgate Market blog discussed above. However, the concern with making a difference locally appears true of citizen news media more generally. Some citizen news-makers talked about how they thought of themselves as helping to 'create' the news as well as simply 'reporting' it. As our interviewee from the Culture Vulture put it, 'We're not waiting for the press release to hit the desk ... We're trying to help create news in a way.' This sort of language seems odd when viewed from the perspective of the professional journalist, who – to quote Dahlgren (2009: 43) again – is seeking to produce 'accurate and impartial renderings of a reality that exists independently of its telling and which is external to the institutions of journalism'. Yet it makes sense from the perspective of the citizen news-maker, who is engaged in the particular community about which he or she writes.

As we have seen, a common complaint about local news from focus group participants was its negative tone: focus group participants were irritated by what seemed to be a focus upon crime, disorder and social incohesion and a disregard for the more positive aspects of their communities. Likewise, several of our interviewees involved in citizen news media talked about how they wished to improve and strengthen the communities they served through their news practices and represent the communities in a positive light. Our interviewee from South Leeds Community Radio described how the radio station aimed to empower and improve the quality of life of local people, while our interviewee from *Kirkstall Matters* said that 'People can post news and it goes out to everybody who lives locally and I think that really does foster a sense of community. I think for quite a long time there has not really been anything like that.'

In summary, the contribution of citizen news-makers to the local news ecology is not limited to producing particular types of story and filling 'gaps' in news provision. We also need to look at the practice of citizen news-making and in particular the types of social relations it enacts. Citizen news media is rooted within particular communities of place, identity and interest, which it simultaneously seeks to contribute to and strengthen. Professional news media, by comparison, still appear more as independent entities, which stand above and apart from these particular communities. Both sets of practices contribute to the local news ecology (Born 2005). Citizen news media can help to represent the shared interests, values and concerns of particular communities. The danger is that they may place too much emphasis on community unity and consensus and downplay differences within communities. The greater reach of mainstream news media can be important, as we note in the next section, in both facilitating communication across communities and groups and linking them with central sources of local decision-making and power.

Citizen news-makers in the news ecology

Rather than view different news media as being in competition with each other, an ecological perspective draws our attention to their distinctive strengths and ways that they may be able to complement one another. But what is the current relationship between citizen news media and traditional news media within a broader ecology? How do they work together, or fail to work together, in producing local news?

While we do not have exact figures, some of the citizen news media in our sample appear to have sizeable audiences: for example, the Culture Vulture appears to be a prominent blog in the city and Radio Asian Fever an important community radio station. However, citizen news media typically tend to attract small audiences, something confirmed by our survey research. While citizens may have more opportunities to contribute to local news today through blogs, social media and in other ways, this does not guarantee being able to reach an audience. We need, as Hindman (2008: 16) notes, to consider 'who speaks and who gets heard as two separate questions'. As Curran (2010: 470) argues, there is a 'tendency to mythologise the role of the Web in "mainstreaming" minority journalism'. Although the web has offered a 'low-cost springboard for some significant new publications, these are mostly niche publications with relatively small audiences'.

Support from mainstream media can be important in providing citizen news-makers with a wider audience. Our interviewee from the Friends of Leeds Kirkgate Market, for example, described how the site received many more visits when their campaign had been mentioned in the *Yorkshire Evening Post* or a local radio programme. However, she described how gaining the interest of mainstream providers in their news content is difficult. Editors tend to be more interested in original stories, rather than stories that have already been covered elsewhere. Given this, she described how she had learnt to send out press releases before writing the story themselves: 'We send out a press release before it goes on the blog because some editors are snobbish and are not interested if it is already out there.' At the same time, some citizen media may be overlooked or disregarded by mainstream media altogether. Our interviewee from Culture Vulture described how traditional news providers either are not aware of the site or decide not to take notice of it: '… the likes of the *Yorkshire Post* either I'm totally not on their radar, or they just ignore us completely, and I don't mind that either, but recently we were up for winning a global social media award and that was the first time after two years that we were ever contacted by the *Yorkshire Post* to find out more about what we were doing'.

In a more recent study of local journalism in Leeds, involving further interviews with local journalists, Firmstone and Coleman (2014: 600) note how mainstream news providers tend not to see citizen news-makers as 'competitors', given the small audiences they attract. Citizen news-makers are instead treated as 'potentially useful sources of information on local issues, in much the same way as journalists nurture contacts in local communities, or at least as a way of seeing what is "going on out there"' (ibid.: 600). At the same time, journalists may be reluctant to rely on citizen news-makers for news or to collaborate with them. As Firmstone and Coleman (2015) describe: '... although the journalists we interviewed did not consider CJ [citizen journalism] producers as competitors, they had not nurtured working relationships with hyperlocal news sites and blogs and did not see CJ producers as a regular or reliable source in news gathering'. They explain that 'Journalists also raised concerns about the validity of using other forms of citizen journalism (CJ contributors, sources and participants) in professionally produced news. They were concerned that information and news available from individual citizens may be at odds with their obligation to produce news according to the professional norms of objectivity and impartiality.'

Whereas traditional news media may be reluctant to direct audiences to citizen news media for these reasons, many of the citizen news media we examined tended to position themselves within a broader conversation in the city and as operating within a cooperative rather than a competitive environment. Citizen news media regularly provide links to traditional or other news providers and sources of information in the news ecology (e.g. council documents or planning applications, YouTube videos, SoundCloud recordings, Flickr photo albums, in addition to the ubiquitous Twitter feeds and Facebook pages). As important as they remain in the news ecology, the mainstream media's apparent transmedia or intertextual blindness belies the fact that they are just one port of call for civic information within the currents and conversations that flow through the city.

Of course, there are exceptions and cases where mainstream media do acknowledge citizen news-makers, suggesting how more productive relationships might operate. We have already mentioned examples of where citizen news media were picked up by professional journalists, but the clearest example during our study of a mainstream provider promoting citizen media in a sustained way was the Guardian Leeds blog, a local initiative run by the *Guardian* newspaper. This ran during our project but was closed down before our monitoring week began. It was run by a single full-time paid journalist. The blog explicitly sought to develop a different model of journalism, which involved collaboration with local citizen news-makers. As the journalist who ran the Guardian Leeds blog explained, the blog did not take a view of the journalist as a 'narrator', but was more about the journalist as a 'curator' of local content:

> What it took forward wasn't a traditional viewpoint of the journalist as the narrator and kind of the know all and he tells you a story and you listen, this was more about the nature of the journalist being a curator, so there has been a curator of news as well as doing what a journalist does which is tells stories, encourage interaction.

The blog sought to make the most of the stories that were available in citizen news media, by distributing them to a wider audience and promoting discussion around them. To do so, the *Guardian* newspaper was able to use its authority and reach, as well as the fact that it was paying a journalist to produce the blog.

The Guardian Leeds blog was considered to be valuable by the other interviewees we spoke to. Our interviewee from South Leeds Community Radio said that 'it's such a shame that they've stopped doing that, it was really well read, it was extremely popular, and that shows that there's a real market for it, it really does, and all sorts of people who I don't think necessarily read the *Guardian* newspaper are reading that, it was local news, well presented, immediate, interesting, but really local, and [the journalist who produces the blog] does a wonderful job of going out and about all over the place and finding out what's going on'.

Given the success and popularity of the Guardian Leeds, a group of Leeds residents decided to try to continue the work it had done, but on a voluntary, citizen-led basis. It was not possible to do everything that the Guardian Leeds blog had done. Nonetheless, it was suggested that the regular round-up of blog content from around

Leeds, which the Guardian Leeds blog had done each morning, had been a particularly valuable feature of the site and that it might be possible to continue this in some form. A new site was therefore set up, run by volunteers, which would include regular round-ups of local news, and would, like the the Guardian Leeds blog, link to and draw attention to citizen news-makers as well as professional news providers. The site was called Beyond Guardian Leeds and ran from May 2011 until December 2013.

It is not only mainstream news media that can help citizen news media to extend their audience. Citizen media also circulates and draws attention to the stories of mainstream media. As argued above, while it is easy to dismiss these practices as insignificant compared with the original production of news, the interpretation and circulation of news may play a role in shaping and constituting what local news is (Goode 2009). One example of this is provided by local community radio. The community radio stations play a crucial role in translating news, as well as other important public information, to specific communities, including communities where engagement with news or reading rates may be low or which do not speak English. Our interviewee from South Leeds Community Radio explained how volunteer presenters use mainstream news:

> Yes and they bring in the *Yorkshire Evening Post*, they bring in what they've heard that's going on round here and what's been reported on the local media, or the national media come to that, so we'll chat about that ...

Our interviewee from Radio Asian Fever notes:

> Then the local news is done by the local journalist Aswanti, here, she does that in three programmes a week. One was yesterday, between six and eight, she did the local round up and then there will be one on Sunday where – it's like *Mock the Week* but it's looking at news, headlines etc., and it's done between two experienced female presenters and they take everything on and then we have generally during the morning show we will pick up the news and the stories as well and that's how we do the local news.

In popular and academic discussions of journalism, the production of original news content is taken to be the 'real' journalism. Other practices are seen as inferior in comparison. Yet clearly practices which interpret and make sense of news for specific communities in particular contexts are also very important in shaping news (Anderson 2010; Goode 2009). Ideally, there would be a feedback loop, whereby mainstream news providers learn by seeing what news becomes through its translation. Unfortunately, though, as we noted above, flows of content in this direction can be more restricted.

Conclusion

In this chapter, we have resisted the reductive tendency to view citizen news-makers through the lens of professional news media. There is no evidence to suggest citizen news-makers are able to replace the work performed by well-resourced professional journalists or are displacing the central news ecology position of the mainstream media organizations, but then judging them in these terms alone is mistaken. Viewed from an ecological perspective, citizen news-makers are producing valuable forms of news at the local level, especially so-called 'hyperlocal' news and news stories connected with particular communities of identity and interest, which can supplement the news stories typically circulated by mainstream journalists. Furthermore, we have argued that the contribution of citizens to local news is not limited to the production of original stories. Citizen news media may also play a role in translating and making sense of news stories, broadening the range of interpretation and discussion around news, and building different types of social relationships around and through news.

Insofar as citizen news-makers do make a distinct and valuable contribution to the news ecology at the local level, critical questions are raised about citizen news media. To what extent are all groups in the city represented? Certain groups are clearly active contributors to local news, but this does not ensure all groups are represented adequately. There is also the question of how groups in Leeds communicate with one another and come to terms with their differences. Mainstream news media, given more significant resources and reach, have a potential role to play here in translating stories across cultural and political distances. But while there are examples of complementary relationships between mainstream new media and citizen media, mainstream media may not only fail to represent differences adequately, but also overlook ways in citizen news-makers could help to enrich their representations. Such disconnections and blockages prevent the possibility of a more productive division of labour being established within the news ecology, a theme which we will return to and develop in our concluding chapter.

7 | 'DOWN THERE IN CHAPELTOWN'

> No American – regardless of his or her racial identity – gets through a day without participating in everyday and mundane instances of 'noticing or sensing a racialized closeness or racialized distance in relation to those we encounter' (Hill 2001: 247). (Gaudio and Bialostok 2005: 65)

Gaudio and Bialostok (2005) refer here to everyday encounters in the American context but their words describe perfectly the northern English city of Leeds. In the focus groups in which word-of-mouth news emerged as a central part of local news (see Chapter 4) and the interviews with local television news editors (see Chapter 5), 'mundane instances' of 'racialized closeness or racialized distance' repeatedly emerged. Such feelings about racial difference felt and spoken about as distance appear to be central to the local news ecology of this multicultural city and the ways in which news travels through it and the ways in which news does not travel, but instead gets stuck. Moreover, it is striking that many of our interviewees thought that local news has a vital role to play in addressing and even countering distances of 'race', ethnicity and class in the city, and this is in terms of the information news delivers, the people news represents and the ideas about groups of people that news communicates. TV news editors, community leaders, newspaper journalists and community radio managers all told us that how news travels (or gets stuck) in the city can foster or help to break down feelings of distance between communities. Moreover, it seems clear that in Leeds right now local news is not helping to break down distances between communities: there are blockages in the news ecology of the city that have to do with how local news does not speak to, and for, the diverse populations of the city (cf Anderson et al. 2015).

In this chapter we explore the role news plays in creating those blockages in the ecology, by shoring up distance based on difference. We also explore the anxieties that such distance breeds. What follows is in three parts. In the first part, we look at how talk of distance stands in for unspeakable anxieties about 'racial' 'others'. We argue that stories help to concretize notions of difference and associated fears, thus helping to create blockages in the news ecology of the city. In the second part, we ask what news organizations might do to address this problem of distance (see also Chapter 5 for a discussion of the role of news organizations). In the third part, we ask what counter-stories might news organizations tell; how far can news as storytelling contribute to removing blockages in the media ecology of the city, thereby enabling new and more (and different) stories to travel in practice.

Difference, distance, storytelling

Across the wide variety of data generated by our research, we encountered a persistent sense of distance and mistrust between communities. Most notably, we encountered anxiety in many of the focus groups where all participants were white, about black and other minority ethnic communities in the Chapeltown area of Leeds. This anxiety emerged as we spoke about the local news story, the annual Chapeltown carnival, which took place during the August bank holiday weekend within our media monitoring week (see Chapter 2). In focus groups with white participants, we encountered a difficulty of speaking about 'race', ethnicity and class and, in these conversations, people alluded to *feelings* of difference by invoking geographical distance to describe parts of the city that were often, in fact, nearby but unknown.

Personal experience and its lack combine to make word-of-mouth news that is both trusted and at the same time unreliable. In those cases where people's actual interaction with people of other 'race', ethnicity and class groups is minimal, it seems as though storytelling plays an important part in fostering dissatisfaction and division; for instance, several of our focus group participants complained that Chapeltown receives a disproportionate amount of public funding:

It's an absolutely fantastic event, having been, and the sense of community and everything is amazing. There is a frustration about the amount of money that is spent down there but ... (Female, Group 1)

Meanwhile, the Coordinator of the Chapeltown Youth Development Centre (CYDC) raised this particular received wisdom about Chapeltown funding in our interview and suggested that as a deprived area of the city, Chapeltown is used to attracting funding. But he suggested that the borders of Chapeltown are, as he put it, 'elastic' – that is, funding that is supposed to be for Chapeltown is not always spent in Chapeltown:

> We call Chapeltown elastic; if there's a shooting in Moortown they'll say Chapeltown. If resources come to Chapeltown it'll go somewhere else. And we know that factually and we see it. Chapeltown is used as a tool to gain mass resources. Whether the work gets done there for young people or for adults in them areas is another thing in itself.

Members of the public from areas of Leeds outside Chapeltown, and the coordinator of a voluntary sector organization in Chapeltown, offer widely divergent views about public funding in Chapeltown. This is interesting for us in the context of the question of how it is that feelings about Chapeltown become fixed via word-of-mouth and other kinds of news. It may be the case that misinformation about Chapeltown, in this case about public funding there, becomes received wisdom in the absence of familiarity with the area and its residents. Exaggerated, stereotypical and anxiety-provoking storytelling can result from distances of race, ethnicity and class. As Bird and Dardenne (2009: 209) note: 'Stories help construct the world, and those in power benefit from constructing the world in specific ways – engaging the audience, but also overshadowing or eliminating competing narratives.' Chapeltown takes on an almost mythical quality in the storytelling practices of those who do not know anyone who lives there and never go there, and this is encapsulated in the repeated use in our focus group interviews of the phrase 'down there' to describe Chapeltown:

> F: It's never really appealed to me to go, and it's not that far away.
> M: I think it's because you know exactly what goes on there, it's not all singing and dancing. (Female and Male, Group 2)

I've been before, I've got pupils who have been part of the
carnival and it's incredibly busy – that was why I didn't go. I
have to be honest as well I was reticent because of all the rioting
etc. However, knowing some of the families that I do *down there*
I don't think it was perhaps fair of me to make that judgement.
(Female, Group 1, emphasis added)

It had come from the police – the police had set up their gold
command, which is something completely different, they tell
their gold command to deal with everything. That had come
from some of the community leaders *down there* as well because
there is a good sense of community *down there*, a real good sense
of community *down there* – we are welcome *down there* now. It's
mainly down to the community leaders *down there* helping and
being part of the community. (Male, Group 1, emphasis added)

Because I was there, the day before, in Chapel Allerton, which
is higher up. And we had family over from Ireland and we were
meeting someone from Moortown and we went *down there* and it
was really intimidating if you was not from that area it was very
intimidating and my mum was going to go and I said there's no
way you're going there. (Female, Group 5, emphasis added)

The coordinator of Chapeltown Youth Development Centre also
notes the use of the phrase 'down there', and attributes responsibility
for the perceptions invoked by the phrase to limited and negative
representations of the area in mainstream media:

I played pro football for ten years full-time. The biggest question
I used to get asked all the time is 'what's it like living down
there'? I says 'it's not a zoo, it's an area'. But I understood some
of their perceptions because all they see factually is the media
coverage, so the media coverage informed them and that's why
they came up with a view that there must be loads going on
down there negative. Not one time did they bring reference to
anything positive.

Here news organizations have a role in enabling or, at least, not
preventing the image of Chapeltown evoked in the phrase 'down

there in Chapeltown'. In this view, news media are responsible for limited, stereotypical perceptions of parts of a city and local news media play a central role in the creation of blockages in the news ecology of the city. News about Chapeltown does not travel to other parts of the city, leaving Chapeltown known only by its stereotyped reputation.

What should news organizations do?

Our interviews with mainstream media representatives suggest that they accept some responsibility for how the communities of Chapeltown are represented in local news:

> We don't, on a daily basis, have a dictionary and say how many people with non-white skins have you had on the news programme today, but it is monitored. We get a report every quarter which gives us an indication of what our portrayal on screen has been and we can compare that with the latest census returns which are ten years old because the last one hasn't come out yet. But it gives us an indication if we are grossly under-representing a community or maybe grossly over-representing a community and happily – oddly enough we got some results last week – we are actually on the right side of the fence on everything.

The editor of ITV's *Calendar* first makes a kind of joke about whether numbers matter: 'we don't … say how many people with non-white skins have you had on the news programme today' but then, in the same breath, indicates that ethnic diversity on screen matters and is taken seriously, 'it is monitored'. He actually does not tell us how he knows 'we are on the right side of the fence on everything'. He both talks about and cannot talk about the problem of representing difference in general. This interview excerpt thus indicates a theme in the interviews with local news providers, wherein the issue is acknowledged to be important, but there is a lack of clarity about what to do next. The editor of *Calendar* goes on:

> Not that we sit down in morning conferences or in meetings and say we must do more stories about the Chinese communities, we

don't, but we have a diversity panel, we are very well connected across the whole of the region, we regularly meet. They suggest stories to us, we do suggest stories to them and then we have a very open debate. We have had some real gems from that. So I am broadly happy with the way that it operates and it is important that there is a measuring system of sorts, however loose it may be, to make sure that we are not doing something that is not actually totally against the grain and missing out large segments of the audience.

Here, again, he indicates the seriousness with which the issue of representation of different communities in the news is treated by *Calendar*. But, at the same time, he avoids telling us what kinds of stories these 'gems' are, or what the 'diversity panel' looks for, or what the problems might be. An editor from BBC Radio Leeds was more forthright:

You only come to us when you want to talk about extremism. You only want to talk to us when there is an incident at the Chapeltown carnival. So I think, yes, that is significant. Because, for me, the diversity has to be embedded in who you talk to about things that are of importance and relevance to a wider audience and it is not an add-on. That's work in progress and that's why I do think community radio has a significant place.

For this editor, there is a problem in that BBC local radio news is not satisfactorily addressing diversity in its representations. Moreover, this problem is seen as having consequences for the kind of local news that is delivered to the city; what information gets put out that allows different communities to talk to each other. She points to the news ecology here, suggesting that where one part of the ecology might not be working as well as it should, another might provide what is missing: 'community radio has a significant place'. However, as we know, and as noted in Chapter 6, community radio stations tend to do important work in serving, reflecting and speaking to and for their particular communities, but not the work of having different communities speak to and know each other. BBC *Look North* editors agree that there is a problem in the representativeness of the city in BBC *Look North* news programmes:

That is a very valid question and I think that there is a danger that if you are doing a TV programme for Yorkshire, you present something which is, how did I hear it put? Preserved in aspic. I think we are very conscious that, as well as having a region with an identity, we have a very, very diverse region. I think we need to do more to reflect that. And it is diverse in hundreds of different ways. So I am talking age, I am talking social class, I am talking ethnic group, I am talking where people live, gender, all sorts of things. And we need to reflect the fact that Yorkshire is a dynamic, diverse community. And we're not always very good at that … So I just think the BBC needs to get its walls down and get more accessible. And that's in terms of ideas of stories in terms of pictures, in terms of 'tell us what you think' and also, frankly, it's teaching us also a thing or two about what our audience want.

But these editors also see the problem in on-screen representation as explicitly linked to the lack of representation of diverse ethnicities within the news staff team:

Again, I think, reflecting on the newsroom, I think we probably are pretty, not representative of the city, or where we might be, and we probably reflect that in our storytelling to a degree. How would I listen to that criticism? I think there is probably an element of truth in it and I suppose the way we would try to avoid being guilty of that is to ensure that our recruitment in the newsroom is actually as broad as possible. Because I think that the way you do get around that is by representing the audience in your newsroom and then you are more prone to reflecting it on air.

We return to this point in the third part of this chapter, when it is raised by our focus group interviewees. Here, we want to note that (some) news broadcasters and (some) audiences agree that the problem of difference and distance is a problem which concerns the representation of diverse communities of the city in the local news itself, but also in who communicates the news; who the storytellers are.

In these excerpts, interviewees focus mainly on questions of representation in local news. What is less explicit in these interviews is the ways in which representation is linked to information about an area and the people who live there, but also to communication *across* areas in the city – that is, across distance. As we have been arguing throughout this book, news is both practice and story. We need to be concerned with diversity of representation in news, but also about the accuracy and range of the kinds of information made available about different communities in the city and about how news helps communities communicate; how news helps the city to talk to itself. Ideas about information and communication are present in the preceding excerpts of interviews with local news providers in Leeds, which focus on the question of representation, but these questions are not tackled quite so explicitly. As the Radio Leeds news editor and the coordinator of the Chapeltown Youth Development Centre both note, news teams only visit Chapeltown for the carnival, asking: did it or did it not pass off peacefully – or for other stories of crime or violence. What this highlights is how negative representation is the status quo in any coverage of Chapeltown, but also that there is a complete lack of *any other information*. If stories do not fit the typical news frame for Chapeltown they are not told. To put it another way, what do we *not* get to know about when it comes to Chapeltown?

I've seen it every year on the news and I think this year was quite a special one I think – I can't remember – we see it on the news every year and they were saying they had troubles in Chapeltown a few weeks ago, generally the day had gone to plan, not too many incidents. (Female, Group 2)

M: I think they just went on a bit too much about the costumes and then they cut to the carnival bit and had the usual three or four people ...

M: And they made a big deal about it after the riots as well because it was a carnival in Chapeltown where there's usually trouble so they made a big deal out of that as well. (Males, Group 5)

F: It had to close early I think and there were less bands on. They couldn't put any steel bands on and the timing was different, that's what I heard. It always says ... if there was an incident that would make a huge ...

What does that suggest to you then when they say 'passed off without incident'?

M: That it's Chapeltown, that's the usual thing …
F: That they were expecting something to … (Conversation, Group 6)

For us the question becomes: what is the (normative) role of local news media in bridging distances of 'race', ethnicity and class in order to enable communication between communities in the city and, ultimately, to break down blockages in the news ecology of a city?

Our focus group participants say they have no sense of local media performing this bridging role; even when they try to it is received as cliché. The pictures of happy carnival-goers are received as a cover for what really goes on 'down there'. Moreover, we encountered mixed views in our focus group interviews as to whether bridging distance is even something that the media should be doing. Media workers absolutely see this as a part of their role, community activists agree. Members of the public expressed a range of views on this subject of the role of the media herein. What does seem to be (largely) agreed upon is that local news media contribute to an *idea* of Chapeltown that, at the very least, does not break down distances of race, ethnicity and class and, at worst, fosters them.

It was, kind of, bright shots, a bit of music and tick some boxes really. (*Calendar*, interview)

Normally we just do a double-page spread with loads and loads of photographs and it's all quite jolly and nice, that's what normally happens and bear in mind the Chapeltown carnival has been going on for donkey's years, they do it every year and we always do a double-page spread […]. I think the fact that it followed the riots this year, if I'm right with my chronology, it followed the riots, therefore there had been concern raised nationally about Notting Hill and the similar sorts of concerns were being raised in Leeds simply because there had been those riots. And, of course, there was a little bit of trouble that had kicked off during the riots in Chapeltown and we'd covered that certainly, we had sort of a looped video going on of some problems in Chapeltown, so this year's coverage may have been a little more on the negative side rather than the positive celebration side. (YEP journalist)

Taken together, these remarks powerfully demonstrate the ways in which repeated media coverage that fits a familiar, established and limited pattern sets up a certain expectation. Consequently, even when there's nothing negative to report, coverage of Chapeltown carnival is framed in such a binary way that a positive report still invokes the negative framework through which inhabitants of white Leeds view Chapeltown: 'not too many incidents', and we learn very little else from the news.

Unblocking the news ecology: new stories, new practices

Our research participants repeatedly proposed two solutions to the problem of distance across the city or blockages in the news ecology of the city. First, they told us that both more, and more varied, coverage of communities in Chapeltown was vital. Second, they suggested enabling communities to represent themselves – that is, tell their own news stories to others:

F: I think someone getting into the heart of their community feed out, rather than look in, from what they think.

How do you get into the heart of a community as a journalist?

F: Go speak to them, the youth, and the elderly. You have to go in and get all their opinions and talk to them. (Female, Group 6)

M: The *Yorkshire Evening Post* choose their own (like with the Carnival), they will send somebody to make their own story, they will send somebody to take the photograph and then use it but not as trying to cover from the—

So what's the difference between the community point of view as you described it and …

M: Well, I think they choose where they go, they don't come around long like as wholehearted as we work for the community. (Males, Group 4)

Indeed, there was a development in the discussion in the focus group with black and other minority ethnic participants, from talking about communities in general, to talking specifically and explicitly about race, racism and ethnicity. Moreover, they talked not only about how local news providers currently address problems of difference, distance and 'race' and racism, but about how those providers *could* and *should* do better in a multicultural and divided city. These focus group participants were interested in how news-makers might improve the ways in which news flows through the city:

> F: We're saying that people who don't know a lot about the culture wouldn't cover it enough. If I know something about Sikh I would cover it more than maybe a white person would, I'm not being racist but I think it's the knowledge of what you're doing and how you [perceive] things and you put it forward to everybody.
>
> F: You would also know your community, you would tailor it. (Females, Group 4)

> *Calendar* did [cover Carnival] but it was for about thirty seconds. (Female, Group 4)

> F: I think they need to recruit more ethnic minority people definitely.
>
> M: I would say it's OK saying they are multicultural without showing it – they should show it as a multicultural society in Leeds and I think it's no good admitting but not showing it and they have got to show it in the programme that Leeds is a multicultural society. When you can see it on the programmes then you can say they are doing something. Even if it has a time space; if they slot a small time for ethnic minorities or to show a multicultural society, it's a starting point. Up to now they haven't done that, if they do this that will be a good start. (Female and male, Group 4)

Indeed, two of our interviewees suggested, in different ways, that the very specific and limited way in which Chapeltown in general, and Chapeltown carnival in particular, are covered by local news media (as a parade that passes off without incident or with the expectation of negative events) means that realities are rarely represented – either about carnival or about the neighbourhood.

> I think, I mean the carnival is no longer a political thing, it's no longer what it used to be. It's a very nice and pleasant party, I don't think there's any politics in there any more, I don't think there's any edge to it – other than hedonism. There's not as much identity of the different West Indian islands coming through that there used to be, I mean it's good fun, it's nice, I enjoy it but ... And I think it's reported in fairly patronizing ways, you know, look at the black people doing their stuff. I think what would be really interesting is if someone reported what actually happens which is, you know, ten thousand people sit in a field, get pissed and stoned and fed up to their eyeballs in a day, you know that's what happens for three days, that's what actually happens. It's probably the biggest bit of hedonism in Leeds and the police don't do anything about, you know, suddenly for three days, drugs are ignored, what's that all about? I mean I have no problem with it [laughs] but it's slightly double standards, isn't it. Licensing laws seem to go out the window, you know, anyone can take in a crate of Red Bull and sell it at two pound a tin. It's weird, it's like a little, it's a little glimpse of almost anarchy. (Community activist and blogger)

> The best coverage we got was the *Guardian*. And the *Guardian* came, care and consideration, good discussion, heard people, looked at the wider perspective of services, to get everybody's views and compile a story. And that wasn't done overnight spontaneously, it was collectively, collaborated information, hearing from the people and the services in [...] And I think at the end of the day it showed Chapeltown in a positive light. So, care and consideration of media is important because – don't use an area as a tool so you can fling crap at it – understand there's real people in real communities that can make a real difference and start respecting and valuing them communities 'cause not everyone is into crime, there's good professionals in our area. We've got a number of sports people; number of barristers; number of doctors that are from the area, that live

in the area. Sometimes that doesn't even get portrayed, it's just like everybody in this area must be doing something wrong. (Coordinator, Chapeltown Youth Development Centre)

In arguing that wider and more varied local news coverage of Chapeltown has a role to play in breaking down distances of 'race', ethnicity and class, we are suggesting that news coverage should move away from a familiar narrative frame which is negative and clichéd and which generates fear. As Farrar (2012) notes, coverage of Chapeltown in 2011 follows an old narrative, and the story could be a different one:

It seems that the Leeds West Indian Carnival HQ in Chapeltown was set on fire because some cars had been smashed up outside a mosque in the same area. That description immediately conjures up the idea that Muslims and African-Caribbeans were going to war in Leeds, particularly when you know that an African Caribbean man was shot by a Muslim, who is now in custody, charged with murder. But this story could follow another script: groups of young men, perhaps not the most consistently law-abiding, move into confrontation when a cross-group sexual liaison gets underway. Men fighting over women is perhaps the oldest story we know. Within a couple of days, local people – mature people, with their long knowledge of protest, the burning of their shops, arrests, court cases, and community 'self-help' in Chapeltown and Harehills – organized a 'peace march'. Combined with effective, and legitimate, additional policing, this activity stopped further disorder from taking place. (Ibid.: 88)

Our focus group participants raised the idea of the negative story frame with which everyone is familiar and, as the coordinator of the Chapeltown Youth Development Centre notes (above), these are, for some people in Leeds, the only stories known about Chapeltown. From this perspective, it is perhaps unsurprising that distance gets created:

I'd be a bit nervous about going to be completely honest with you, I mean I like the idea of different races and communities coming together but you're always frightened when you're in a

crowd like that, things can happen, can't they, you're frightened
of getting robbed or stabbed, maybe we read too much into it ...
(Female, Group 2)

You can create negative attitudes, can't you, that news
predominantly focuses on bad negative things because they are
the ones that catch your attention rather than good news which
can go by the wayside. So they all tell you the negative bad
things happening in communities as opposed to the good things,
so it forms your attitudes even on a relaxed level like 'I don't
like them because of this and this'. You don't actually know the
sense of good that happened, like you say with the Chapeltown
carnival there could be other things that happen that don't get
focused on. (Female, Group 1)

F: I've always felt a bit nervous about taking the children
   somewhere like that but I have friends who have been and
   taken the children and they say it's fantastic.

Why?

F: Because there has been trouble in the past.

What is the connection between the way it's reported and what you
associate with it because presumably you make these associations
because you hear something – what is it that you've been hearing?

M: Chapeltown has a reputation. You don't ever hear about
   Chapeltown in the news for a positive reason. It is only ever
   there when there has been a stabbing, or a shooting or a
   police officer or a drugs raid and that is part of the problem.
   (Conversation, Group 3)

But you also talked about how the way it's reported is negative ...?

F: Yes
F: They don't tell us about the good things, it's always about the
   bad things like there has been a shooting or a stabbing, etc.,
   but you get that everywhere but they paint Chapeltown with
   that brush and I think it's wrong. (Females, Group 4)

Thus focus group participants indicate their awareness that news providers 'paint Chapeltown with that brush' and their anger that this is the case and that essentially the people who live there are stereotyped in ways that other communities in Leeds are not. Indeed, when moving on to news providers, the focus groups particularly single out local news providers for being at fault in terms of this poor representation:

> M: I think different papers understand different groups and represent different groups. I think across the spectrum, again nationally rather than locally, there is probably good representation of all age groups, sexes, minorities, so on and so forth. Locally I would say probably not.
> M: Yes, I was talking locally.
>
> *You think not – who is not represented?*
>
> M: Apart from the Chapeltown festival which is one day in the sun and the rest of the time it's all negative.
> M: If someone gets stabbed or shot – nothing positive, all negative.
> M: That news doesn't really sell, though.
> M: That's the problem.
> F: I do quite a bit of sports coaching in Chapeltown, it's a really good vibe, it's really positive, there are lots going on, lots of community spirit but that doesn't really come across in that.
> M: A couple of drugs raids that gets in the papers.
> (Conversation, Group 6)

Of course, the problem of negativity in the news has been widely discussed and is not limited to coverage of black and minority ethnic communities. As an editor of *Calendar* notes, 'most places we go something bad has happened, we're news':

> I went down to Chapeltown with the recent disturbances and I think I was still producing it, and there were people who came up and said 'you only come up here when something bad has happened'. I said, to be fair we have done quite a few … and there's a guy that we were doing quite a lot of stuff with, who is a community worker up there, and I said, to be fair most places we go something bad has happened; we're news. (*Calendar*, interview)

Thinking about deployments we sensed that potentially that it could have been (given what had happened a couple of weeks before in Chapeltown) and a lot of people in one area, it wouldn't be unfair to say we were anticipating there would be a possibility there would be a bad news story there. (*Look North* deputy editor)

In response to this defence, which relies on accepting the idea that news is by definition bad, we want to suggest that it is time to revisit the problem of the negative story frame in news. Moreover, we want to suggest that the excitingly varied news ecology of the contemporary city might provide opportunities for countering the long-standing problem of negative news, by offering, as it does, opportunities for a diversity of voices to be heard in much more rich, rounded and interesting ways. An elderly Sikh man in one of our focus groups began to think through ways to improve representation, reinventing BBC Access programming initiatives of old for the era of diversified media and diversified local news:

F: Compared to ... for the community side of things, time slots are only about ten minutes if that and then you have got your weather twice.

M: There is another way I was thinking. Thursday you've employment, if you did Wednesday it would be all community programmes, if you do it that way at least they can have a better slot – then at least you have a fair chance ... like if anyone wants to see employment they will [...] Thursday, and if you are only interested in community it's on Mondays/Wednesday – whichever, you could do it that way, at least you are trying to do something ...

F: It's a start – if people wanted to know more about the carnival they should film more of it – show a bit of it but the rest of it on the internet.

F: If they could say if you want to see more, go on the internet. (Conversation, Group 4)

However, there is a problem with the above suggestion that 'if you want to see more, go on the internet'. Compounding distances created and shored up by a familiar negative framework in news stories about

Chapeltown is the idea, expressed strongly in our focus groups and community media interviews, that people consume media that speak to their own lives and the people in those lives:

> During the general election, you know you were saying about newspapers being political party – the *Daily Mirror* were Labour and *Express* […] If you believed in the Labour Party you wouldn't buy a newspaper that was pro-Conservative, would you? You'd buy that and read all about what you agree with. (Female, Group 1)

> F: My in-laws come and watch Star news every day – I miss the music when they are not there – then I try and tell them you need to know what's going on here as well – let's watch something else but they could watch it every day, all day.
> F: We got involved when Sherpa was on *Big Brother* – otherwise I wouldn't. (Females, Group 4)

> They [mainstream local news providers] don't understand the communities so how can they provide for it and that's what it is. And they don't provide. They haven't got provisions for the South Asian community, yet the South Asian community is the biggest community after the white community, yet we've got no provision for it here. Why? This is the provision for it and this is because we have given them a voice, because we have allowed them to own this as theirs, because that is what it is, and they fully support it. It is being supported by local business, by local sponsors, donations; it *is* the community, and if you had come in a week earlier, on the tenth, you would have seen the whole of the community in here when we launched into here, into the new premises here. (Manager, Radio Asian Fever)

It has been widely observed that the contemporary fragmented and diversified news environment can mean that we do not see representations of 'others' in the city, or beyond. As a result, local news media practices can compound distances of 'race', ethnicity and class in the city. Madianou (2009) has emphasized the ways in which the news excludes groups and communities as much as it includes. We draw attention to the affective nature of the responses of the focus group we conducted with black and minority ethnic members of the public in Leeds. We suggest that the anger and frustration expressed in that conversation is a visceral response to the very fact of exclusion from the local news media. The news creates distance by reporting only repeated, limited and clichéd stories. In this way, we suggest, silencing is also a news practice. Moreover, in an age when we can select our news sources, as our focus group participants point out (above), ignoring might be a news practice too. Writing in 2003, Couldry (2003: 51) notes: 'Perhaps we are entering an era in which many of us will want to look more closely at where and to what end we obtain news about the world.' We can say the same for news about the city; many of us will want to look more closely at where and to what end we obtain news about the city. We want to end this discussion of 'racial', ethnic and class distance by emphasizing that the news ecology of the contemporary city might be an opportunity; our interviews with a broad range of stakeholders suggest the will is there to *use* news media to break down distance in the city. The question is: how is this apparent goodwill to be transformed into meaningful outcomes?

They invite you to the door of the cave and say 'Shout here' but no one's listening or responding. (Coleman and Firmstone 2014)

Unlike passive spectators, destined to receive as given the decisions that govern their lives, democratic citizens are supposed to be able to not only hold to account those making such decisions, but also contribute to and challenge them. To be regarded as democratic, a local news ecology should not merely afford opportunities for finding out what is going on, but provide meaningful opportunities for citizens to perform as autonomous political agents, capable of engaging in purposeful collective action.

Unlike bureaucratic forms of public communication, which perform a functional role in maintaining political boundaries, a democratic news ecology is sensitive to a diversity of voices, perspectives and potential political outcomes. Public communication becomes more than a one-way process whereby local government communicates its messages to citizens and citizens are free to submit recommendations to decision-makers. Democratic engagement calls for an ethical commitment to communicative reciprocity, which entails a motivation on the part of actors to listen to and learn from one another. The record of local governments rising to this communicative challenge has been disappointing. An important reason for this has been confusion about what local democratic engagement means in practice. While happy to support and even promote it at a rhetorical level, local governments are confused by discrepant expectations of what the experience of 'being engaged' is supposed to entail.

This chapter aims to add to our understanding of the dynamics of the relationship between the engagement strategies of local government, local journalism and citizens' experiences by exploring an example of engagement that became a major local news story during the week of our intensive study: the closure of adult care homes. In August 2011, the council decided to close down three residential care homes and four day centres for the elderly. Local authorities all over the UK were struggling to deal with the cataclysmic effects of the 2008 financial crash, which resulted in cuts to local services amounting to over a third of their budgets. Leeds Council leader Keith Wakefield declared that 'These cuts were thrust upon us without any consultation. They are an ideologically-driven attempt to undermine local government' (*Guardian*, 11 February 2011). Talk of cuts to local services can easily descend into statistical abstraction. It is not numbers that injure people, though, but hard decisions about priorities. We explore one such decision and the way that it was communicated to citizens in the local news ecology in the following five sections of this chapter. First, we set out the range of understandings of the concept of engagement and perceptions of the characteristics of successful engagement. Having painted a picture of a system of local representation straining to adapt to new technologies and expectations of public participation, we then consider the council's public communication about the decision to cut services. Third, we give an overview of the media coverage of the announcement to see how the decision was framed and what this suggests about the kinds of public engagement at play in the decision-making process. Fourth, we reflect on what the practices and role perceptions of local journalists tell us about the way that local news represents and engages the public. Finally, we draw on our focus groups to explore citizens' perspectives on local decision-making and the role of local news in engaging the public in civic practices.

What does public engagement actually mean?

With a view to understanding how local news ecologies can facilitate public engagement, we conducted twenty-three face-to-face, semi-structured interviews with people representing differing functions and levels of responsibility within Leeds City Council. These included elected council members from all three main parties (councillors), communications and public engagement specialists, parish councillors, and heads of directorate and front-line workers from two areas of service delivery, youth and children's services and leisure services. These were selected with a view to exploring how public engagement might be thought of in distinctive ways in relation to different service contexts, policy drivers and public expectations. In addition, we interviewed a range of other key actors, including journalists from the mainstream local news media (TV, press and online) as well as producers of non-mainstream forms of local digital journalism, community activists and local NGOs. We asked them about their understanding of why the council needed to engage with the public, as well as for examples of when such engagement worked well or failed. We set out some selected findings from these interviews in order to provide a backdrop to the example about the decision to close some council care homes which this chapter focuses on.[1]

When asked why local government needed to engage with citizens, our interviewees referred to a diverse and sometimes inconsistent range of notions of public engagement that can be grouped into three main concepts. First, public engagement was understood as a process of public education, informing rather than interacting with citizens. Second, it was seen as being about consulting the public, either as a broad entity or as specific groups or mini-publics. Third, more commonly alluded to than advocated, public engagement was understood as a process of empowerment whereby citizens moved from being recipients of council decisions and services and became partners in their production.

The elected council representatives (councillors) seemed to be of the view that public engagement entailed explaining the council to bewildered citizens. For one councillor, the main benefit of public engagement was that 'The public will hopefully have a better understanding of what the council can and cannot do'. Asked to say what public engagement strategies should aim to achieve, this councillor said: 'I think our job is to explain why we do certain things and what benefits come out of it'. Making citizens aware of how and why their representatives act in particular ways certainly accords with norms of democratic transparency, but is it engagement? Council communication strategists also placed great emphasis upon the informational aspect of public engagement, but for them there seemed to be a much clearer link between public understanding and expanding the scope for autonomous civic action. According to a

---

1 A detailed discussion of the findings can be found in Coleman and Firmstone (2014).

Communications Team member:

> Without really effective engagement, I think we'll continue to
> have people complaining about 'Well, I didn't know where to
> go and how to do it' – that sort of thing; so, the more that we
> get people understanding what councils can and can't do, what
> you can do yourself to help yourself ... people are going to better
> understand the types of support, the levels of support that are
> available.

A second articulation of the need for public engagement moved
beyond merely disseminating or sharing information and focused
upon listening to and learning from the experiences and expertise
of local citizens. As one councillor put it, 'There are occasions when
I think you've got to start listening more to local opinion. There
are too many decisions made by officers who do not live in an area,
nor totally understand the area, or the consequences of some of the
decisions that are made that affect an area.' The enjoinder to 'start
listening' is significant, for it suggests that communication between
representatives and the represented has yet to reach the most basic
level of communicative reciprocity. Local governments are under
increasing pressure to ensure that citizens have an opportunity
to comment on policies and strategies before they are agreed and
implemented. Failure to do so can result in expensive legal challenges
and political embarrassment. One motivation to consult, therefore,
is to avoid the negative consequences of failing to do so, and in these
circumstances public engagement can often seem like a tick-box
activity. Beyond this bureaucratic rationale, two other motives for
consulting the public became apparent.

The first was to extend democratic accountability beyond the
electoral mandate, so that preferences are not simply stated at
the ballot box and presented to the council as a blank cheque for
legitimacy, but are rearticulated and revised through an ongoing
conversation. One councillor explained, 'In the good old days
councillors would say, "Well, you elected me and that's it; just go
away and I'll sort it out." And we make a decision based on what I
think, but not necessarily what you think.' For this councillor, 'In an
ideal situation [effective consultation] means that we've given people
the opportunity to engage with us; we have listened to the comments

that they have made; we then reflect back on those comments and then issue a revised document … highlighting which areas changed as a result of the consultation, but also pointing out which areas haven't changed, and the reasons why it wasn't deemed feasible.' In this sense, consulting with citizens becomes a way of redefining the representative relationship; of rooting local democracy in something closer to an ongoing conversation than a fleeting and sweeping mandate. Interestingly, this was the most common reason given by non-council interviewees for the council needing a public engagement strategy. For example, one local BBC journalist told us that 'they've got to have one, because the whole purpose of local authorities is not to have their views imposed upon the public. In theory we're a democratic process, so they've got to engage with the electorate.' A local newspaper journalist stated: 'It's elected, you know, there are elected members – elected by the taxpayer – and so it is accountable to people, to the public and therefore needs to engage with the public to show that it is doing its job.'

As a Council web team member put it:

> I think it's having that two-way conversation with residents
> and stakeholders on what we're doing. We're quite a faceless
> organization, with us being so big, and I think that it's really
> important that we understand how well we're doing and what we
> feel we're doing right and what's wrong and how we can improve
> and where people can get involved with influencing how we run
> services …

Managing such a communicative relationship is difficult. It entails more than having a council Facebook page or an email address at the end of policy documents. A member of the directorate in charge of running the council's museums and galleries described how, for him, effective public consultation means recognizing that the users of a service should be encouraged to define its resource priorities and cultural rationale, and this involves a fine balance between offering people 'a completely blank sheet, where they haven't got the faintest idea what might be possible' and 'some options or some guidance, without actually controlling'. The value of making this work is that a new kind of relationship emerges between people and public institutions: 'The public gains from this because it actually feels it's having a say … and people are taking notice, and it's a relationship, not a one-off meeting-type consultation.'

There were rare moments when interviewees alluded to a third sense of public engagement – as a form of empowerment that shifts traditional relationships between government and citizens – and distinguished between this reconfiguration of the terms of governance and more traditional forms of information dissemination and consultation. Citizen empowerment was hardly ever raised as a direct aspiration, but as a potential outcome of other political changes, such as the need to persuade communities to take on responsibilities once resourced and managed by government, or the central government's drive towards 'localism'. One interviewee suggested that some councillors felt uncomfortable with any notion of engagement that resulted in a diminution of politicians' authority: 'When it starts to shift – potentially, on some of the localism stuff, about who makes decisions – then it will be interesting to see what councillors want out of engagement.' At least one of the councillors we interviewed said that he was beginning to change his mind about devolving decision-making to citizens:

> If you'd have asked me twenty years ago I might have said I'm not sure whether citizens – this is going to sound terrible on the tape – are fit to take power. As I've got older, I've got more relaxed … and, in some ways, I now say to people, 'Well, look, if you really, really, really want to do this, and you've actually thought through what you want, then are you prepared to accept the consequences?'

In one sense, this rhetorical question goes to the core of democratic theory. Are citizens fit to make autonomous decisions about matters most likely to affect them? Are there appropriate mechanisms for thinking things through? Our interviewees were consistently silent about the potential of public deliberation, despite this being a major theme in the theoretical literature about democratic engagement (Carpini et al. 2004; Hajer 2005; Fung 2009; Coleman 2012; Coleman et al. 2015).

What makes engagement successful?

Each of our interviewees was asked to begin by giving an example of a successful and a failed attempt to engage with citizens – and to say why they think these outcomes came about. While all actors were able to give examples of what they perceived to be successful engagement strategies, several were reluctant to provide examples of failed attempts.

The ways in which interviewees perceived success related closely to the differing conceptions of public engagement outlined earlier. Where they regarded engagement as a means of nurturing public understanding of the council, its policies and its constraints, they tended to evaluate success in informational terms. Engaged citizens, in this sense, were conspicuous when they understood what the council did and why they had to do it: 'The more you engage with people and the more you make them understand what you're actually about, the less likely they are to knee-jerk in their reactions' (Communications Team). A key means of developing such understanding seemed to involve managing public expectations. As one member of a service directorate put it:

> I think that's one of the big problems that I think sometimes the council has, that it's not very good at managing expectations. It's like if you [citizens] want to get anything done in the council, all you've got to do is contact your local councillor, preferably a couple of local councillors, and they will ensure that, whether it makes any sense or not, whether it's a priority or not, it will get dealt with.

The desire to ensure that citizens do not hope for more from the council than it can possibly deliver was linked to a growing recognition, strongly expressed in several interviews, that the relationship between local state and citizens is changing as a result of budgetary pressures and that the public is going to have to take responsibility for aspects of its well-being about which it had hitherto looked for state support. Successful engagement in this sense was expressed in terms of citizens learning to be 'self-sufficient': 'We now very commonly transfer assets to local organizations ... these resources are really expensive. We can't continue to operate them and ... the solution is that we give up something, which is giving up an asset, and they [the public] take on the responsibility to run the resource' (Communications Team).

If successful public engagement amounts to little more than teaching citizens to understand and accept the new constraints facing local government, what is the difference between this and public relations? Interviewees from the Communications Team were aware that most of what they were doing could hardly be called public engagement: 'Engagement is really only engagement if it's a two-way process. You can't just tell people stuff and assume you've ... Our team isn't really set up for public engagement; it is set up for media. Although we recognize there is this wider role in the public, our role is actually specifically with the media.' Interestingly, they point out that other people within the council do not always recognize this and sometimes think that sending out a message through the press office constitutes engaging with the public. One member of the press office commented that 'people use the service we provide in the press office to sort of tell people stuff, but they can't just assume that's engagement ... what we do relies on people actually reading the newspaper or watching the TV or whatever, so you can't replace local, direct engagement with what we do'. For the majority of citizens, communication with the council happens only when something goes wrong in their own lives and when they felt disappointed that an anticipated level of service has been reduced, or when faced with a new situation calling for institutional support. Some of the most concrete examples of successful engagement related to specific issues of service provision where engagement was focused on citizens who had a vested interest in a particular service. For example, the process around the closure of adult care facilities for the elderly and disabled was deemed to have been successful because the council 'took its time to do more than consultation, to engage with local people and get them involved in discussing the solutions ... People really had the opportunity to be heard and voice their opinion' (Communications Team). Similarly, a member of a council directorate described the success of engaging disabled children in decisions to award contracts to companies to provide services for them.

The most common examples of successful public engagement involved efforts by the council to communicate directly with specific groups of people, particularly those regarded as excluded, marginalized or without a strong political voice. More than one interviewee spoke of the 'Vision for Leeds' project as a model exercise because of the way that it 'broadened the amount of engagement and voice' by successfully connecting target groups. Councillor A explained how he was involved in a 'state of the city' exercise 'where all the partners come and talk to the councillors. And we had one section where the youth came and talked about their aspirations and visions for the future. Wow, did that really go down well.' A member of the web communications team explained how they had sent out 'lots of questionnaires and surveys that went out to different groups, right from schools to ethnic minorities to staff members and the public in general, to … try and get an idea of what they think the priorities are for us to resolve over the next ten, fifteen, whatever it was, years'. Clearly, the more specifically targeted and resource-intensive engagement exercises were more likely to be deemed successful than more general attempts to involve the mass of represented citizens in discussions on the broad political and cultural questions that shape top-line policies and determine overall council priorities.

Many of the examples of failure stemmed from exercises in which the council began to involve citizens only at a point when policy proposals had already been formulated or, worse still, agreed upon. In these cases, citizens often felt that the main decisions had already been made and their contribution to the engagement process would not make any difference. A parish councillor gave the example of an exercise in which parish councils were invited to contribute to local neighbourhood plans, but the city council 'steamed ahead, regardless of the plans that it had asked local parish councils to come up with'. Her concern was that the council lacked integrity in asking for people's views and then going ahead with its own plans without leaving adequate time for such input to be considered. In several cases, citizens participated actively in policy consultations – and were invited to engage at a point when their views could have affected decisions – but they were left feeling that, despite their input, the council had not really listened to them. As one local political blogger put it, 'They invite you to the door of the cave and say "Shout here" but no one's listening or responding. The council has had to take a lot of flak for that, to be honest.' At risk here is political efficacy: people's belief in their ability to influence their government (internal efficacy) and in the government's willingness to be influenced by people like them (external efficacy) (Campbell et al. 1971; Milbrath 1965; Sullivan and Riedel 2004).

In other cases, there was a more basic failure of communication between citizens who had bothered to engage and the council itself. Where there is a lack of feedback, either in the form of clear information or policy action, citizens are left wondering why they had ever been asked to contribute their opinions. A member of a council directorate identified this as problem that had been reported several times in consultations that he had helped to run: 'No feedback ever happens. So what we tend to hear … is "I've been consulted all the time, but nobody ever tells me what happens as a result of those consultations."' An interviewee from another council directorate reported similar citizen dissatisfaction with feedback:

> There was a lot of ill-feeling about the previous experiences
> that the groups have had with council consultation, which in
> their eyes consisted of … a meeting, they'd give their views,
> then they'd hear nothing, and five years later something would
> happen which the council would claim related to their views,
> and which usually didn't bear any relation.

More than lip-service – serious attempts to ensure successful engagement

Despite this lack of clarity and substantial definition, there was a widespread perception among interviewees, including those outside local government, that the council had expanded and improved its methods of engagement with the public over the last decade. While consultation has long been a statutory requirement for councils, in the past this was often addressed in an entirely reactive fashion by announcing plans in the local newspaper, holding public meetings and responding to complaints and protests. The council considers that it now routinely consults citizens likely to be affected by forthcoming decisions that will concern them; has plans for public engagement built into all proposals for change; and sees its website and emerging social media strategy as a crucial part of its new proactive approach to relationship-building with citizens. The council's relatively recent reorganization of its structure of service provision into local area committees is seen as an important means of opening up opportunities for citizens to become engaged close to their homes and workplaces. A member of the Consultation Team told us that 'There's a lot of thinking about how and where we deliver locally based engagement'. The shift from a centripetal notion of engagement, in which the council buildings, elected representatives and permanent officials were at the centre and citizens came to them, to a centrifugal notion of engagement taking place within the communities and networks, virtual as well as physical, in which people feel most at home and where problems are actually experienced, is an important step in the reconceptualization of public engagement. Anecdotal accounts from interviewees suggested that citizens feel much more comfortable and efficacious when they are asked to engage with the council within their own spaces than when expected to enter the alien orbit of institutionalized politics.

Crisis, cuts and consultation

Thus far we have painted a picture of a system of local representation straining to adapt to new technologies and expectations of public participation. How do such systems deal with the need to gain public support for tough decisions about priorities necessitated by unwelcome cuts to the budgets of local governments? In our example the council had held an official consultation to invite the public to submit their views about the proposed closure. The results of the consultation were made available to a committee which published the final recommendations to the council midway through the week we studied. We now explore how the council communicated the recommendation and consider how their public relations strategy shaped the framing of the decision in the local news media. The concept of framing is broader than agenda-setting. The latter refers to the kind of stories that are included in 'the news' and how they are prioritized. Framing refers to the field of meaning within which a story is set. Some stories, for example, are framed as 'natural disasters', others as 'malicious acts' and others as a consequence of competing 'political values'. The kind of meaning ascribed to stories influences, but does not wholly determine, the ways in which they are received and acted upon by media audiences. In the case of the care home closures, the councillor in charge of adult health and social care was reported by the BBC as saying that 'I fully accept that our customers have found some of our proposals upsetting'. The daughter of an eighty-eight-year-old care home resident who had lived in one of the care homes for ten years and would now have to move stated that 'The cost in human lives is going to be phenomenal and a lot of these people can't fight back'. 'Upsetting' is the kind of reaction one might have to an inevitable event. 'Fighting back' suggests political choice and agency. Every political story entails a semantic battle for the moral high ground. In this sense, government press releases are moral missives, journalistic storytelling is a way of framing what is decent and efforts by campaigners to attract public attention are calls for moral recognition.

The press release/the council's side of the story

The council presented its message about the decision via an overtly positive press release on the morning of the announcement on 30 August 2011. The press release headline framed the closures as a 'reshaping' of council-run services: 'Council asked to approve plans to reshape residential and day care service for older people'. The language focuses on opportunities and options for the future rather than closures and the contentious nature of the decision. For example, 'the recommendations will transform current day and residential services so that they focus more on delivering specificity care' and 'this has given us a fantastic opportunity to re-evaluate what we currently do'. The details of the decision are set out midway down page two of the press release where it is announced that four (out of twelve) day care centres under review will close, three (out of eleven) residential homes will close with two more due to close once replacement homes have been built. In addition, it noted that a further eight residential homes remained under review. The existence of local citizen-led campaigns to fight the closures was absent from the narrative. This part of the story was largely omitted and is only vaguely acknowledged in a statement from the councillor responsible for adult health and social care. Her statement, which was widely quoted in newspapers, referred to the decision as a 'difficult process' and acknowledged that the decision included some proposals that people found 'upsetting'.

The choice of language gives the decisions a sense of legitimacy in two ways. First, the recommendations are constructed as emerging independently from the council. The references to an unnamed report, which was actually commissioned by the council, suggest that the recommendations comprise 'expert' wisdom. Second, the press release emphasizes the input of 'the public' to the recommendations by highlighting 'feedback from the citywide consultation about the future of adult social care in Leeds, and the more detailed consultation with the people living in the six residential care homes and four day centres which were earmarked for possible closure earlier this year'.

Although the consultation is mentioned on several occasions, no space is given to specific public inputs to or recommendations from the consultations. Indeed, the voice of the people affected by the decision is almost entirely absent from the press release. The press release gives no indication of how, if at all, the consultation was taken into account in the decision-making process. This leaves the question of who was listened to, and how. This is not to say that the consultation was not effective in influencing the report. In fact, much of the news coverage suggested that the consultation and views of campaigners were successful in convincing the council to delay the closure of several care homes. By not giving participants in the consultation a voice in the press release, the council missed a valuable opportunity to illustrate the success of its public engagement activities on this occasion.

The news story

How much of the council's message was picked up by journalists and how did the press release become evident in news coverage? The press release was clearly used as a principal source of information by the three local newspapers that covered the story. Several sections of the press release were reproduced verbatim within local press reports about the closures, although the tone of the press release did not shape their overall framing and headlines. In particular, sections of the councillor's statement were quoted to present the council's commentary on the decision. Newspapers seemed to have made independent decisions to frame the decision as either negative (*Yorkshire Evening Post* – 'Clashes over care homes closure plan', 31 August 2001 and 'The axe falls', 30 August 2011) or positive in terms of the outcome of the citizen-led campaigns (*Morley Observer* – 'People power', 31 August 2011). The daily *Yorkshire Evening Post* (YEP) published stories on the closure the day before the announcement, on the day of the announcement and for two days after (29, 30, 31 August and 1 September 2011). The YEP's page-seven story the day before the announcement focused on criticizing the councillor responsible for adult social care for cancelling a meeting at one of the care homes under review at short notice (29 August 2011). On the day of the press release the headline focused the story on the six care homes and four day centres that were to close. The full story framed the decision as ignoring the voice of the people and the inputs they made to the public consultation: 'Council bosses are preparing to press ahead with the controversial closure etc. ...' and 'the closure plans will be a blow to campaigners ...' (30 August 2011). The YEP's framing of the decision as controversial continued the next day, albeit lower down the agenda on page fourteen, and pointed to the disagreements between councillors about the decisions rather than the impact of the decisions on residents (31 August 2011). Only two of the five weekly newspapers in our study included the story in their next edition after the announcement. The *Morley Observer*'s front page was dominated by a photo of the residents from the Morley care home which had fought a campaign against the closures (31 August 2011). An article on page three framed the issue as a triumph of active citizenship – 'People power helps save Knowle Manor'. Focusing only on the outcome of the decision for Morley, the article framed the decision to delay closure of the care home until a replacement was built as a victory for the residents, and omitted the implications of the decision for other care homes in the Leeds area which were not as positive. An editorial in the same issue celebrated the success of the residents' campaign and the efficacy of their engagement in the consultation: '... the Council clearly listened to what the many objectors had to say. But the real victory is that of the residents of Knowle Manor, who refused to give up and go quietly.' The *Wharfdale Observer* framed the decision slightly less positively owing to the mixed outcome for two care homes on its patch – one was to be closed and one had been given a reprieve until a privately funded alternative could be found (1 September 2011). Both weeklies featured photos of residents whereas the YEP used photos of the homes and centres to be closed.

In contrast, our analysis of broadcast news content showed that neither the content nor the framing of the press release was reflected in local radio or TV news coverage. The conventions of broadcast journalism provide one explanation for this. For example, it is difficult to create a broadcast news package entirely from a press release owing to the requirement for journalists to get direct quotes from sources on camera or audio rather than rely on the reproduction of written quotes. The story was covered by BBC *Look North*, BBC Radio Leeds and ITV *Calendar* on the day of the announcement.

BBC *Look North* also featured the upcoming announcement in its early evening bulletin the day before and BBC Leeds covered it the day after. The framing of Radio Leeds' coverage on the day of the announcement changed through the course of the day. It started with a focus prior to the report's release on the potential effects of the closures on residents, then changed to bulletins which included interviews with campaigners to highlight the human impact of the decision, and finished with reports towards the end of the day which were more positively framed to highlight the campaigners' success. The announcement was the top story in almost every on-the-hour bulletin throughout the day. Throughout the morning the journalist's summary of the story was accompanied by a clip from one of several different campaign groups. Journalists labelled the decisions as a 'victory' for the campaigners, but the campaigners talked about the need to 'continue fighting'; suggesting an *us versus them* relationship. Once the decision had been announced by the council, a clip of a councillor explaining the difficulties involved in making the decision was also included. The headlines of the *Look North* reports (it was the top story at lunchtime but down to third by 6.30 p.m.) framed the decision positively by introducing it as being 'welcomed by campaigners' and suggesting that the council had made a 'U-turn'. The main story was presented as a pre-recorded package at both 1 p.m. and 6.30 p.m. which gave space to all viewpoints. It began by explaining that the closures had sparked several campaign groups to fight against the decision, gave the main councillor a voice to explain the decision, emphasized the success of the campaigners, who were delighted that the council had 'listened to them' and felt they 'had won', then finished with two comments from councillors who opposed the decisions and remained concerned about the future of several care homes. In comparison to the radio reports the TV reports gave less emphasis to the consequences of the decision and more prominence to the role of the campaign groups in opposing the plans. Albeit after the potential for active engagement had ended, the broadcast news gave space to a diversity of voices and opinions on the topic, thus performing a democratically useful role. The news media's inclusion of a broad range of voices and focus on the success of campaigners serves another vital role in facilitating successful engagement: as a source of feedback on the efficacy of the public's engagement in the decision-making process.

While this review of content goes some way to explaining the disconnect between the council's preferred narrative and the broadcast coverage, it does not explain fully the relationship between such council-led communication and news content in the news ecology. In order to understand more about the production of news within the Leeds news ecology, we interviewed the BBC journalists who covered the story on Radio Leeds and BBC *Look North*.

Local journalism and engaging the public

Talking to the journalists enabled us to take an innovative approach to observing the relationship between journalistic practices, role perceptions and the content of news. While a large body of research makes a valuable contribution to our knowledge of this relationship, few studies have combined tracking the production of a story with in-depth interviews to explain the processes behind the construction of a news story. We followed each stage of the story's production from its origin as a press release to its production by journalists and finally to the resultant news coverage. We asked BBC journalists to explain their involvement in the production of the story in order to explore practices, role orientations, journalists' relationships with the council and, ultimately, the way that local news represents and engages the public.

The interviews revealed that the council's press release was not the initial source for the story and, more importantly, that the aim of the press release to frame the decision in positive terms was ignored. The tactics of press officers to structure press releases in ways that provide a 'cushion' around straight facts are clearly well understood by journalists. Journalists described a practice of decoding and deciphering press releases in order to find the information that they needed:

I just ignored the entire chunk of waffle at the top and went straight for the meat to discover exactly what they'd decided to do. It was quite an interesting press release. Because they had obviously backtracked or done a U-turn or however you'd like to put it, on the three homes that we [*Look North*] had been so heavily involved in supporting. (*Look North* journalist)

But also getting down to the nitty-gritty and looking farther down and realizing that in among the good stuff, they were burying an awful lot that actually hadn't come out. (*Look North* journalist)

I don't think anyone in the building where I work looked at that particular release as anything but a bit of spin or a bit of sugar to make some unpleasant medicine slip down a bit easier. (Radio Leeds journalist)

Press releases do not always hold as much power over the construction of news as is suggested by proponents of the concept of 'churnalism' (Davies 2008); and the spinning of news. In the case of BBC coverage of the care home closures, the press release played a minor role as a source of news. Both journalists had been following the case for several months before the report was published and had cultivated several key sources for different angles on the story over this time. The story had originated from a phone call made to the television journalist by a worker in one of the care homes six months earlier when the council had first indicated some homes might have to be closed. The journalist then got in touch with members of the public who had formed several distinct campaign groups against the closures because they had relatives in the affected homes. These members of the public then became key sources for both BBC journalists as the issue developed over the next few months, during which time the council held two consultations which contributed to the report's recommendations.

Out of those six care homes, two of them had extremely vocal campaigns behind them: the one in Morley and the one in Otley. Our sources of information really came through those people and I guess their information came to them through speaking to staff at the homes that cared for their family members. (Radio Leeds journalist)

In addition, the journalists obtained a leaked copy of an internal council document which alerted them to potential shortcomings in the planned public consultation. The document and concerns raised by affected families about the unlikely efficacy of the consultation exercise motivated the journalists to closely follow the consultation process and hold the council to account. One further explanation for the low impact of the press release relates to the communication strategy of the council press office. As is common before a major announcement, journalists were invited to a media briefing on the morning that the report was due to be considered by the council committee. The press release was not issued until after the briefing, when the BBC journalists had already obtained the key information, thus rendering the press release superfluous.

The role of journalists in the news ecology

The journalists' descriptions of events leading up to the coverage of the council's announcement illustrate some interesting findings about the roles that journalists see themselves as fulfilling in the news ecology.

The first of these was to represent the interests of the public by holding their elected leaders to account on their behalf. One of the journalists explained how stories such as the closures enable local news media to fulfil one of its key democratic roles of giving local people a voice:

An awful lot of people who are facing a political juggernaut and have absolutely no idea how to tread those waters do come [to us] for a voice. I suppose that's kind of what we've provided here. (*Look North* journalist)

The fact that following the situation with the care homes, I was absolutely inundated with emails and texts and phone calls from people just saying, 'Thanks for your help'. Whether it be people that didn't get the outcome that they wanted, but knew that they could still pick up the phone to me at every step of the way and make sure that people are still watching or they did get the outcome that they wanted. In that situation I think people are now contacting us and knowing that if they send us an email or a tweet or post something on the Facebook site that they're worried about, that we will come and give them a voice. (*Look North* journalist)

The local BBC journalists felt that it was their task to hold the council to account. One way of doing this was to make them aware that they were being watched at every stage in the process. As soon as the tip-off was received from the care home worker, and throughout the consultation process, the journalists felt that their conspicuous presence played a role in making the council think about the consequences of its actions:

> I think we were certainly successful in making them [the council] think about the decision that they were making [...] But by catching them out on meetings that they'd already had with developers and with giving a voice to protesters and allowing them to really pinpoint the fact that there weren't homes which people could go into in those areas, it did feel like we certainly made them work harder at the consultation process than they might otherwise have done. Whether or not we influenced their decision in any way, I would doubt. But whether or not the public opinion that we highlighted influenced their decision in any way, it's distinctly possible. (*Look North* journalist)

In this context, 'public interest' journalism entails enabling citizens to be taken seriously when they find themselves in conflict with a much better resourced and institutionally powerful political opponent:

> They [affected members of the public] were setting up a number of protest groups and they were holding a number of public meetings themselves, rallies and that kind of thing. And they were all asking questions [of the council] and they felt that they weren't getting answers to a lot of the questions. And of course in our position we can bring them [the council] into the studio and put them on the spot and demand those answers.
> (*Look North* journalist)

But there were significant limits to this representative role. Although it was clearly important to both journalists that local news gives the public the opportunity to have their opinions heard by a mass audience, they were also very clear about their obligation to present issues in what they understood to be a fair and balanced way. Neither of the journalists felt it was their place to support public campaigns or to 'take sides':

> I think we've reflected their views. I don't think it was ever our

place to support those people other than to try and broadcast the most accurate information we could as quickly as possible. I don't feel we took sides on it, because certainly the scripts I wrote and the ones others wrote did whenever possible make it clear that Leeds as a council has to save £90 million worth of savings due to the cuts, so that did figure heavily in the scripts and all the pieces etc. that we broadcast. (Radio Leeds journalist)

So it was a matter of taking a look at the entire story and speaking to people from all the different backgrounds and angles. And yes, in a way we did support them, but we never at any point took their side, as it were. We were always very careful to ensure that we gave both sides. (*Look North* journalist)

Journalists gave a clear sense of their role as informers and educators, who provide the public with the information they need to make decisions, rather than attempt to influence the decision-making process. When asked whether Radio Leeds could play a role in encouraging people to get involved in consultations, the journalist's response highlighted the ambiguity of journalistic neutrality:

We sort of purvey information to people in West Yorkshire and I guess we made people aware that those consultations were going on. In terms of us actually trying to mobilize people to participate in that process, I don't believe we did. I think ultimately we just again present the facts and let the listener decide whether that's something they want to become personally involved with. (Radio Leeds journalist)

When asked later on in the interview about the role of local journalism, this journalist made an interesting point about the way that local radio can play an important role in communities. Rather than pursuing a campaign agenda or taking sides with members of the public on specific issues, the journalist described how providing balanced, truthful and trustworthy news is a crucial way of gaining the trust of the public:

I think ultimately the very trust you crave from the audience

I think you'd lose that by trying to be more on their side than anyone else's. I think it just comes down to trust, and if people can tune into their local radio station and believe what you're saying to them, then you are on their side and you are a part of the community, and there's no actual need for any kind of agenda or anything beyond that. (Radio Leeds journalist)

Both journalists want to be seen by local citizens as trusted sources of information. When asked how they would like local people to see them, both talked about the important role of local journalists in helping to explain issues to people and to make some issues that are perceived as complex clearer for the public. This is particularly true when covering local government decision-making bodies, budgets and consultations, which are notoriously complicated and are seen as difficult to make sense of:

I think in terms of the general public, it's trying to be a point of reference and try and make things clear for people. Because consultations and budgets, they're confusing and often shrouded in gobbledegook. And it's just really trying to inform people and educate people a little bit, but trying to do it on a really clear basic level. (*Look North* journalist)

I think every reporter here politics aside feels it is a part of their duty to explain. I think we all just see ourselves as completely objective, and I think if you tried to do the job in any way other than that you'd only make things more difficult for yourself. (Radio Leeds journalist)

Citizens or spectators?

Given the outcome of our research, we are left with a strong impression of a council that wants to engage with citizens, but is not at all sure what engagement means or how to make it work; and journalists who do have a serious commitment to 'the public interest', but are torn between the tasks of empowering citizens who want to confront political authority and being constrained by a principle of impartiality which curbs their capacity to represent the least powerful in society. But what about local citizens themselves?

In our focus groups (see Chapter 4) we asked participants what they knew and thought about the care home closures (given that the story had been so recently prominent in the local news); how they thought voices like their own should be able to contribute to such policy decisions; and how well they felt represented by local politicians and media. From our analysis of the focus group transcripts, we offer five observations about citizens' perspectives.

First, few focus group participants claimed to know much about the care home closures, but equally few claimed to know nothing about them. This is an important observation. Citizens are rarely completely inattentive to news stories. Once reminded, they often express a semi-conscious awareness of them. But unless the story affects them directly they tend to tune out; to regard this as the latest in a long narrative of 'necessary cuts' or 'heartless austerity', depending upon their values. Except for those affected by a news event, it is not the details of stories which stick in people's minds, but a cumulative picture of what local life is like.

Second, political decision-making is surrounded by deep suspicion. This is almost a default reaction. When we asked focus group participants how they felt about policy consultations, they were almost entirely sceptical. As one male participant explained, 'I think a lot of people think that no matter what they say or do those decisions will be made by a few people in a room anyway'. He was followed immediately by another man who stated that:

> I think sometimes decisions are made before we find [out] about them. My feeling is that certain things have already been decided and it doesn't matter if you are against it or whatever – it's going to happen and that is the way it is. (Male, Group 1)

In a different group a male participant expressed the view that:

> Lots of decisions are made behind closed doors, so what was the point of a consultation anyway? The whole consultation might be a paper exercise. (Male, Group 6)

There were occasional differences of opinion about the efficacy of consultations, as in the exchange between these two men:

> M: I don't think it matters why the decision was made, you're

not going to change the decision. Knowing why it was made is absolutely irrelevant.

M: I disagree with that on the basis that if people know why a decision has been made by the council and a large number of people disagree fundamentally with that decision you can change the decision because we live in a democracy. (Conversation, Group 4)

But even here, the second speaker did not elaborate on how such changes could be brought about – and not once did anyone cite working with the local media as a means of challenging bad decisions.

This relates to a third common observation: that the local media do too little to explain how and why decisions are made – to put them into context and set out the policy options. Local news seems to be framed in terms of effects and, while such stories often provide powerful reasons for people to pay attention and empathize with victims of certain decisions, they do not explain how or why the decision was made. So, headlines tended to appear out of the blue, rather like news of natural disasters, leaving people feeling disconnected from the process of decision-making. In the case of the care home closures – or, for that matter, the council's major spending review – the local media might have performed a more productive role had they encouraged people to engage with and comprehend a range of different policy options. By failing to support the consultative process and then highlighting its deficiencies, local media could be seen to have contributed to the failure of local political communication.

Despite these shortcomings, a fourth observation from the focus groups was that people seemed to be attuned to linking issues together. When we asked about the care home closures they linked it to an equally recent national news story: the collapse of a leading private care home provider, leaving over 30,000 elderly people with uncertain futures. In turn, the alleged financial mismanagement of the private care home chain was connected in focus group discussions to the long-term mismanagement of Leeds United football club. Discussion of the limitations of consultation led several participants to mention other consultations, such as the one that preceded the decision to close the Leeds children's heart unit. We found it interesting to note how citizens were making these significant and relevant connections to issues being dealt with nationwide.

Finally, we were struck by the extent to which a 'them' and 'us' perspective dominated people's talk of both the council and the local media. As has been argued in previous research focusing on the same city:

> When we encountered distrust in the news – which we frequently did – it was because people felt that their expectations were not shared by news producers; that they were being told stories that were not properly explained; that their lives were being reported in ways that were not adequately researched; or that they could find more useful, reliable or amusing information elsewhere. Public trust in the media was lost when they were imagined and approached in ways that ignored or deviated from their everyday experiences. (Coleman et al. 2009: 2)

The above quotations refers to what people *felt*. While such feelings do not fully reflect the reality of efforts made by journalists to speak for, to and with local people – and of the council to engage with them – they point to a significant fracture in the local democratic relationship. If a news ecology is to be regarded as more than a transmission belt for the dissemination of passing stories, as a foundation for the enactment of efficacious civic practices, there is quite evidently something wrong. In a period of profound economic instability in which the very functions of local government are having to be reinvented, there would seem to be only two directions in which to go. One is towards even greater technocratic management of cities, with citizens squeezed out of decision-making in accordance with the ruthless logic of neoliberalism. The other is towards an ethos of co-governance in which the rational allocation of values is increasingly determined, in collaboration with communities and civil society, and where public communication comes to focus much more upon mutual deliberation and inclusive recognition.

9 | LOCAL NEWS: A DIFFERENT STORY

What has our study revealed about news in the mediated city? The evidence that we have presented throughout this book suggests that news is rather more than a commodified package to be delivered to a consuming population. When Dewey (1916: 5) stated that 'There is more than a verbal tie between the words common, community, and communication' he had in mind a theory of how publics come into being and are sustained by common knowledge and a shared sense of belonging. Cities are not only the sites of news circulation, but the subjects of the news that is circulated and the outcomes of the narratives that emerge. In short, the city is imagined through the stories that we tell about it and it is enacted through the practices that we pursue as we tell those stories.

At its best, news binds us together; reflects our lifeworlds; invites us to explore and even celebrate our differences; allows our disagreements to be founded on common understandings of what we disagree about; empowers us in our common quest for dignity and efficacy in the face of otherwise unaccountable authorities; gives substance to the pronoun 'us'. The more local the news, and the more fluently and inclusively it circulates, the more likely we are to feel the benefits of the ties that it generates.

By employing a broad range of research methods to investigate the news ecology of one major British city – in many respects, typical of late-modern, post-industrial urban spaces across the globe – we have been able to make a number of specific, empirical observations, among the most significant which are that:

- There is a great appetite for local news. It is not regarded by people as a mere optional extra – a passing add-on to the national news. People have a strong desire to know what is going on in the areas where they live and work. This stretches from interest in hyperlocal to regional stories (Chapter 3).
- Despite the virtual ubiquity of the internet and some of the more outlandish claims made about how it is displacing mainstream

media, people still trust and turn to television, radio and the local press to find out the main local stories that concern the areas that they live and work in (Chapter 3).

- Even though only a minority of people in our city went online to find the news from non-mainstream providers, many look to the internet as a key source of supplementary and explanatory information. If they want to know more than the mainstream local media offer, they go online (Chapter 3).
- People also pick up and reflect upon a lot of local news via interpersonal conversation. It is in everyday talk between people from the school gates to chats between neighbours that trusted narratives emerge and circulate (Chapter 4).
- Unlike national and global news, which continue to be dominated by elite actors, in local news the voices of non-elites are widely heard and reported (Chapter 2). Local producers seem very eager to feature 'ordinary' people. Sometimes this is at the expense of holding elite actors to account (Chapter 5).
- Much mainstream local news content fluctuates between 'celebratory' (somewhat folksy) accounts of 'our area' and anxious accounts of local disorder (Chapter 2). As a result, the 'tone' of local news is rather unbalanced.
- Local news does not provide people with enough in-depth civic or political information and analysis. Compared to national political stories, local politics tends to be under-scrutinized (Chapters 2, 3, 4 and 8).
- While local voices are widely featured in local news stories, the voices heard and stories told lack sufficient diversity. Different communities and groups within the city tend to be unevenly represented – and misrepresented – often through framing biases that cast certain populations as inherently troublesome. The under-representation of certain groups has long been acknowledged by mainstream news practitioners, but minority audiences are frustrated at the failure to represent them fairly (Chapters 2, 4 and 7).
- As national stories are picked up by local media, messages are often diluted and local contexts are inadequately explored (Chapter 5).
- Many mainstream local media producers and journalists have a strong sense of public purpose and claim to be committed to providing authoritative analysis and democratic accountability,

but such objectives are not sufficiently realized. Local democracy is weakened by a failure to nurture effective channels of mediated civic agency (Chapters 5 and 8).

- The emergence of alternative media practices offers opportunities for new journalistic relations, not least because such practitioners are often embedded and invested in particular communities (Chapter 6).
- New media practices should not be seen as being in competition with mainstream journalism. They often produce outcomes that mainstream local media do not even try to achieve (Chapter 6).
- Elected city governments are trying to establish more direct relations with citizens, but, despite a widely used rhetoric concerning digital engagement and networked communities, their communication with citizens remains sporadic, exclusive and often untrusted (Chapter 8). Non-governmental mediators are better placed to develop citizen-to-government and citizen-to-citizen connections and there are exciting examples of them doing so (Chapters 2, 6, 8 and 9).

Some of these findings will relate more to Leeds than to other cities; some will be more relevant to the time of our empirical research than to the present. Overall, however, we think that they tell a story of local news in a context of volatile uncertainty. It is understandable that some writers about local news offer an account of despair and demise, peppered with yearnings for a nostalgic era of municipal confidence, while others grasp on to hopes of a coming communitarian revival, facilitated by bits and bytes. But conventional stories of deficit ('the end of the local newspaper') and regeneration ('hyperlocal news creators to the rescue') miss the point. Before we can consider the health of local news we need to think carefully and critically about what it is and what it does. Rather than allowing our observations to be overdetermined by fixed assumptions about what news is, we need to explore what Bourdieu (1992: 229) refers to as the 'construction of the pre-constructed object' (see also Fairclough et al. 2003: 99–102). This entails asking a set of open questions about what local news is, the types of practices that make it up and the kind of stories that emerge from these practices. Exploring the broad range of practices involved in producing, circulating and consuming news within a culturally diverse city has enabled us to recognize the various ways in which individuals and groups find out, follow and discuss local issues and events (Darnton 2000; Rantanen 2009).

Unlike studies which have focused upon the revitalizing effects of digital technologies, we have chosen not to ignore mainstream news institutions *or* to conclude that all the news practices we came across are equal. While we started by rendering the 'social as flat as possible' (Latour 2005: 16), this was only in order that we might then better appreciate the value of different practices and the distinctive contribution they make to the local news ecology. For it is precisely as an uncoordinated but interdependent set of practices that a news ecology can be identified; its ecological quality derives from the often non-visible linkages and synergies that contribute to the heterogeneous coordination of the city.

The news as social practice

The concept of 'practices' is a commonplace in social theory, central to the work of Bourdieu (1977, 1992), Giddens (1979, 1984) and others (see Schatski and Knorr-Cetina 2001; Swidler 2001; Reckwitz 2002). It has more recently begun to be discussed by media theorists who are interested in the diverse, often creative ways in which people generate, share, make sense of and act upon media content (Couldry 2004; Bräuchler and Postill 2010). The term 'practice' is used in several different ways, but definitions tend to share an emphasis upon ordered and recurrent social activity. In general terms, practices can be defined as recurrent social activities that are 'distinctively "the same" across time and space' (Giddens 1984: 3). As Rhodes and Bevir (2015: 75) put it in their innovative study of the machinery of state as a set of practices, 'A practice is a set of actions ... that exhibit[s] a pattern, perhaps even a pattern that remains relatively stable across time.' But what 'binds' these patterned activities together? Shatzki (1996: 89) points to three linkages: '(1) understandings, for example, of what to say and do; (2) explicit rules, principles, precepts, and instructions; and (3) "teleaffective" structures embracing ends, projects, tasks, purposes, beliefs, emotions, and modes'. Shove and Pantzar (2005), who place particular emphasis on the role of objects and materiality in holding practices together, suggest that 'practices involve the active integration of materials, meanings, and forms of competence' (see also Law 1994). Relating to the above, but at a more general level, Giddens's (1984: 25, 1–41) theory of structuration refers to 'rules' (informal and formal) and 'resources' (material and symbolic) as the key structural features of practices that actors draw upon as 'both the medium and outcome' of their activities. We follow Giddens (ibid.) in emphasizing 'rules' and 'resources' as the main structural aspects of practices, although, for descriptive purposes, we broke these general categories down in our account of news to refer to more specific aspects of particular practices, such as different forms of local news production, distribution and reception.

The concept of practices focuses our attention 'neither on the experience of the individual actor nor the existence of any form of social totality, but on social practices ordered across time and space' (ibid.: 2) As such, the concept allows us to be attentive to diversity and local context in our account of news (in a way that much news research arguably fails to do), but without, at the same time, relinquishing the ambition to make sense of broader social patterns and relationships that are not reducible simply to the behaviour and choices of individual actors (Warde 2005).

Analysing media practices empirically can be boiled down to two concrete research questions which we have tried to pose in this study: 'What types of things do people do in relation to media? And what types of things do people say in relation to media?' (Couldry 2004:141). In other words, our empirical task has been to investigate what different individuals and groups *do* in relation to local news and how, as competent and knowledgeable actors (Giddens 1984: 5–6), they described these activities. For example, reading the local evening newspaper is a different type of news practice, involving a different set of rules and resources, to engaging with local news via social media or, for that matter, television or radio. Likewise, producing independent and probing investigative journalism is a different type of news practice, involving different rules and resources, to commenting on or circulating news via a blog or community newsletter. Just as importantly, by looking at local news through the lens of practice and listening to how people themselves categorize and evaluate the practices with which they are engaged, we think we have developed a better understanding of the *value* of news media for different individuals and groups and of the various roles that diverse media channels play in the news ecology.

Most news journalism, as Silverstone (2005: 196) notes, takes a 'transmission approach to the communicational infrastructure of news'. News media are conceived as conduits that transmit information from producers to audiences (Carey 1989). The focus then is on how content is produced (chosen, framed, and so on) by journalists and on what effects, if any, this content has on the knowledge, beliefs and actions of citizens, who are viewed as being variously informed, persuaded and otherwise shaped by the news content they receive. There is no question that this approach to news is important. It raises critical questions about the varying power of media organizations, through their access to different resources, to determine what information and issues circulate in the public sphere (Habermas 2006). This includes the question of whether ordinary citizens have any opportunity to participate and to raise their own agendas in their own terms.

However, important as these questions are, the prevalence of this perspective on news has obscured other ways that people engage with news that may be equally valuable and important. Rather than understanding news only as information transmission and exchange, we may, following Carey's (1989: 18) 'ritual view' of communication, view it in terms of 'sharing', 'participation' and 'association'. Viewed this way, while information transmission and acquisition remain important, they do not exhaust the ways in which citizens engage with news practices or capture fully their social value and role. Existing political communications research, as Jones (2005: 376–7) argues, tends

> ... to emphasize the importance of 'information' as the central component of mediated citizenship. But as proponents of the ritual view of communication argue, there are many reasons why citizens engage in communicative acts that are either unrelated or tangential to the desire to be informed. Ritual acts of communication facilitate a sense of identification, community/sociability, security/control, expression, pleasure/entertainment, distraction, and even possession. A cultural approach to mediated citizenship foregrounds the ways in which citizens utilize media for these ends, as well as how certain media facilitate these feelings or behaviors more than others.

A major advantage of the concept of practice is that it is flexible enough to capture the non-instrumental aspects of news that might,

in the long run, perform as important a role in coordinating the city as more conventional dissemination of transient headlines and stories that are intended to provide a daily first draft of history. As Warde (2005: 136) explains, 'practice theories comprehend non-instrumentalist notions of conduct, both observing the role of routine on the one hand, and emotion, embodiment, and desire on the other'. So, when our focus group participants tell us that they look to the local media to remind them what it feels like to live in their particular neighbourhoods, or when our content analysis shows that much mainstream news tends to 'celebrate' the distinctive character of the locality, these do not reflect a failure by news-makers or audiences to focus on the civic import of 'serious news', but constitute news practices in their own right – practices that affirm and enrich civic attachment.

Our purpose in discussing practice theory has been to develop a sense of the role and value of the different news media that form part of the media ecology at local level. This applies both to established and to emerging news practices. Consider, for example, the local evening newspaper. As we have seen in the preceding chapters, readers may value this daily delivery of news into their lives because of the informative content it provides. They might want to know what the local council has been up to or what films are showing at the cinema or whether the police have managed to solve a crime in the next street. But they may also value it because it provides a way to identify with their local community; to express pride or contentment in the neighbourhood where they live or work, or because of the particular experience of using a print medium (Fenton et al. 2010: 22–3). Likewise, consider heated debates about the value of online citizen media. Such debates have tended to focus narrowly on information provision (Baker 2002). While some commentators, such as Benkler (2006: 264–5), suggest that online 'peer production' can supply the types of information citizens require, others emphasize the extent to which online story-sharing and discussion depend on and are fuelled by content produced by professional journalists (Curran 2010; Pew Research Center 2010). This is clearly an important debate, but, as we argued in Chapter 7, the narrow focus on the production of original content and information excludes other ways that we might understand the value of news practices that are taking shape online. Their value may reside, not so much in information provision and acquisition, but in the new relationships and modes of participation and engagement they make possible (Baker 2002: 297–307). If the claim that citizen news-makers can replace the products of professional journalism appears questionable from the perspective of the political economy of media (ibid.; Garnham 2000; McChesney 2003), Benkler's (2006: 213) suggestion that people feel a 'qualitative change' when engaging with online media – 'represented in the experience of being a potential speaker, as opposed to simply a listener and voter' – seems to be important in accounting more fully for the value of online news practices.

What we have said about practices thus far has left unanswered the crucial question of the relationship between different news practices at local level. How, if at all, do these divergent practices connect to one another? This is a question that an ecological policy for local news is uniquely well placed to answer. Despite the fact that some practices 'anchor' or 'order' other practices (Couldry 2004: 122) and possess greater resources, reach and power, it would surely be a mistake to think of a news ecology in singular and holistic terms. It is better perhaps to think in terms of 'modes of ordering' (Law 1994: 20–2) rather than a single communications order. It is that challenge that we turn to later in this chapter, but first we need to say more about an important characteristic of news practices: the generation, narration and circulation of stories.

The news as storytelling

Much easier to comprehend than the notion of social practice is the idea of news as storytelling. Stories are the common currency of most accounts of journalism. For example, David Manning White's (1950) seminal study of 'gatekeeping' considered how certain social narratives are allowed to become news stories while others are dismissed; studies by Gans (1979), Golding and Elliott (1979), Schlesinger (1978) and Tuchman (1972, 1978) discuss how newsroom routines and norms generate certain kinds of news story; McCombs and Shaw's (1972) pioneering study of agenda-setting examined how certain stories come to dominate the news; Entman's (1993) work on framing considers how news stories are placed within a field of meaning, thereby influencing the ways in which people make sense of them; studies of news ideology, such as those produced by the Glasgow Media Group (1976, 1980) and

Hall et al. (1978) interrogate the ways in which hegemonic beliefs are reproduced through the narrative bias of news stories; studies of news events focus upon stories around which publics congregate (Boorstin 1961; Dayan and Katz 1992). In all of these diverse accounts of journalism the news story stands as the pivotal object of analysis.

Clearly, this story-centric perspective has brought much of crucial importance to scholarly understanding of the news. But our study suggests that the emanation of news stories from mainstream media institutions is only one part of the picture. While mainstream news media still produce a lot of information about local matters, the ease and speed with which audiences are able to access local information directly from 'non-news' organizations or social peers has radically diminished their reliance on news media for a master narrative of local life. As discussed in the preceding chapters, journalists perceive that audiences are increasingly turning to them for campaign-oriented news, drama or interpretation rather than information. Our focus groups showed that local news was relied upon as a consistent link in the chain of public communication while, paradoxically, it was often less trusted than the local grapevine. Our content analysis showed that mainstream news outlets favour the topics of crime and culture over information on local policy and public services. Our rich, complex and sometimes contradictory findings suggest that news is at once communication, information and representation. News as stories that inform is not enough – as well as receiving accounts of 'what's going on', people want to engage communicatively with those accounts and to feel represented by and within them. In response to this observation, we want to problematize the news story, moving from the story as noun and object to storytelling as verb and expression of urban subjectivity.

In addressing the recurrent stories in the news – the pre-existent stories the 'news' fits into, and the myths the news reconfirms and repeats – Bird and Dardenne (2009: 206) suggest a conception of news as storytelling: 'In the sense that myth comforts, news also comforts, and provides a sense of control'. They refer to work in the 1980s by Knight and Dean (1982), drawing on Carey and ritual (1982), on seeing news as ritual not at the level of the individual story, but at the level of the news in society performing a ritual function engaged in by both public and journalists. Bird and Dardenne refer to 'mythical archetypes' in the news and point to the argument that news is the main vehicle for myth in contemporary culture. The discussion of Chapeltown in the news, in Chapter, 8, certainly makes sense in this light. Bird and Dardenne explain the myth idea in the context of news, but present an important critique focused on the idea of the mythic archetype and the timelessness (ahistorical, apolitical) that this implies. They argue that the application of mythic archetype to news cannot account for the particular contexts to which we would want to attend in analysing the news: 'The "universalist" approach pays scant attention to differences in time and place that produce particular cultural moments and narratives, rooted in particular histories' (Bird and Dardenne 2009: 207). 'A "story" is different from a simple chronological account, because it seeks coherence and meaning; a story has a point, and it exists within a cultural lexicon of understandable themes' (ibid.). While this suggests the power of the producer of the news, at the same time we are suggesting, as Jonathan Gray's work highlights, that the news becomes meaningful only as the audience makes sense of it. Gray (2007) positions online news consumers as 'fans' who bring news stories to life in lively discussions centring on hard, political news: '[Politics] must matter to the individual and must be consumed emotionally to some degree if it is to become meaningful to its viewers' (ibid.: 80). In their discussion Bird and Dardenne summarize the research in the area of news as storytelling, noting that storytelling is as complex as myth: 'Story, we have discovered after two decades, is not less complex. Scholars productively explored myriad texts to discover image, representation, mythic and traditional theme, and other qualities of myth and story' (Bird and Dardenne 2009: 211). They place particular value on the narrative approaches in journalism scholarship, and in the fruitful enquiry into alternative or peripheral forms of journalism (including reality television, for instance). Barbie Zelizer suggests that anxieties constantly surround an effort to define the news story and to exclude that which is not news:

> Journalism's coexistence with the academy rests on various sources of existential uncertainty that build from this tension. The most obvious uncertainty stems from the pragmatic questions that underlie journalism's practice, by which its very definition is tweaked each time supposed interlopers – blogs, citizen journalists, late night TV comedians or reality television – come close to its imagined borders. (Zelizer 2009: 30)

What seems clear from this brief review of the literature in this area is that in practice the news story and news as storytelling overlap – that is, the news is both news story and storytelling as it is made meaningful through people's practices. Our study supports this direction of thinking; we see people using a range of sources, platforms and styles to tell stories about where they live. Many people still turn to the mainstream media in the hope of becoming more visible (as in the case of communities involved in the Chapeltown carnival) or to amplify their voices (as in the case of victims of cuts in council expenditure). Some turn to the internet, exchanging messages on Facebook, tweeting and posting videos on YouTube. Some never produce such material, but act as active nodes in local networks of content distribution. People talk to one another about the latest goings-on, sometimes supplementing mainstream media accounts with their own experiences and opinions, sometimes contributing to those accounts by sharing what has become known as user-generated content. Some call into local radio phone-ins, write letters to the newspaper or become celebrated locally as the source of jokes about the latest institutional cock-up. People and their stories move between old and new media platforms. Both matter. They matter differently.

Emergent practices in the news ecology

Practices of local storytelling have become messier and less coherent than ever before. Without clear centres of authoritative narrative and interpretation of the kind that once had greater presence, knowing who or what to trust has become more difficult. The problem of trust and epistemological authority has become mixed up with a related problem of economic failure. The old economic model of 'making news' seems not to work very well, but a new model has yet to become apparent. Accounts of the decline – even imminent demise – of local news production and dissemination are abundant:

> The latest print circulation figures for Britain's regional newspapers appear to show an industry driven to the precipice and staring at imminent extinction. Sales are in freefall – down by an average of 13.5 per cent year-on-year in the first half of 2014. (*The Independent*, 31 August 2014)

... in the first years of the 21st century, accelerating technological transformation has undermined the business models that kept American news media afloat, raising the possibility that the great institutions on which we have depended for news of the world around us may not survive. (Kaiser 2014)

In the past decade, as a percentage, more print journalists have lost their jobs than workers in any other significant American industry. (That bad news is felt just as keenly in Britain where a third of editorial jobs in newspapers have been lost since 2001.) The worst of the cuts, on both sides of the Atlantic, have fallen on larger local daily papers at what Americans call metro titles. A dozen historic papers have disappeared entirely in the US since 2007, and many more are ghost versions of what they used to be, weekly rather than daily, freesheets rather than broadsheets, without the resources required to hold city halls to account or give citizens a trusted vantage on their community and the world. (*Guardian*, 21 March 2015)

These are alarming reports, but, like many others coming from a range of different countries, they tend to focus on the problem through one particular institutional prism: that of market failure. This is true of many areas of social policy in contemporary, late capitalist societies. First, services, goods and opportunities are conceived as being viable only if they can be made commercially successful, i.e. profitable to investors. Then some sort of problem is identified that renders public provision a poor investment. And finally, huge efforts are made to conceive of strategies through which services, goods and opportunities can be delivered cheaply, with a minimum of skilled or creative human input and through the 'management' of consumer expectations, i.e. teaching people to hope for less than their parents and grandparents had regarded as basic elements of the social fabric. A variety of media economists and policy-makers have come up with policies intended to make local news more *marketable*. Regardless of the economic or political feasibility of these schemes, we wonder whether they are conceived within too narrow a framework. In thinking about news as practices of storytelling, it becomes clear that the nature of the current institutional arrangements whereby local news is 'produced' by a 'media industry' in which lots of competing entities are seeking to tell 'the story' amounts to more than an economic malfunction. It is an obsolete model of cultural practice. It fails to acknowledge the increasingly distributed and networked nature of contemporary meaning-making. Before turning to our own tentative thoughts about policy, let us return briefly to the city of Leeds to explore some emergent practices that have little to do with making local news profitable and much to do with a shift in the way that people are telling stories and sharing knowledge. Here are four quite different initiatives that have emerged within the city that cast some light upon the potential for a reconfigured division of labour within the news ecology:

The Leeds Citizen The Leeds Citizen is a website that has been published using Wordpress blogging software since July 2011. It has been described as a 'single-handed mission to bring accountability to Leeds civic life'. Harcup (2015: 7), who has monitored this initiative, observes that it does not 'offer much in the way of what might commonly be regarded as "news" ... making little or no attempt to keep up with major events or to cover the tales of crime, human interest, weather or sport that unfold daily in any major city', but argues that 'there is a case for it to be seen as sharing the much-trumpeted potential of such sites 'to foster citizenship, democracy and local community cohesion' while 'producing news which fulfils the watchdog function of holding local elites to account'. In short, the Leeds Citizen does not seek to duplicate the work of other news providers, but does set out to fulfil a democratic function that more traditional media fall short in performing. Quentin Keane, the pioneer of this initiative, explained to Harcup (ibid.:10) that 'It's not driven by an ideology of any sort but it's driven by trying to work out how power works, work out how things work, how all the different forces in the city operate'. This is a specific journalistic practice, different from reporting stories or providing a platform for local opinions, but arguably more vital than ever in an era when socio-economic power has become so diffuse and unaccountable. The council might release data on its expenditure or consultation documents on intended policies, but working through these and making them meaningful for citizens who are neither economists nor policy experts is a particular role that could otherwise slip between the institutional cracks of 'journalism as usual'. There is also evidence that this initiative has expanded practice by forcing the local council to revise its rules regarding the right of people attending its meetings to record what is being said. As Keane explains to Harcup (ibid.: 12):

> There were rumblings here and there nationally about people being thrown out for trying to record meetings. But for me, there was the nonsense side of it – that this was an anachronistic thing that I ended up with a bee in my bonnet about – but the other one was terribly practical. I haven't got shorthand, I go to these council meetings and I always want to be as accurate as I possibly can be. I was going to council meetings, trying to get quotes in longhand, not daring to use them because there was no way of going back and checking that they were accurate. So it made my attendance at council meetings, apart from saying they voted this and they voted that, it was seriously limiting.

Keane requested permission from the council to make audio recordings of meetings, solely for his own purposes. He was refused several times, but after he publicized these refusals (including in one national newspaper), the council gave in. New practices often test limits in precisely this way. In response to citizen journalism of the kind practised by the *Leeds Citizen*, established protocols governing the relationship between journalists and politicians need to be rethought (Firmstone and Coleman 2015b). When, for example, a local blogger was invited by the council to attend a media briefing alongside mainstream journalists and then published the story before the embargo had passed, the council was left uncertain as to whether they were dealing with an errant journalist or a disruptive impostor. As one communications officer put it:

> That then leaves us with that quandary: we'd like to treat you the same, because actually I'm all for openness, transparency, let xxx have it in the same way. However, if you expect to be treated the same, you need to behave in the same way [...] there's a set of behaviours that come along with that [acting in a journalistic role], a set of responsibilities, on our side but also on yours. (Firmstone 2016)

The City Talking Reconfiguring of the conventional political communication pyramid between politicians, journalists and citizens

(Gurevitch et al. 2009) might turn out to be one of the most delicate manoeuvres arising from the new news ecology. In thinking it through, it would seem to make sense not to regard initiatives like the Leeds Citizen as rivals to the mainstream local news media. *The City Talking* (TCT) newspaper began in 2009 as a Facebook page launched by Lee Hicken as a reaction to a feeling among his contemporaries that local media in the city were not effectively representing them and the conversations they were having about Leeds. TCT has gone from strength to strength, with the launch of a monthly print edition distributed free across the city in 2013, a website, Twitter presence, and expansion of the brand to four other Northern cities in 2015 (Sheffield, Manchester, Liverpool and York). Hicken described the motivations and strategies of TCT in a recent research interview (Firmstone 2016).

Three features of the TCT's practice characterize their distinctive addition to the news ecology. First, despite calling itself a newspaper, the TCT's practices differ from traditional understandings of news journalism. Hickens defined TCT's output as 'news features', not 'news', and the contributors as 'storytellers' who do not identify as journalists. Similarly to the Leeds Citizen, TCT aims to add something that is missing to the news ecology rather than replace the old functions of the mainstream media. Hicken states:

> Unless something dramatically changes I don't ever see us
> as a 'breaking news, this just happened, more to follow brand'.
> Frankly with how media works these days there's no need
> for it. Anybody can get anything from Facebook, from
> Twitter, from whatever instantly anyway. What we're looking
> at is why did it happen and what happened afterwards and
> exclusive stuff, so if we do feel that there is something that
> we can explore that somebody else is not exploring that's
> where we'll go.

TCT's team of 'storytellers' are drawn from a diverse range of backgrounds – photographers, fashion designers, film-makers and English literature – with trained journalists conspicuous by their absence. The creative desire to tell stories about Leeds in an engaging way is a strong influence on their practice. As Hicken puts it:

The future for us is print in terms of the beautiful storytelling, photography, 10,000 word features and film. That's where it's at. We use this term all the time of 'depth and beauty'. Because a lot of us are from the fashion and visual background, we always want everything to look great. Even if it's not telling a beautiful story we still want it to look really interesting.

Second, TCT believes in the future of printed newspapers as a valuable source of storytelling practice for local citizens. While local newspapers across the UK have been turning from daily to weekly publications, trying to increase their readership through digital editions or closing down, TCT has defied economic logic and launched itself as a free monthly print newspaper. The website aims to drive people towards the print edition rather than vice versa, and the full version of the paper is available only in print.

Third, TCT has formed relationships with other established news media in the city. It has been distributed as a monthly supplement to the *Yorkshire Evening Post* (YEP) since September 2014. This provides YEP readers with access to news produced according to a set of practices far from those of the mainstream YEP, and TCT with access to a wider audience.

The Voice of Leeds summits The Voice of Leeds summits are a joint initiative by the Leeds Community Foundation (LCF), an independent agency that builds partnerships with charities to tackle local problems, and the *Yorkshire Evening Post* (YEP). The summits were preceded by a survey in which the newspaper's readers were invited to highlight issues in the city that need attention in the form of human and financial resources. In part, this was an attempt by the newspaper to reconnect with its readers; in part it was an attempt to put local communities and pressure groups in touch with potential funders of changes that could not be brought about without publicity and external support. During 2015 a series of monthly summits brought key stakeholders together to discuss issues that had been raised, such as social isolation, youth unemployment, digital inclusion, domestic violence, arts & culture, food poverty and dementia. The summits were attempts to create broad conversations reaching beyond the usual political channels. Again, this kind of practice is not in competition with the other forms of public involvement that the local council and mainstream media promote (from phone-ins to policy consultations), but seems to offer a rather less managed, exclusive and factional approach to public discussion. From LCF's perspective, the discussions have been valuable in that they have attracted a broad range of inputs from NGOs, local communities and the local council. The YEP argues that the summits provide an opportunity to engage with readers at a time when audiences for local news are fragmenting and the reputation of journalism has been damaged by recent scandals. The YEP's managing editor described the importance of such engagement practices as strategies to prove the continuing value of local newspapers by showing readers that 'we care, we are responsible and we are accountable':

> So what this has allowed us to do is to re-engage with key parts of the City, with key stakeholders in the City and also to demonstrate to our readers our commitment to standing up for the City in terms of – and that's not just a notional we champion Leeds, but I do really mean that. We are supporters of the City of Leeds. We want it to be a success. (YEP managing editor, cited in Firmstone 2016)

It is only one provisional discursive space, but, as with all practice, it allows participants to experiment with ways of articulating problems, thinking about inventive approaches to meeting local challenges and learning to hear voices that are not typically part of the policy debate.

The BBC The BBC has announced plans to invest part of its licence fee funding in a service that reports on councils, courts and public services. Locally produced audio and video content will be released for immediate use by local news organizations. Speaking about this initiative before the House of Commons Media, Culture and Sport Select Committee, the BBC director general, Tony Hall, stated that:

> We have been trying ... to work out ways about how we can jointly with local newspapers tackle a shared problem, namely how we ensure that local democracy and our local communities are properly reported on. In fact, some time over the last year I

went up to Leeds to look at how BBC live in online terms was working with local newspapers there. One newspaper editor said to me, 'Look, we have talked about this for a long time. We are now sitting in the same room,' and I thought, 'That is good. That is the kind of open BBC we want.' (Oral evidence to the committee, Question 83, p. 30, 15 September 2015)

Here again is an example of a change in practice. Rather than starting from the competitive position of several news organizations trying to be best at 'covering local democracy' – and often doing so quite poorly because there is so much to report and explain – the challenge that is given priority here is how to make local democracy genuinely accountable and relevant to communities it is supposed to represent. (Of course, some media organizations baulk at what they see as an anti-competitive attempt to buck the market.) Regardless of the commercial objections, the task of opening up democracy is unlikely to be executed well by a single storyteller. By its very nature, democracy is most likely to flourish when it is translated into a plurality of narrative modes and explanatory idioms.

Of course, there is no certainty that any of the emergent practices we have outlined will be effective or sustainable in the long term. In all likelihood, some will evolve into more embedded news practices and others will transpire and offer civic sustenance to parts, if not all, of the city. And, of course, in hundreds of other cities similar, if not more innovative, initiatives are springing up. Our main point in noting these emergent practices is to suggest that the commercial lens is not the only one through which to perceive the state of local news. None of the practices we have outlined emanate from the logic of the marketplace – and some appear to be going against that particular grain. As several scholars have argued, ecological synergy and market rationality are often in tension with one another (Rees 1992; Söderbaum 1999; Dolsak and Ostrom 2003). Solving the problem of making local news commercially viable entails a different approach from the challenge of enriching (non-valorized) civic resources – often referred to as externalities. The enhancement of such resources may well depend upon a convergence of practices that have hitherto been ignored as valueless or artificially disaggregated by market norms which pay more regard to economic than civic integration.

Thinking about local news ecologically

Often, seemingly intractable problems are made harder to tackle by placing too great a burden upon a single term. In such circumstances, it makes sense to unpack the overladen term and pay attention to its constituent elements. The term 'news', as in 'the crisis of local news', would be a good candidate for such deconstruction. From a civic perspective, we might identify four key functions of local news:

- To provide tools, skills and content that will allow publics to witness themselves and their lifeworlds.
- To provide tools, skills and content that will help diverse publics to make sense of one another.
- To monitor, facilitate and connect public deliberation on matters of common interest and concern.
- To provide tools, skills and content that will enable citizens to understanding the multifaceted and often discreet workings of power, and to hold the powerful to account in ways that can make a difference. (Coleman and Ross 2011)

Each of these could be regarded as distinctive areas of mediation. For example, the opportunity to be witnessed and encounter others is increasingly being performed by individuals and communities, using low-cost technologies. But because there is a danger of such news being narrowly consumed by people in search of others like themselves, there is an important role for aggregators to curate these accounts and distribute them across the city. Local newspapers and radio stations as curators and aggregators could add important value to the diverse and dispersed witness accounts that citizens are now able to produce. But local media organizations might see this as a diminution of their role as originators of news content – and this in turn might challenge their business model of being (at least potentially) the central voice of the city. Before ecological benefits can be realized, then, the various contributors to the first of the civic outcomes listed above need to arrive at some kind of a settlement. The same is true of the second outcome. Here again, there is an important aggregative and integrative role to be performed by mainstream local journalists, but they need to understand that they are not the only ones with expertise and commitment to contribute to the project of making communities and publics mutually visible and intelligible. The council devotes considerable resources to the same project; so do a range of schools, colleges, youth services and arts organizations. At the moment, each and every collaboration between these common actors has to be negotiated within an atmosphere of pressured competition. An ecological news policy would reward an effective division of labour in relation to this objective. The third objective – deliberation – calls for some honest thinking on the part of several currently major actors. At the moment, most initiatives relating to city-wide policy debate are led by the council or by interest groups. All the evidence suggests that citizens do not trust political actors to lead such initiatives. Could an independent space – a local commons, online and/or offline – be established so that people feel less prone to manipulation? But if it is, the council – and especially its elected representatives – would need to engage with it, mainstream media organizations would need to publicize it and explain what is going on within it, and as many non-mainstream media as possible should be encouraged to make their own official and unofficial contributions to it. Finally, holding power to account needs to continue to be a key responsibility of the mainstream local news media, but, given the vast range of issues around policies that interest some if not all or many people, citizen journalists should be given full access to proceedings and records that will help them to hold power to account.

Of course, civic objectives do not exhaust the functions of local news. News provides entertainment, local pride, a sense of security, broadened horizons of imaginative possibility and everyday sociability. As with civic outcomes, ecological divisions of labour could enhance the mediation of each of these. But for that to happen there needs to be a new ecological settlement; a more efficient post-industrial way of facilitating joined-up storytelling across the city.

Critics might argue that all of this is already happening. And, in small, uncoordinated ways, it is. Where it happens, it enriches the quality of local news and the strength of the city as a storytelling network (Yong-Chan and Ball-Rokeach 2006). But planned ecological news synergies remain rare – and often press against the boundaries of commercial logic. A second criticism would be that we are naive. We do not live in a planned economy; market competition is not only the norm, but becoming more ideologically embedded by the day. It is indeed true to say that an ecological conception of news as a common good runs counter to the increasing drive towards the commodification of everything. We would argue, however, that even in terms of conventional economic orthodoxy, externalities matter, insofar as they support sociocultural cohesion and democratic ends. As Baker (2002: 49) argues:

> If the press deters misdeeds, everyone positively affected by the absence of the misdeed benefits. 'Deterrence' means, however, that the media has no 'expose' – no product – to sell to its audience and hence no opportunity to internalise the benefits it produces. The deterrence can be correctly described as either a (positive) externality or a pure public good – that is, not only is its use nonrivalrous but beneficiaries are nonexcludable [...] Even when the media can 'sell' an expose (or sell more papers generally because of its enhanced reputation), usually these sales will dramatically under-internalize the benefits. The economic prediction must be that, to the significant detriment of the country, the market will encourage the media grossly to underproduce these benefits.

It surely makes more sense to share the cost of producing such externalities than to allow them to fail. It is not our aim in this book to produce a precise policy blueprint for such ecological collaboration, but we are encouraged by Fenton et al.'s (2010: 47) proposal for the introduction of independent 'local news hubs'. They argue that 'the facilitation of citizen involvement in feeding and shaping stories, and an emphasis on collaboration rather than competition is best suited to the digital age' (ibid.: 47). Local news hubs would be designed to facilitate such collaboration, providing a space where the different actors involved in the local media ecology can collaborate with one another and share resources, ideas and information. As they describe, the news hubs 'would be a place where local people could collaborate with local paid-for journalists who work for local news media that may be published or broadcast elsewhere but that have a newsroom in the hub and hold regular news surgeries with the local community' (ibid.: 47). In addition, the news hubs would 'mean that community media and mainstream media link up more readily and share training and facilities as well as cross-promoting content and contribute to community renewal' (ibid.: 47). Importantly, Fenton et al. (ibid.) emphasize the need for the news hubs to be well funded so that they are sustainable. They advocate the use of foundation grants, local government funding and tax incentives in addition to advertising revenue and placing requirements on the largest media companies (which may have benefited from changes in local media ownership rules) to support the hubs (ibid.: 48).

Beyond the economic policy arguments, we conclude our study with a more normative reflection, rooted in the empirical research we have conducted in one particular city. People, we would argue, care more about the vibrancy, diversity and efficacy of the stories that define them than the dividends that accrue to those who invest in their depiction. The sustainability of civic democracy cannot be left to the vagaries of the marketplace.

APPENDIX 1: CONTENT ANALYSIS CODING SCHEMA (WITH INSTRUCTIONS FOR CODERS), DISCUSSED IN CHAPTER 2

1. **Story ID**: (this is generated automatically for each record)
2. **Date**: (date of publication/broadcast, e.g. 11/07/2011). For weekly/monthly publications, put first date.
3. **Time**: (e.g. between 6.00–7.00 a.m.) – select from list box. For broadcast news headlines at 8 a.m., use 8 a.m.–9 a.m. For newspapers, use 'N/A'.
4. **Media Outlet**: (radio, TV, newspaper, website)

VARIABLES Media outlet

Outlet number	Media form	Media outlet name
1	Radio	Radio Aire
2	Radio	BBC Radio Leeds
3	Radio	Asian Fever
4	Radio	South Leeds Community
5	Radio	East Leeds FM
6	Radio	Radio Jcom
7	Radio	Branch FM
10	Television	BBC1 Yorkshire
11	Television	ITV *Calendar*
20	Website	southleeds
21	Website	holtparktoday
22	Website	culturevulture
23	Website	beyondgdnleeds
24	Website	blotr Leeds
25	Website	theleedscitizen
26	Website	northleedsnews

27	Website	*Kirkstall Matters* (from new.kirkstall)
30	Newspaper	*Yorkshire Post*
31	Newspaper	*Yorkshire Evening Post*
32	Newspaper	*Wharfedale Observer*
33	Newspaper	*Wharf Valley Times*
34	Newspaper	*Weekly News Leeds*
35	Newspaper	*Morley Observer*
99	Other	Other

5. **Geographic location**: Does the item focus its **primary** attention on an international/national/regional/Leeds city/hyperlocal story? Hyperlocal would be an area within Leeds (e.g. Chapeltown). You can use the map at www.leeds.gov.uk/maps/leeds_wb.html for a guide to what falls within the Leeds City Council wards.

6. **Headline/ summary**: text box to note headline or give short summary of the story.

7. **First head/Front page**: Tick box to indicate if the story appears on either the front page of the newspaper, is the main story on a webpage or the first item on broadcast news. Otherwise leave unticked.

8. **News in brief:** Tick box to indicate a 'news in brief/news file'-type item, or for broadcast media an item short in length (usually with an anchor-only piece to camera with possible images and no other speaking contributors). For print media, 'news in brief' is usually an item less than around 60 words; for broadcast media, it is usually around 30 seconds or less.

9. **Story type**: code as descriptive for straight news, or one of the 'explanatory' options for where **substantial** explanation is provided by other quoted sources or, alternatively, by the reporter (possibly as comment, contextualization or analysis). Non-news items may be 'preview/review' or 'curatorial' (bringing together multiple media stories).

   a. Descriptive: straight news reporting (who, where, when)
   b. Explanation from source: includes contextual or explanatory work from cited/ quoted sources. I.e. answering the 'why' question in substantial form.

  c. Reporter explanation: includes contextual or explanatory work by the reporter. Reporter provides explanation, answers the 'why' question, rather than simply presenting views from other sources.

  d. Preview/review: for items that preview or review an event (this is quite common in the community blogs).

  e. Curatorial: For items that gather together various media stories (quite common in some blogs, and also indicative of a digital storytelling form, with multiple hyperlinks).

  f. Not codeable: for rare occasions when the coder is unable to code in either category. Should only be used as a last resort.

10. **Good/bad news**: This is recorded on a three-point option bar – only one option can be selected.

  a. **Celebratory**: Celebratory of Yorkshire/Leeds: its character(s), heroes/achievers, scenery, reasons for local pride/products, charity achievements, cultural events, positive nostalgia, people/places overcoming obstacles/disadvantage. Coders should bear in mind this is not simply 'good news' but celebratory in nature.

  b. **Neither celebratory or disorder**: If the item is neither explicitly celebratory nor focusing on disorder issues. This is likely to be the most common option.

  c. **Disorder**: Crime and corruption, rape, fires, accidents, bad weather (e.g. floods or drought), drunkenness and disorder in town, environmental degradation.

11. **Orientation to conflict or consensus**

  a. Difference of opinion noted: (more than one view on the subject is presented)

  b. No recognition of opinion diversity: one source with sense of balance

  c. Explicit consensus: multiple sources in agreement

  d. Not relevant

12. **Prominent story topic**: one subject only selected from variables

13. **Subsidiary story topic**: one subject only selected from variables

VARIABLES Story topic

Topic number	Story topic type
1	Politics
2	Crime/legal
3	Business/economy
4	Culture/entertainment
5	Sports
6	Government cuts/spending
10	Education
11	Youth/young people
12	Environment/transport
13	Welfare
14	Health
15	Community relations
16	Human Interest
17	Housing
18	Charity event/related
20	Armed forces
21	Scandal
22	National event (incl. local impact)
23	International event (incl. local impact)
24	Other topic
99	Not sure/N/A

This can be amended during the pilot phase.[1] At the moment we have gone with one exclusive topic for each of these measures (i.e. one prominent story topic and one subsidiary story topic).

This has advantages (the database has a single value rather than multiple values in each measure, and so later analysis is simpler). It means that the coder might have to make a harder decision in choosing a primary story topic. However, the option to code for a 'subsidiary topic' makes this less difficult, and perhaps less artificial. Coding for a subsidiary topic could even

---

[1] In the piloting phase, we added 'human interest' and 'charity event/related'. We also split the 'youth' and 'education' codes.

be optional – in other words, only selected if the story really is difficult to categorize as a single subject.

Please note: 'Politics' should be selected for significant references to political authorities (MPs, parties, councillors) and political activities.

14. **Actors quoted**: For all types of actor given direct access to speak.
15. **Actors cited**: For indirect citations – not actually shown/heard speaking in broadcast material and not in 'speech marks' in print.

Both measures use the following variables:

VARIABLES Actors

Actor number	Actor type	Notes
1	Politicians/elected councillors	
2	Council workers/public officials	Any non-elected council workers
3	Community representatives	If they have a named role in community group
4	Police	
5	Reps of other causes	Other interest groups, campaigners
6	Public sector (medics, teachers)	
7	Private sector/business	
8	Experts/academics	
9	Trade unions/federations	
10	Media worker	Only code for other media, not own correspondent
11	Ordinary people: adults	
12	Ordinary people: youth	
13	Celebrity	
14	Other	
30	Not applicable/no quotes	

16. **Presence of key stories**: This will be 'not applicable' for most stories, but a note is made for the presence of two key stories for which project team members are to conduct more detailed analysis. We will be able to track occurrence and prominence over all media forms.

    a. Residential care homes closure: This story follows Leeds City Council's announcement of closures of a number of homes. The exact number of homes to be closed changed throughout the day – please note the number mentioned in the news item in 'further comments'.
    b. Leeds carnival: This is the Chapeltown carnival.
    c. Not applicable: Most stories will come in this category.

17. **Type of political story**: Only code for stories with 'politics' or 'government cuts/spending' as a 'prominent' or 'subsidiary' story topic. Otherwise code as 'N/A'.

    VARIABLES Political story type

Political story number	Political story type
1	Ordinary person with grievance/demand/issue
2	Campaigner with grievance/demand/issue
3	Report of improved development in service provision
4	Report of problems in service provision
5	Policy considered/consultation by political authority
6	Confrontations of reporters and political decision-makers
7	Other debates/controversy
10	Not applicable

18. **Intertextuality**: Text box for coder to note explicit reference to other media – this could be social media such as Facebook or Twitter; other local media which have possibly broken a story; national or international media of any kind. Explicit mentions

could help us to track how stories travel across mediascape – or at least the moments where it is acknowledged.

19. **Further comments**: Text box for coders to make any comments that they think could be of interest, or difficulties with the news item. This might be an interesting visual image, a moment of clear disdain from a reporter, or an otherwise surprising occurrence.

APPENDIX 2: DATA FOR CHARTS PRESENTED IN CHAPTER 2

DATA FOR FIGURE 2.1

	BBC1 Yorkshire		ITV *Calendar*	
Crime/legal	24	24.5%	14	23.7%
Other topic	11	11.2%	12	20.3%
Culture/entertainment	17	17.3%	4	6.8%
Government cuts/spending	13	13.3%	4	6.8%
Sports	7	7.1%	4	6.8%
Human interest	2	2.0%	8	13.6%
Environment/transport	3	3.1%	3	5.1%
Health	5	5.1%	0	0.0%
Politics	3	3.1%	2	3.4%
Business/economy	2	2.0%	2	3.4%
Charity event/related	2	2.0%	2	3.4%
Education	2	2.0%	1	1.7%
Housing	3	3.1%	0	0.0%
National event (incl. local impact)	3	3.1%	0	0.0%
Armed forces	0	0.0%	2	3.4%
Community relations	0	0.0%	1	1.7%
Youth/young people	1	1.0%	0	0.0%
Scandal	0	0.0%	0	0.0%
International event	0	0.0%	0	0.0%
Welfare	0	0.0%	0	0.0%
N/A/not sure	0	0.0%	0	0.0%
Total	98	100.0%	59	100.0%

DATA FOR FIGURE 2.2

	BBC Radio Leeds		Radio Aire	
Crime/legal	24	20.3%	15	27.3%
Culture/entertainment	17	14.4%	7	12.7%
Other topic	12	10.2%	5	9.1%
Human interest	11	9.3%	4	7.3%
Government cuts/spending	11	9.3%	2	3.6%
Business/economy	8	6.8%	3	5.5%
Politics	6	5.1%	3	5.5%
Armed forces	3	2.5%	4	7.3%
International event (incl. local impact)	7	5.9%	0	0.0%
Health	3	2.5%	3	5.5%
Housing	4	3.4%	2	3.6%
Environment/transport	3	2.5%	2	3.6%
Sports	4	3.4%	0	0.0%
Charity event/related	3	2.5%	0	0.0%
Education	0	0.0%	3	5.5%
Welfare	2	1.7%	0	0.0%
Scandal	0	0.0%	1	1.8%
Youth/young people	0	0.0%	1	1.8%
National event	0	0.0%	0	0.0%
Community relations	0	0.0%	0	0.0%
Total	118		55	

DATA FOR FIGURE 2.3

Story topic/newspaper	YEP	
	'n'	percent
Culture/entertainment	95	24.7%
Business/economy	54	14.0%
Charity event/related	45	11.7%
Crime/legal	38	9.9%
Other topic	20	5.2%
Health	19	4.9%
Environment/transport	18	4.7%
Government cuts/spending	16	4.2%
Human interest	14	3.6%
Education	12	3.1%
Sports	12	3.1%
Housing	8	2.1%
Youth/young people	8	2.1%
Politics	7	1.8%
Armed forces	6	1.6%
Community relations	5	1.3%
Welfare	5	1.3%
National event (incl. local impact)	2	0.5%
International event (incl. local impact)	1	0.3%
Scandal	0	0.0%
Not sure/N/A	0	0.0%
Total	385	100.0%

REFERENCES

ABC (2015) Audit Bureau of Circulations, online, www.abc.org.uk/.

Aldridge, M. (2007) *Understanding the Local Media*, Maidenhead: Open University Press.

Aminzade, R. (1992) 'Historical sociology and time', *Sociological Methods & Research*, 20(4): 456–80.

Anderson, C. W. (2010) 'Journalistic networks and the diffusion of local news: the brief, happy news life of the "Francisville Four"', *Political Communication*, 27: 289–309.

— (2013) *Rebuilding the News: Metropolitan journalism in the digital age*, Temple University.

Anderson, C. W., S. Coleman and N. Thumim (2015) 'How news travels: a comparative study of local media ecosystems in Leeds (UK) and Philadelphia (US)', in R. K. Nielsen (ed.), *Local Journalism: The Decline of Newspapers and the Rise of Digital Media*, London and New York: I. B. Tauris.

Atkins, J. and A. Finlayson (2013) '"… A 40-year-old black man made the point to me": everyday knowledge and the performance of leadership in contemporary British politics', *Political Studies*, 61: 161–77.

Baker, C. E. (2002) *Media, Markets and Democracy*, Cambridge: Cambridge University Press.

Ball-Rokeach, S. J., Yong-Chan Kim and S. Matei (2001) 'Storytelling neighborhood paths to belonging in diverse urban environments', *Communication Research*, 28(4): 392–428.

Barnett, S., G. N. Ramsay and I. Gaber (2012) *From Callaghan to Credit Crunch: Changing Trends in British Television News 1975–2009*, London: University of Westminster.

Bauman, Z. (2000) 'Time and space reunited', *Time & Society*, 9(2/3): 171–85.

Baym, N. K. and D. Boyd (2012) 'Socially mediated publicness: an introduction', *Journal of Broadcasting & Electronic Media*, 56(3): 320–29.

BBC (2003) 'Look North is 35!', BBC Bradford, online, 25 March, www.bbc.co.uk/bradford/features/look_north_anniv.shtml.

— (2013) 'Child heart surgery at Leeds had to stop, says NHS boss', *BBC News*, online, 29 March, www.bbc.co.uk/news/health-21974053.

Benkler, Y. (2006) *The Wealth of Networks: How Social Production Transforms Markets and Freedom*, London and New Haven, CT: Yale University Press.

Bennett, W. L. (1990) 'Toward a theory of press–state relations in the United States', *Journal of Communication*, 40: 103–25.

— (2008) 'Changing citizenship in the digital age', in W. L. Bennett (ed.), *Civic Life Online: Learning How Digital Media Can Engage Youth*, MIT Press.

Beyond Guardian Leeds (2015) 'About', online, beyondgdnleeds.wordpress.com/about/.

Bird, S. E. and R. W. Dardenne (2009) 'Rethinking news and myth as storytelling', in K. Wahl-Jorgensen and T. Hanitzsch (eds), *The Handbook of Journalism Studies*, Abingdon: Routledge.

Boorstin, D. J. (1961) *The Image: A Guide to Pseudo-Events in America*, New York: Harper Colophon.

Born, G. (2005) 'Digitising democracy', *Political Quarterly*, 76: 102–23.

Bourdieu, P. (1977) *Outline of a Theory of Practice*, Cambridge: Cambridge University Press.

— (1992) *The Logic of Practice*, Cambridge: Polity Press.

Bräuchler, B. and J. Postill (eds) (2010) *Theorising Media and Practice*, Oxford: Berghahn Books.

Braudel, F. (1980) *On History*, trans. S. Matthews, Chicago, IL: University of Chicago Press.

Campbell, A., G. Gurin and W. E. Miller (1971) *The Voter Decides*, Greenwood Press.

Carey, J. (1989) 'Interactive media', in W. Donsbach (ed.), *International Encyclopedia of Communication*, vol. 2, Wiley-Blackwell.

Carey, J. W. (1982) 'The mass media and critical theory: an American view', *Communication Yearbook*, 6: 18–33.

Carpentier, N. and B. Cammaerts (eds) (2007) *Reclaiming the Media: Communication Rights and Democratic Media Roles*, Bristol and Chicago, IL: Intellect.

Carpini, M. X. D., F. L. Cook and L. R. Jacobs (2004) 'Public deliberation, discursive participation, and citizen engagement: a review of the empirical literature', *Annual Review of Political Science*, 7: 315–44.

Castells, M. (1989) *The Informational City: Information technology, economic restructuring, and the urban-regional process*, Oxford: Blackwell.

— (1994) 'European cities, the informational society, and the global economy', *New Left Review*, 204: 18.

— (2008) 'The new public sphere: global civil society, communication networks, and global governance', *Annals of the American Academy of Political and Social Science*, 616(1): 78–93.

Chan, J. K.-C. and L. Leung (2005) 'Lifestyles, reliance on traditional news media and online news adoption', *New Media & Society*, 7: 357–82.

Coleman, S. (2012) 'The internet as space for policy deliberation', in F. Fischer and H. Gottweis (eds), *The Argumentative Turn Revisited: Public Policy as Communicative Practice*, Durham, NC, and London: Duke University Press.

Coleman, S. and J. G. Blumler (2011) 'The wisdom of which crowd? On the pathology of a listening government', *Political Quarterly*, 82: 355–64.

Coleman, S. and J. Firmstone (2014) 'Contested meanings of public engagement: exploring discourse and practice within a British city council', *Media, Culture & Society*, 36: 826–44.

Coleman, S. and K. Ross (2010) *The Media and the Public: Them and Us in Media Discourse*, Oxford: Blackwell-Wiley.

Coleman, S., S. Anthony and D. E. Morrison (2009) *Public Trust in the News: A Constructivist Study of the Social Life of the News*, Reuters Institute for the Study of Journalism, University of Oxford.

Coleman, S., A. Przybylska and Y. Sintomer (eds) (2015) *Deliberation and Democracy: Innovative Processes and Institutions*, New York: Peter Lang.

Conboy, M. (2009) *Journalism: A Critical History*, London: SAGE.

Costera Meijer, I. (2010) 'Democratizing journalism? Realizing the citizen's agenda for local news media', *Journalism Studies*, 11: 327–42.

— (2013) 'When news hurts: the promise of participatory storytelling for urban problem neighbourhoods', *Journalism Studies*, 14(1): 13–28.

Couldry, N. (2003) 'Beyond the hall of mirrors? Some theoretical reflections on the global contestation of media power', in N. Couldry and J. Curran (eds), *Contesting Media Power: Alternative Media in a Networked World*, Boulder, CO: Rowman and Littlefield.

— (2004) 'Theorising media as practice', *Social Semiotics*, 14(2): 115–32.

— (2010) *Why Voice Matters*, London: SAGE.

Couldry, N. and T. Markham (2006) 'Public connection through media consumption: between oversocialization and de-socialization?', *Annals of the American Academy of Political and Social Science*, 603.

Couldry, N., S. Livingstone and T. Markham (2010) *Media Consumption and Public Engagement: Beyond the Presumption of Attention*, Basingstoke: Palgrave Macmillan.

Crisell, A. (2002) *An Introductory History of British Broadcasting*, London and New York: Routledge.

Cross, K. A. (2010) 'Experts in the news: the differential use of sources in election television news', *2010*, 35: 413–29.

Curran, J. (2010) 'The future of journalism', *Journalism Studies*, 11: 464–76.

— (2012) 'Reinterpreting the Internet', in J. Curran, N. Fenton and D. Freedman (eds), *Misunderstanding the Internet*, London and New York: Routledge.

Dahlgren, P. (2009) *Media and Political Engagement: Citizens, Communication and Democracy*, New York: Cambridge University Press.

Darnton, R. (2000) 'An early information society: news and the media in eighteenth-century Paris', *American Historical Review*, 105.

Davies, N. (2008) *Flat Earth News*, London: Chatto & Windus.

Dawson, S. (2012) 'What is the future for Kirkstall Matters?', *Kirkstall Online*, online, 21 February, new.kirkstall.org.uk/893.

Dayan, D. and E. Katz (1992) *Media Events: Live Broadcasting of History*, Cambridge, MA: Harvard University Press.

Dewey, J. (1916) *Democracy and Education*, New York: Free Press.

— (1927) *The Public and Its Problems: An essay in political inquiry*, Penn State University Press.

Dewey, J. and M. L. Rogers (eds) (2012) *The Public and Its Problems: An Essay in Political Inquiry*, University Park, PA: Penn State University Press.

Dickens, L., N. Couldry and A. Fotopoulou (2015) 'News in the community? Investigating emerging inter-local spaces of news production/consumption', *Journalism Studies*, 16(1): 97–114.

Diddi, A. and R. Larose (2006) 'Getting hooked on news: uses and gratifications and the formation of news habits among college students in an internet environment', *Journal of Broadcasting & Electronic Media*, 50: 193–210.

Dolsak, N. and E. Ostrom (eds) (2003) *The Commons in the New Millennium: Challenges and Adaptation*, Cambridge, MA: MIT Press.

Entman, R. M. (1993) 'Framing: toward clarification of a fractured paradigm', *Journal of Communication*, 43: 51–8.

Fairclough, N., S. Pardoe and B. Szerszynski (2003) 'Critical discourse analysis and citizenship', in H. Hausendorf and A. Bora (eds), *Analysing Citizenship Talk: Social positioning in political and legal decision-making processes*, Amsterdam: John Benjamins.

Farrar, M. (2012) 'Rioting or protesting? Losing it or finding it?', *Parallax*, 18: 72–91.

Fenton, N. (ed.) (2009) *New Media, Old News: Journalism and Democracy in the Digital Age*, London: SAGE.

— (2011) 'Deregulation or democracy? New media, news, neoliberalism and the public interest', *Continuum*, 25: 63–72.

Fenton, N., M. Metykova, J. Schlosberg and D. Freedman (2010) 'Meeting the news needs of local communities', www.mediatrust. org/uploads/128255497549240/ original.pdf.

Firmstone, J. (2016) 'Mapping changes in local news', *Journalism Practice*.

Firmstone, J. and S. Coleman (2014) 'The changing role of the local news media in enabling citizens to engage in local democracies', *Journalism Practice*, 8: 596–606.

— (2015a) 'Rethinking local communicative spaces: reflecting on the implications of digital media and citizen journalism for the role of local journalism in engaging citizens in local democracies', in R. K. Nielsen (ed.), *The Uncertain Future of Local Journalism*, London and New York: I. B. Tauris.

— (2015b) 'Public engagement in local government: the voice and influence of citizens in online communicative spaces', *Information, Communication & Society*, 18(6): 680–95.

Flavian, C. and R. Gurrea (2007) 'Perceived substitutability between digital and physical channels: the case of newspapers', *Online Information Review*, 31: 793–813.

Franklin, B. (ed.) (2006) *Local Journalism and Local Media: Making Local News*, Abingdon: Routledge.

— (2013) *The Future of Newspapers*, Abingdon: Routledge.

Friedland, L. A. (2001) 'Communication, community, and democracy: toward a theory of the communicatively integrated community', *Communication Research*, 28(4): 358–91.

Frisby, D. and M. Featherstone (1997) *Simmel on Culture: Selected writings*, London: SAGE.

Fung, A. (2009) *Empowered Participation: Reinventing urban democracy*, Princeton, NJ: Princeton University Press.

Gans, H. (1979) *Deciding What's News*, New York: Pantheon.

— (1999) 'Deciding what's news', in H. Tumber (ed.), *News, a Reader*, Oxford: Oxford University Press.

Garnham, N. (2000) *Emancipation, the Media, and Modernity: Arguments about the Media and Social Theory*, Oxford: Oxford University Press.

Gaudio, R. P. and S. Bialostok (2005) 'The trouble with culture', *Critical Discourse Studies*, 2: 51–69.

Giddens, A. (1979) *Central Problems in Social Theory: Action, Structure and Contradiction in Social Analysis*, Basingstoke: Palgrave Macmillan.

— (1984) *The Constitution of Society: Outline of the Theory of Structuration*, Cambridge: Polity Press.

— (1990) *The Consequences of Modernity*, Cambridge: Polity.

— (1991) *Modernity and Self-identity: Self and society in the late modern age*, Stanford, CA: Stanford University Press.

Glasgow Media Group (1976) *Bad News*, London: Routledge and Kegan Paul.

— (1980) *More Bad News*, London: Routledge and Kegan Paul.

Golding, P. and P. Elliott (1979) *Making the News*, London: Longman.

Goode, L. (2009) 'Social news, citizen journalism and democracy', *New Media & Society*, 11: 1287–1305.

Goodwin, P. (1998) *Television under the Tories: Broadcasting Policy 1979–1997*, BFI Publishing.

Gray, J. (2007) 'The news: you gotta love it', in J. Gray, C. Sandvoss and C. L. Harrington (eds), *Fandom: Identities and Communities in a Mediated World*, New York: New York University Press.

Greenslade, R. (2004) 'Have the regional takeovers run out of steam', *Guardian*, 29 November.

Gurevitch, M. and J. G. Blumler (1990) 'Political communications systems and democratic values', in J. Lichtenberg (ed.), *Democracy and the Mass Media*, Cambridge: Cambridge University Press.

Gurevitch, M., S. Coleman and J. G. Blumler (2009) 'Political communication – old and new media relationships', *Annals of the American Academy of Political and Social Science*, 625(1): 164–81.

Habermas, J. (2006) 'Political communication in media society: does democracy still enjoy an epistemic dimension? The impact of normative theory on empirical research', *Communication Theory*, 16: 411–26.

Hajer, M. A. (2005) 'Setting the stage: a dramaturgy of policy deliberation', *Administration & Society*, 36(6): 624–47.

Hall, S., C. Critcher, T. Jefferson, J. Clarke and B. Roberts (1978) *Policing the Crisis: Mugging, the State and law and order*, London: Macmillan.

Harcup, T. (2015) 'Alternative journalism as monitorial citizenship? A case study of a local news blog', *Digital Journalism*, 1–17.

Hargreaves, I. and J. Thomas (2002) 'New news, old news: an ITC and BSC research publication', www.ofcom.org.uk/static/archive/itc/uploads/New_News_Old_News_An_ITC_and_BSC_research_publication.pdf.

Harju, A. (2007) 'Citizen participation and local public spheres', in B. Cammaerts and N. Carpentier (eds), *Reclaiming the Media: Communication Rights and Democratic Media Roles*, Bristol and Chicago, IL: Intellect.

Hebe Media (2011) 'LOL! Leeds Online', *Hebe Media*, online, 28 July, hebemedia.squarespace.com/everything-blog/2011/7/28/lol-leeds-online.html.

Heider, D., M. McCombs and P. M. Poindexter (2005) 'What the public expects of local news: views on public and traditional journalism', *Journalism & Mass Communication Quarterly*, 82(4): 952–67.

Heritage, J. (1985) 'Analyzing news interviews: aspects of the production of talk for an "overhearing"', in T. A. van Dijk (ed.), *Handbook of Discourse Analysis: Discourse and Dialogue*, London: Academic Press.

Hindman, M. (2008) *The Myth of Digital Democracy*, Princeton, NJ: Princeton University Press.

Huckfeldt, R. and J. Sprague (1987) 'Networks in context: the social flow of political information', *American Political Science Review*, 81(4): 1197–1216.

— (1995) *Citizens, Politics and Social Communication: Information and influence in an election campaign*, Cambridge: Cambridge University Press.

Independent (1995) 'Obituaries: Phil Sidey', *Independent*, 25 October.

Iveson, K. (2007) *Publics and the City*, Wiley-Blackwell.

Jones, J. P. (2005) 'A cultural approach to the study of mediated citizenship', *Social Semiotics*, 16: 365–83.

Kaiser, R. G. (2014) *The Bad News about the News*, Brookings Institution.

Kaniss, P. (1991) *Making Local News*, Chicago, IL: University of Chicago Press.

Kirkstall Matters (2011) *Kirkstall Matters*, 108, Autumn/Winter, online, issuu. com/kirkstallmatters/docs/km108/ 1?e=6497900/6551825.

Knight, G. and T. Dean (1982) 'Myth and the structure of news', *Journal of Communication*, 32: 144–61.

Knorr-Cetina, K., T. R. Schatzki and E. von Savigny Schatzki (eds) (2001) *The Practice Turn in Contemporary Theory*, London: Routledge.

Kovach, B. and T. Rosenstiel (2006) 'The elements of journalism: what newspeople should know and the public should expect', *Science*, 608(1): 251–69.

Latour, B. (2005) *Reassembling the Social: An Introduction to Actor-Network-Theory*, Oxford: Oxford University Press.

Law, J. (1994) *Organizing Modernity*, Oxford: Blackwell.

Law, J. and J. Urry (2004) 'Enacting the social', *Economy and Society*, 33(3): 390–410.

Lee-Wright, P., A. Phillips and T. Witschge (2011) *Changing Journalism*, London: Routledge.

Lenhart, A. (2012) 'Teens, smartphones & texting', Pew Internet & American Life Project.

Lenhart, A. et al. (2010) 'Social media & mobile internet use among teens and young adults. Millennials', Pew Internet & American Life Project.

Lewis, J., R. Brookes, N. Modell and T. Threadgold (2006) *Shoot First and Ask Questions Later: Media Coverage of the 2003 Iraq War*, Oxford: Peter Lang.

Lewis, J., A. Williams and B. Franklin (2008) 'A compromised Fourth Estate? UK journalism, public relations and news sources', *Journalism Studies*, 9: 1–20.

Lippman, W. (1922) *Public Opinion*, New York: Macmillan.

Lum, C. M. K. (ed.) (2006) *Perspectives on Culture, Technology and Communication: The media ecology tradition*. Cresskill, NJ: Hampton Press.

Madianou, M. (2009) 'Audience reception and news in everyday life', in K. Wahl-Jorgensen and T. Hanitzsch (eds), *The Handbook of Journalism Studies*, Abingdon: Routledge.

Manning, P. (2001) *News and News Sources: A Critical Introduction*, London: SAGE.

McChesney, R. W. (2003) 'The problem of journalism: a political economic contribution to an explanation of the crisis in contemporary US journalism', *Journalism Studies*, 4(3): 299–329.

— (2012) 'Farewell to journalism? Time for a rethinking', *Journalism Practice*, 6: 614–26.

McCombs, M. et al. (2011) *The News and Public Opinion: Media effects on civic life*, Polity.

McCombs, M. E. and D. L. Shaw (1972) 'The agenda setting function of mass media', *Public Opinion Quarterly*, 36: 176–85.

McLeod, J. M. et al. (1996) 'Community integration, local media use, and democratic processes', *Communication Research*, 23(2): 179–209.

McLeod, J. M., D. A. Scheufele and P. Moy (1999) 'Community, communication, and participation: the role of mass media and interpersonal discussion in local political participation', *Political Communication*, 16(3): 315–36.

McNair, B. (1996) *News and Journalism in the UK*, London: Routledge.

Mejias, U. A. (2010) 'The limits of networks as models for organizing the social', *New Media & Society*, 12(4): 603–17.

Milberry, K. (2012) *Media Ecology*, Oxford: Oxford University Press.

Milbrath, L. W. (1965) *Political Participation: How and Why Do People Get Involved in Politics?*, Rand McNally.

Mitchelstein, E. and P. J. Boczkowski (2010) 'Online news consumption research: an assessment of past work and an agenda for the future', *New Media & Society*, 12: 1085–1102.

Morley Observer (2011a) 'People power helps save Knowle Manor', *Morley Observer*, 31 August.

— (2011b) 'A real victory for residents', *Morley Observer*, 31 August.

Nardi, B. A. and V. O'Day (1999) *Information Ecologies: Using technology with heart*, Cambridge, MA: MIT Press.

Nielsen, R. K. (ed.) (2015) *Local Journalism: The Decline of Newspapers and the Rise of Digital Media*, London and New York: I. B. Tauris.

Ofcom (2009) *Putting Viewers First: Ofcom's Second Public Service Broadcasting Review*, Ofcom.

— (2015) *Public Service Broadcasting in the Internet Age: Ofcom's Third Review of Public Service Broadcasting*, Ofcom.

Oliver, P. E. and D. J. Myers (1999) 'How events enter the public sphere: conflict, location, and sponsorship in local newspaper coverage of public events', *American Journal of Sociology*, 105(1): 38–87.

Oxford Economics (2011) *Housing Market Analysis July 2011: A report for National Housing Federation*, www.oxfordeconomics.com/publication/open224393.

Paek, H.-J., So-Hyang Yoon and D. V. Shah (2005) 'Local news, social integration, and community participation: hierarchical linear modeling of contextual and cross-level effects', *Journalism & Mass Communication Quarterly*, 82(3): 587–606.

Pavlik, J. V. (2004) 'A sea-change in journalism: convergence, journalists, their audiences and sources', *Convergence: The International Journal of Research into New Media Technologies*, 10: 21–9.

Pew Research Center (2010) 'How news happens: a study of the news ecosystem of one American city', Pew Research Center, online, 11 January, www.journalism.org/2010/01/11/how-news-happens/.

Radcliffe, D. (2012) 'Here and now: UK hyperlocal media today', *Nest*, online, 29 March, www.nesta.org.uk/publications/here-and-now-uk-hyperlocal-media-today.

Radio Today (2011) 'Martin Kellner on radio's future', *Radio Today*, online, radiotoday.co.uk/2011/10/dqf-martin-kelner-on-local-radios-future/.

Rantanen, T. (2009) *When News Was New*, Oxford: Wiley-Blackwell.

Reckwitz, A. (2002) 'Toward a theory of social practices: a development in culturalist theorizing', *European Journal of Social Theory*, 5: 243–63.

Rees, W. E. (1992) 'Ecological footprints and appropriated carrying capacity: what urban economics leaves out', *Environment and Urbanization*, 4: 121–30.

Rhodes, R. and M. Bevir (2015) *The Routledge Handbook of Interpretive Political Science*, London: Routledege.

Ross, K. (2006) 'Open source? Hearing voices in the local press', in B. Franklin (ed.), *Local Journalism and Local Media: Making the Local News*, London and New York: Routledge.

Scannell, P. (ed.) (1991) *Broadcast Talk*, London: SAGE.

Schatzki, T. R. (1996) *Social Practices: A Wittgensteinian approach to human activity and the social*, Cambridge: Cambridge University Press.

Schlesinger, P. (1978) *Putting 'Reality' Together: BBC News*, New York and London: Methuen.

— (1990) 'Rethinking the sociology of journalism – source strategies and the limits of media centrism', in M. Ferguson (ed.), *Public Communication – the New Imperatives: Future Directions for Media Research*, London: SAGE.

Self, D. (2005) 'Meet Dave 'n' Sue', *New Statesman*, 28 February.

Seymour-Ure, C. (2003) *Prime Ministers and the Media: Issues of Power and Control*, Oxford: Wiley-Blackwell.

Shah, D. V., R. Nojin Kwak and R. Lance Holbert '"Connecting" and "disconnecting" with civic life: patterns of Internet use and the production of social capital', *Political Communication*, 18(2): 141–62.

Shirky, C. (2009) 'Not an upgrade – an upheaval', *CATO Unbound*, online, 13 July, www.cato-unbound.org/2009/07/13/clay-shirky/not-upgrade-upheaval.

Shove, E. and M. Pantzar (2005) 'Consumers, producers and practices', *Journal of Consumer Culture*, 5: 43–64.

Sidey, P. J. (1994) *Hello Mrs Butterfield: The Hilarious Story of 'Radio Irreverent', the First Two Years of BBC Radio Leeds*, London: Kestrel.

Silverstone, R. (1999) *Why Study the Media?*, London: SAGE.

— (2005) *The Sociology of Mediation and Communication*, London: SAGE.

Simmel, G. (1922) *The Web of Group-affiliations*, trans. R. Bendix, Glencoe, IL: Free Press.

Söderbaum, P. (1999) 'Values, ideology and politics in ecological economics', *Ecological Economics*, 28: 161–70.

Stamm, K. R. (1985) *Newspaper Use and Community Ties: Toward a dynamic theory*, Praeger.

Stillwell, J. and P. Shepherd (2004) 'The "haves" and "have-nots": contrasting social geographies', in *Twenty-first Century Leeds: Geographies of a Regional City*, pp. 127–46.

Strate, L. (2006) *Echoes and Reflections: On media ecology as a field of study*, Cresskill, NJ: Hampton Press.

Street, J. (2011) *Mass Media, Politics and Democracy*, Basingstoke: Palgrave Macmillan.

Strömbäck, J. and L. W. Nord (2006) 'Do politicians lead the tango?: a study of the relationship between Swedish journalists and their political sources in the context of election campaigns', *European Journal of Communication*, 21: 147–64.

Sullivan, J. L. and E. Riedel (2004) 'Political efficacy', in N. J. Smelser and P. B. Baltes (eds), *International Encyclopedia of the Social and Behavioral Sciences*, Elsevier.

Sweney, M. (2012) 'Circulation slide continues for regional evening papers', *Guardian*, online, 29 February, www.theguardian.com/media/2012/feb/29/circulation-slide-continues-regional-evening-papers.

Swidler, A. (2001) 'What anchors cultural practices', in K. Knorr-Cetina, T. R. Schatzki and E. von Savigny (eds), *The Practice Turn in Contemporary Theory*, Routledge, pp. 74–92.

the leeds citizen (2015) 'About', theleedscitizen.wordpress.com/about/.

Thompson, E. P. (1971) 'The moral economy of the English crowd in the eighteenth century', *Past & Present*, 50: 76–136.

Thompson, J. B. (1995) *The Media and Modernity: A social theory of the media*, Stanford, CA: Stanford University Press.

Thorson, E. (2008) 'Changing patterns of news consumption and participation', *Information, Communication & Society*, 11: 473–89.

Thrift, N. (2008) *Non-Representational Theory: Space, politics, affect*, London: Routledge.

Tuchman, G. (1972) 'Objectivity as strategic ritual: an examination of newsmen's notions of objectivity', *American Journal of Sociology*, 77: 660–79.

— (1978) *Making News: A Study in the Construction of Reality*, New York: Free Press.

Virilio, P. (2005) *The Information Bomb*, vol. 10, London: Verso.

Warde, A. (2005) 'Consumption and theories of practice', *Journal of Consumer Culture*, 5(2): 131–53.

Wharfedale Observer (2011) 'Home reprieved – until private sector steps in', *Wharfedale Observer*, 1 September.

White, D. M. (1950) 'The gate keeper: a case study in the selection of news', *Journalism Quarterly*, 27: 383–90.

Williams, A., D. Harte and J. Turner (2014) 'The value of UK hyperlocal community news', *Digital Journalism*, 3: 680–703.

Williams, B. A. and M. X. Delli Carpini (2011) *After Broadcast News: Media regimes, democracy, and the new information environment*, Cambridge: Cambridge University Press.

Yong-Chan, K. and S. J. Ball-Rokeach (2006) 'Community storytelling network, neighborhood context, and civic engagement: a multilevel approach', *Human Communication Research*, 32: 411–39.

Yorkshire Evening Post (2011a) 'Councillor under fire for failing to attend care home', *Yorkshire Evening Post*, 29 August.

— (2011b) 'Axe falls on Leeds care homes', *Yorkshire Evening Post*, 30 August.

— (2011c) 'Clashes over care homes closure plan', *Yorkshire Evening Post*, 31 August.

— (2011d) 'Thank you for all the support', *Yorkshire Evening Post*, 1 September.

Zelizer, B. (2009) 'Journalism and the academy', in K. Wahl-Jorgensen and T. Hanitzsch (eds), *The Handbook of Journalism Studies*, Abingdon: Routledge.

INDEX

Note: *n* following a page number denotes a footnote.